Image and Representation

Also by Nick Lacey

NARRATIVE AND GENRE
MEDIA INSTITUTIONS AND AUDIENCES
INTRODUCTION TO FILM
BLADE RUNNER
SE7EN

Image and Representation

Key Concepts in Media Studies

Second Edition

Nick Lacey

Curriculum Leader, Film and Media
Benton Park School, Leeds

palgrave
macmillan

First edition 1998
Second edition 2009

Published by
PALGRAVE MACMILLAN

Palgrave Macmillan in the UK is an imprint of Macmillan Publishers Limited,
registered in England, company number 785998, of Houndmills, Basingstoke,
Hampshire RG21 6XS.

Palgrave Macmillan in the US is a division of St Martin's Press LLC,
175 Fifth Avenue, New York, NY 10010.

Palgrave Macmillan is the global academic imprint of the above companies
and has companies and representatives throughout the world.

Palgrave® and Macmillan® are registered trademarks in the United States,
the United Kingdom, Europe and other countries

ISBN-13: 978–0–230–20335–8
ISBN-10: 0–230–20335–3

This book is printed on paper suitable for recycling and made from fully
managed and sustained forest sources. Logging, pulping and manufacturing
processes are expected to conform to the environmental regulations of the
country of origin.

A catalogue record for this book is available from the British Library.

A catalog record for this book is available from the Library of Congress.

Contents

List of Tables

List of Figures

Acknowledgements

The author wishes to thank the following, without whom, etc.: Kevin Atkins, who made sure everything, more or less, made sense; Richard Duckworth, who showed me that some of it didn't make (some) sense; Henrik Bicat, who made the computer make sense of something it shouldn't have; Alex and Kate for not turning my computer off at crucial moments; my wife for looking after the kids; my students for test-driving the material – and no, you can't have any of the royalties; my mother-in-law, for helping look after the kids; Roy Stafford for letting me use the *in the picture* spread and his enthusiasm for the subject; Len Masterman for his exceptionally useful comments; Keith Povey and Eileen Ashcroft for their editing and excellent suggestions; Everton FC for not getting relegated and winning the Cup; Brian Bicat for talking Brecht; Dave Croft for being Dave Croft; Catherine Gray, Frances Arnold, Jo Digby and Nancy Williams at the publishers.

And in the second edition: thanks to Phil Day, Mellissa Houlding, Megan Fenwick and Chris Mann, but most of all to Babs.

NICK LACEY

The author and publishers would like to thank the following for permission to reproduce copyright material:

The Howling family for 'Mother and Child Cooking' by L. Howling; Richard Smith for the use of his picture 'Poll Tax Riots in London'; Palgrave Macmillan for the use of the website homepage; SuperStock Ltd for the use of *Book of the Dead: Princess Entiu-ny & Osiris*; Roy Stafford for the centre-page spread of *In the Picture*; IPC Media Ltd for the front cover of *Loaded*; Columbia Pictures Corporation for film stills from *Gilda* and *The Wild One*, courtesy of the Kobal Collection; Emap Elan Ltd for the front cover of *More!*, January 2008, and

March 1995; MGM/Pathé for the film still from *Thelma and Louise*, courtesy of the Kobal Collection; Vestron/MGM/United Artists for the film still from *Blue Steel*, courtesy of the Kobal Collection; the artist and Metro Pictures for 'Unititled Film Still no. 21' by Cindy Sherman; Faber & Faber Ltd for the quotation of T.S. Eliot's *The Waste Land*.

Every effort has been made to trace all the copyright-holders, but if any have been inadvertently overlooked the publishers will be pleased to make the necessary arrangement at the first opportunity.

Introduction to the First Edition

The British Film Institute report *Primary Media Education: A Curriculum Statement* 'proposed six areas of knowledge and understanding as the basis for ... curriculum development' (Bowker 1991: 5):

> WHO is communicating, and why? WHAT TYPE of text is it? HOW is it produced? HOW do we know what it means? WHO receives it, and what sense do they make of it? HOW does it PRESENT its subject? (ibid.: 6)

These 'signpost questions' lead to the following key concepts:

1. media agencies
2. media categories
3. media technologies
4. media languages
5. media audiences
6. media representations.

These key concepts inform the structure of this book, and two others, on introductory Media Studies. By concentrating on these approaches to the subject I hope to give the student the basic skills they require for post-16 education, whether in their final years at school/college or in the first year of Media Studies degrees at undergraduate level. It is intended that the books be used as a back-up to teacher/lecturer input.

There is an artificiality in splitting these concepts, for without technology there would be no media; without language we would not understand representation, and so on. However, for pedagogical purposes the categories are very useful.

The adaptation I have made follows the emphasis given by current syllabuses, but as it is dealing with key concepts of the subject, this book should be relevant to any future media syllabus that I can imagine. The adaptation is as follows:

1. media agencies – media institutions
2. media categories – genre
3. media technologies – remains as a category but is not dealt with separately, but in relation to each of the other categories, except in this volume, because narrative and genre refer to how texts are *structured* while technology *mediates* this structure
4. media languages – image analysis and narrative
5. media audiences – audiences
6. media representations – representations.

I have paired the adapted concepts to illustrate clearly the interconnectedness of the categories without attempting to encompass the massive intellectual field of the subject in a single book.

The structure of this book

Many students in post-16 education come to Media Studies with little or no previous experience of the subject. Although there is a plethora of books available, most of them are too academic for those who are still at school – and some are too complex even for those who are doing a degree course.

Many textbooks have an implicit model of their audience as being an intellectually static individual. This textbook differentiates between the pre- and post-16 student, a difference that represents not just twenty months of study but, for most, the rapid intellectual development of 16–18-year-olds. A consequence of this is that the key concepts are dealt with, first, at a basic level, appropriate for students at the beginning of the course. The following chapters introduce more advanced theories, such as ideology and semiotics, which are then applied to the concept. The book could form part of the structure of a two-year course, with more advanced chapters being used in the later stages. Be aware, however, that it is likely that most advanced level students will find at least some parts of this book difficult, though undergraduates should have few problems with it.

The subject matter of Media Studies is the artefacts that influence us every day of our lives: advertising, movies, videotapes, CDs, the internet and so on. It investigates how the media operate, what are their rules, conventions and ideological purpose, and what are the artefacts' meaning for us in the early years of the twenty-first century.

Unlike many subjects, Media Studies is exceptionally wide in its scope, without the narrow specialization of which other qualifications are accused.

Media Studies gives us a crucial understanding of our world. It should also be a lot of fun.

The examples I have used are a mixture of contemporary and classic (in the sense of being part of a canon) with an emphasis on film that reflects my own interests and, in my experience, those of most students. However, these are not meant to supersede teachers' own preferences. Besides, students best understand the key concepts through discussion of their own experiences of media. Although this book can be read in isolation, it is intended to complement the other volumes in the series: *Narrative and Genre* and *Media Institutions and Audiences*.

One final note of caution: while this text is obviously usable as a reference book, the later chapters do refer to material discussed earlier, and this may cause confusion if sections are read in isolation.

Introduction to the Second Edition

The media have undergone an upheaval caused by the arrival of new technologies since the first edition of this book was published. The internet, in particular, has 'changed everything' and is a medium, so it can be studied in the same way as can television or cinema. However, the changes wrought by the internet, particularly the advent of Web 2.0, have challenged the subject of Media Studies: are the key concepts sufficient to analyse 'we media'? Do we need Media Studies 2.0?

The existence of this book indicates that we (that is, Nick Lacey and Palgrave Macmillan) believe that the key concepts are robust enough to deal with the changes wrought by multimedia and the interactivity made possible by new media technologies. While there is no doubt that there has been a change in the way we access, and create, texts, fundamental issues of media language and representation remain vital. While there are sections of this book that remain virtually unchanged, particularly Chapter 2, much of the rest of the book has been altered, either because of the changing media landscape or in order to improve on the first edition. In addition, there are new sections (such as section 3.5 New media technologies) and an attempt to broaden the texts considered in the first edition – such as comics in section 1.12 Images in sequence. The separate chapter on technology has been dropped.

Of course, I've used this opportunity to update sections. In some cases, such as in section 5.5 Gender in magazines: *More* and *Nuts*, I've also, in this case, included the 1998 analysis of *More!*, as this serves to highlight how the magazine has changed over a decade; these changes are seen to be symptomatic of how representation of gender has altered. Chapter 5 is also informed by the post-feminist perspective that has gained ground since the first edition.

The internet, in particular, has made it far easier both to access texts and writings about these texts (indeed the tide of information unleashed by the Net can be overwhelming). Consequently, there is a much wider use of other sources in this edition.

Another seismic shift since 1998 has been the arrival of DVD. The audience's seemingly insatiable desire to own both old films and television shows has resurrected many texts, making it much easier to contextualize contemporary productions historically. In addition, DVD has encouraged the viewing of films in their correct aspect ratio, and the abomination of 'pan and scan' has almost been consigned to history.

In the spirit of 'we media', I'd be delighted to receive comments (positive as well as negative) about this book; you can contact me via www.nicklacey.org.uk.

CHAPTER

1 Introduction to Textual Analysis

1.1 'Seeing is believing'

Of our five senses, it is sight that gives us the most detailed information. It is, for most people, more important than hearing, taste, smell or touch. The majority of us rely on it to such an extent that we neglect the other senses. 'Seeing is believing' is such a powerful idea that many people accept it as true. However, in Media Studies things aren't so simple.

As R. L. Gregory points out:

> We are so familiar with seeing, that it takes a leap of imagination to realise that there are problems to be solved ... From the patterns of stimulation on the retinas we perceive the world of objects and this is nothing short of a miracle. (1966: 9)

Gregory is concerned with the biological processes of perceiving the world around us. Media Studies, when analysing texts, concerns itself with the factors that influence how we understand our world.

Texts are created in order to communicate a message. Even straightforward holiday snapshots attempt to convey what it was like to be at a particular place at a specific time. However, whether we understand what was intended to be conveyed by a photograph depends upon how we, as the audience, interpret the image.

1.2 Interpreting the world around us

It is obvious that you – the reader – have a greater understanding of the world than a young child has, because you have had more experience of the world and a formal education. This demonstrates that we have learnt to understand the world; understanding does not come naturally. The fact that this understanding is learnt means that the particular society we are born into has a

6

great effect on us. People born into different societies have a different understanding of the world, because they learn about it in different ways.

In the initial stages of textual analysis it is helpful simply to describe what we see, using terms as neutral as possible. At this stage of analysis we are simply engaging in the process of describing what we are seeing and/or hearing; this is analysis at the level of denotation (see also section 2.2). For example, if we describe a particular colour as 'red', this is denotation; we may associate this colour, however, with passion or danger (this association happens at the level of connotation, which will be dealt with later in the chapter). Theoretically, at the level of denotation almost everyone will describe an image in exactly the same way, but this is not necessarily the case – an artist may perceive the colour to be *vermillion*, say, which suggests that even denotation is affected by an individual's understanding of the world.

EXERCISE 1.1

In order to demonstrate how we interpret our world, I am going to ask you to do something that appears contradictory: imagine the image shown in Figure 1.1) is a real situation. You are facing this group of six men in Newcastle at about six o'clock on a Saturday evening in July, when the photograph was actually taken. None of them is talking to you. You are waiting for a bus at a bus stop.

Figure 1.1   Facing a group of six men

- Make a note of what your feelings would be if you were confronted by this group, before you read my interpretation.
- If you have done this in a classroom situation, compare your interpretation with those of other students. The fact that everyone doesn't have the same feelings demonstrates that each person has interpreted the image for themselves.

See Box 1.1, which describes how I would have interpreted what was happening if I were in that position.

Box 1.1   Interpreting the world

The group of six men are young, but not very young (late 20s/early 30s), so they may have a degree of social responsibility; they're waiting for a bus (possibly can't afford the taxis that are available); their appearance is casual (all are wearing jeans), neither scruffy nor smart; they're unlikely to have spent the day shopping as they aren't carrying any bags (an unlikely activity for a group of men in any case); they may have been to a sporting event (not football in July, though) and are now on their way home; four of them are facing me, a fact I find threatening (the use of the word 'confronted' in the exercise probably led you to assume that the situation was potentially violent; what difference would it have made if I'd written 'in front of this group' or 'with this group' do you think?).

In order to reach this interpretation of the situation I have used a whole series of assumptions, such as the fact that it is a norm of our society that older people tend to be more responsible. I have used the setting (time and place) and my understanding of clothing codes (if they were all wearing dinner jackets or tramps' clothing, my understanding of the situation would be very different) to guess their reasons for being there. My knowledge of the potential for inner-city violence, gained through news reports, warns me that the situation is potentially dangerous to me.

If I had suffered violence in the past in a similar situation, I would probably be scared. If they were six women, or men I knew, then I wouldn't be afraid at all. If I were a woman, then I imagine the situation would be even more threatening.

Any interpretation of the world that we make depends on who we are and our previous experiences in life. What should be clear is that we *interpret* what our eyes are seeing all the time.

If we consider the situation further, and look at the body language of each individual in the photograph, we find we have more (coded) information that we can interpret. From left to right:

1. looks slightly disbelieving ('How did we miss that bus?') or perhaps surprised
2. has a cheerful expression on his face but, while undoubtedly male, wears his hair in a pony-tail, which is not conventional
3. partially obscured by person 4, so difficult to draw any conclusions
4. again very calm – if anything, he has a cheerful expression
5. looks angry and mean, and is staring straight at me! His arms are at his side as if he's ready for anything!
6. thoughtful ('What shall we do now we've missed the bus?'), or possibly has an itchy chin.

If everyone had the same expression as No. 5 I'd have been very worried, but overall they seem a harmless group.

Because there is no verbal communication between me and the group, I have used their body language to interpret what they might be thinking. These codes are part of non-verbal communication (NVC).

1.3 Non-verbal communication (NVC)

In assessing the young men individually, I have been reading their body language, which is one aspect of non-verbal communication (NVC). NVC is a particularly important channel of communication which all human beings use – with the exception of those who are severely mentally ill or have developmental disorders – often unconsciously.

Michael Argyle, in *The Psychology of Interpersonal Behaviour* (1983), describes eight aspects of NVC:

- facial expression
- gaze
- gestures and other bodily movements
- bodily posture
- bodily contact
- spatial behaviour
- clothes and appearance
- non-verbal aspects of speech (for example, tone of voice or grunting agreement).

Each of these aspects has its own code with which, as fully socialized members of Western society (that is, from northern Europe, North America or Australasia), we are all quite familiar.

EXERCISE 1.2

Using any photographs of people, such as those in a family album, describe the meaning of as many codes of NVC as you can.

Because we all understand the codes of NVC, to a greater or lesser extent, there is little point in explaining them in detail here. However, it is worth pointing out that while most people assume such codes to be based on common sense, psychological experiments have shown that most of them are, in reality, culture-specific. This means that they too, like language, are learned. Just as we learn language as a child, we also learn how to communicate non-verbally; then we spend our lives using NVC without even thinking about it, just as we can usually speak without having to consider consciously what we want to say.

A few examples of NVC

- *Facial expression.* Eyebrows are important features in facial expression (indeed, I used them in assessing the mood of characters No. 1 and No. 5 in the photograph in Figure 1.1). Argyle describes the following meanings of eyebrows: fully raised = disbelief; half-raised = surprise; normal = no comment; half-lowered = puzzled; fully lowered = angry (1983: 33).
- *Gaze.* This term is used to describe the focus of a person's look and is a particularly powerful form of NVC. When the gazes of two people's meet, this is known as *eye contact*, which can be particularly meaningful. We are familiar with the cliché of lovers gazing into each other's eyes, and the manic stare of a psychopath. When analysing images, we should be particularly interested in gaze: are the people in the image looking directly at the audience, at each other, or out of the edge of the frame?

  To test the power of gaze, the next time you're engaged in conversation with someone, just look into their eyes and wait for their, and your own, reaction (don't choose someone with a violent disposition to practise this on, though).
- *Gestures.* Another experiment you might like to try is engaging in conversation without moving your hands. It is exceptionally rare for someone who is explaining not to make gestures with their hands. Once

you are conscious of the gestures you are making as you talk, the effect can be quite comic. In a classroom situation, watch your teacher's hand movements and if they ask 'Are there any questions?', say: 'Why do you move your hands like that?'

- *Posture.*   This also communicates much information, from the slovenly pose of the lazy student to the erect stance of an officious teacher.
- *Body contact.*   This is restricted in many Western societies (I'm sure it is also in many non-Western societies, but I cannot speak about them with any confidence) as it conveys a high degree of intimacy unless it happens in a professional context – at the doctor's, for example – or forms part of etiquette, like shaking hands. Both the professional context and etiquette possess their own sets of codes that define what is permitted.
- *Clothes and appearance.*   Whether we like it or not, the clothes we wear make a statement about us. We may be hysterically fashionable or the person who has no sense of how to combine colours. Uniforms are formal declarations, often of authority; types of clothing may be associated with a sub-culture (for example, leather-jacketed bikers). Even our haircut makes a statement – from the long-hair of hippies (man!) to the shaven heads of the skinheads.

Because these non-verbal rules are learned, they change as society changes. This is also true of language; one of the reasons the literature from more than 100 years ago can be difficult to read, at least at first, is because the meaning of some words has changed. In *Keywords* (1976) – a particularly interesting text for Media Studies students – Raymond Williams describes how the meanings of certain terms have altered.

Similarly, different cultures have different norms. A Venezuelan friend found the rules of spatial behaviour in Britain difficult to come to terms with at first, as the British require more body space than is conventional in South America. When he returned home, however, he found he was backing away when holding a conversation. In terms of his non-verbal behaviour he had become a fully-fledged, insular Brit.

We spend every second of our waking lives unconsciously interpreting the information our senses receive from our environment. This interpretation is possible because we automatically follow the codes we have learnt in order to give meaning to the world, whether these are linguistic or non-verbal. If we had to do all this decoding consciously, we would probably go mad from information overload.

Incidentally, the men in the image in Figure 1.1 were half-way through a stag day (the thoughtful one is, appropriately, the 'stag'). Despite this, they weren't threatening. At the time, they were waiting for the eighth member of their party, having spent the day losing money at the racetrack. I was, in fact, standing in the imagined position, taking the photograph.

We must next consider the difference between interpreting the world around us and analysing images.

EXERCISE 1.3

Using the above information, interpret any non-verbal behaviour in an advertisement of your choice, and use your own experience to decode anything else that is being communicated.

1.4 Textual analysis

The word 'photography' is from the Greek, meaning 'writing with light'. While we would not question the need to read writing, we often do not realize that we also have to read images. We might assume that, because photographs usually look like the 'real world', they simply reflect reality and so all we need to do is to look at them to understand them. The first objective in Media Studies should be to move from this passive 'consumption' of images to an active reading of them. This is *textual analysis*.

The object of textual analysis is to understand how the meaning of a text is created (whether it be a novel, a film, a TV programme, an image, a web page or anything else). In the context, or discourse, of Media Studies, text means any artefact that contains information communicated via a medium. So text is not, as it is traditionally understood, merely written material: *Coronation Street* is considered just as much a text as Charles Dickens' *Oliver Twist*, and *The Simpsons* TV programme is as much a text as *The Times* newspaper.

When analysing texts, whether they are advertisements, films, television and so on, it is common to distinguish between their form and their content. This distinction can be applied to any text, whether it is an image-based text (such as a film), a written one (a novel) or a combination of words and images (such as magazines).

- Form refers to the medium of the text: for example, books, films, music
- The content is what is in the text. For example, Suzuki Kozi's novel *Dark Water* was originally published in 1996 and followed by graphic novel and film versions in 2002. While these are, narratively, essentially the same, the form inevitably changes how the text is experienced.

Whilst it is assumed that the texts considered in the next section are created using a camera, all the points made can be applied just as easily to images that are drawn or computer-generated. Initially, we shall concentrate on aspects of images to be analysed without specific reference to their meaning; however, it must be borne in mind that, during analysis, these aspects are only interesting because of the meanings they generate.

1.5 Form

Although information about how a text was created can be very useful, that information is often not available. In most analyses, it is sufficient to assume that all the information we require is available in the text.

Framing

When analysing images, the formal aspects are almost wholly related to the image's frame.

We are accustomed to seeing frames on paintings, even if we pay no attention to them, but we often consider that snapshots – such as that shown in Figure 1.1 – do not have a frame. This is not the case. All images have frames – the frame is the boundary between the image and what surrounds it: the image's edge.

The frame defines the position from which the image is perceived. It's the border between the space we are allowed to see, and what is out of our sight. The relationship between on-screen and off-screen space is particularly important in film and television and will be discussed later.

The formal aspects that the frame does not determine are: the depth of field (what is in focus) and the quality of film (or related technology, such as video) used to create the image.

Frame dimensions and shape   All frames have a shape: an A4 piece of paper measures 211mm x 298mm and its shape depends on whether it is portrait or landscape. For example, a picture of a man and woman together that is long and narrow (portrait) will emphasize their closeness more than a wider frame (landscape) that allows the viewer to see more detail of what is around them.

Image dimensions are usually given in ratios, rather than in height and width, because the same image can vary enormously in size. If you get your photographs printed it is common to get larger prints of those you particularly like: the print will have changed in size but the ratio between the top/bottom and sides will have remained the same.

The Academy ratio is 1:1.37; this means that the image is one-third longer than it is high, so 1m in height = 1.37m in width, and 5m in height = 6.65m in width, and so on. This ratio has historical precedents in painting.

Figure 1.2   Academy ratio (1:1.37)

For many years the standard format of television was 4:3 (the same ratio as 1:1.33). During the 1950s, as a way of competing with TV, films started to be made in wide-screen formats, but when they were shown on television, part of the original image was cut off. Contemporary wide-screen TVs are 16:9 (1:1.78), roughly the same dimension as most films. However, films in formats such as CinemaScope still require black bands at the top and bottom to 'letterbox' the frame.

Figure 1.3   CinemaScope (up to 1.2.66)

Similarly, we are all used to seeing different-sized television screens, but just because we are watching a portable TV doesn't mean that we don't get the same picture as on the 127cm wide-screen television in the lounge; it's just a smaller version of the same image. What doesn't vary is the relationship between the image's height and width; this is called the *aspect ratio*. The standard cinema film dimension for many years was the *Academy ratio*, named after the Hollywood Academy that standardized it in the 1930s.

Angle   The angle of vision refers to the camera's angle in relation to the vertical; the most common is the 'straight on' position. Otherwise, the camera will be at a high (clearly above the object) or low (below the object) angle.

- *A low angle* is often used to indicate a position of power. The audience is forced to look up at a character and, as such, low angles are used conventionally to represent heroes.
- Similarly, a *high-angle* shot necessitates the audience looking down at a character (or object) and suggests that the character is in a subservient position. It should be stressed that just because a high-angle shot is used, it doesn't necessarily mean that the person is in a subservient position; this is merely a convention, and the true meaning is determined by the context. A shot that is directly over the scene is a *bird's-eye* view shot.

High angle

Low angle

Figure 1.4 High- and low-angle shots

Figure 1.5 Level canted left and right

Height   Height is obviously the height at which the shot is taken. The most common height is at eye-level, just under 2 metres.

Level   The level refers to the camera's horizontal angle. As with the vertical angle, the norm is 'straight on', or zero degrees. However, the camera can also be canted on its side to the left or right, so the shot could appear as in Figure 1.5.

Distance   Finally, distance simply refers to the distance of the object from the camera. There are seven categories (the descriptions in parentheses are given as examples):

1.   extreme long shot (a landscape)
2.   long shot (a group of people)

Figure 1.6a Long shot   **Figure 1.6b** Close-up

3. medium shot (one or two people)
4. medium close-up (part of body)
5. close-up (face)
6. extreme close-up (part of face).

Look at Figure 1.6, for example, which shows the same person shot in long shot and close-up. It isn't necessary to define these precisely: one person's medium close-up might be another's medium shot; it's their function, which I shall consider later, that matters.

EXERCISE 1.4

Using the advertisement you used for Exercise 1.3, add all the formal aspects present to your analysis.

Depth of field   This refers to the distance between the nearest and furthest area from the camera that is in focus. Deep focus photography will have the whole scene in focus, whereas a more conventional style will highlight objects within the frame by having the background out of focus. The depth of field can be altered during the shot – a rack focus – and so change what is in (and out) of focus; this technique is an example of 'intensified continuity' – see below.

A soft focus effect can also be created by using special lenses or filters that prevent the appearance of hard edges in the image. This can be used to give a glamorous, or romantic, look to a scene.

Lens type   The standard single-lens reflex for still cameras is 50–55mm for 35mm film and is commonly held to approximate human sight. Wide-angle lenses, which are used for deep focus photography, make the scene appear deeper than it actually is, so objects in the frame seem to be further away than they are in reality. An extreme wide-angle lens gives a 'fish-eye' effect, in which everything is distorted.

A telephoto lens creates the opposite effect, pulling objects closer together; for example, athletes running toward a camera can seem to be running in a very tight group until a cut to a side shot shows the actual distance they are apart.

The stock, or type, of film   This refers to the speed at which the film responds to light. A fast stock will tend to produce grainy images and is used in low light or to shoot fast-moving objects, while a slow stock will give a fine-grained image but will require plenty of light.

A slow stock is the norm in cinema, though digital cameras are increasingly being used. For television, digital video (DV) and, increasingly, high definition (HD) is used. These are formats that are much cheaper to use than film and can offer very similar picture quality.

The mobile frame   All we have considered so far are still images, but many images we see are moving, whether in the cinema or on television. Indeed, the word cinematography means 'recording movement'. The mobile frame could encompass all the elements described so far in one shot, though this would be highly unlikely.

There are seven types of moving images:

1. *Pan* (short for panorama), in which the camera moves horizontally from a static position. A pan could move through the 360 degrees of a circle. A pan that moves very quickly, blurring the scene, is a *whip pan*
2. *Tilt,* where the camera moves up or down, in effect a vertical pan
3. *Cant,* where the static camera tilts left or right
4. *Dolly,* in which the camera moves on tracks, giving a particularly smooth movement. This can be forward into a scene or backward out of it (a push in or out), or run parallel to the action (tracking)
5. *Crane,* in which the camera is moved on a device that can move up, down and laterally
6. *Handheld,* which gives the frame a shaky look, particularly when it moves; often used to indicate a subjective shot (that is, we are seeing in the same way as the character)
7. *Zoom (telephoto)* is technically not movement at all. The camera stays still and the focal length is altered during the shot, taking the viewer closer

(the zoom), or further away (wide angle) from the object. What doesn't change, though, is the aspect – we are still looking at the object from exactly the same position.

These are the main formal features that should be investigated in any analysis of the mobile frame.

To state whether an image is, say, a high-angle shot, from floor level, tilted to the right, tracking left is, however, only the first part of the analysis. It is considering the text at the level of denotation. Analysis does not simply describe the features of a text but also shows what they *mean*. But before we consider the meaning of the formal aspects of the text, we should investigate the second component of analysis: content.

1.6 *Mise en scène*

The term *mise en scène* means literally 'put on stage' and is used in Film Studies to demonstrate the film director's control of everything that appears in the film frame. When analysing *mise en scène* we must assume that everything in the picture has been put there for a reason; it is a series of codes waiting to be interpreted.

There are three main components of *mise en scène* analysis: the subject, the lighting and the setting of the image.

The subject

The subject of an image may be a person, or a number of people; in fact, it can be anything that is foregrounded. It may represent reality or be something completely abstract. It may be the only thing within the picture or there may be many subjects, making it difficult to work out what is, in fact, the subject of the image.

When trying to make sense of the subject we bring our cultural knowledge, our understanding of social rules, to bear on it. For example, we know that a vehicle with four wheels on a road is most likely to be a motor-car; however someone who has never heard of such an item would be unable to name it. If the subject is a person, then we would consider all the aspects of non-verbal communication (NVC) as we did when analysing Figure 1.1.

The positions in which subjects are placed form the image's composition. The main subject of an image is usually placed one-third of the way across the image from either edge; this convention arises because the 'natural' position for a subject – the middle – would divide the image in half, which can be aesthetically displeasing. In conjunction with this, the horizon, if present, should be placed either one-third or two-thirds up the composition. This convention is called the 'rule of thirds'. (Applying these rules to your own photography will give it a more professional look, if that's what you desire).

The lighting

The lighting of an image may be daylight or, more usually, additional lighting. Light can be used in numerous expressive (coded) ways. For example, with the use of filters, daylight can be made to look like moonlight (a technique called *la nuit americaine*). Alternatively, lack of light – in the form of shadows – might be used to conceal someone or something.

The lighting in many of the images you will study will not be natural, and even if it is 'natural' lighting – that is, the light used is what is available – for the purposes of analysis it is still assumed to be making an expressive point. After all, in most cases, the producer chose not to use artificial light, or chose that particular position in relation to the sun.

There are three main aspects to the study of lighting:

1. where the lighting is coming from: front, side, back, above or below?
2. is the lighting of equal intensity? (this is unlikely)
3. the colour of the light.

The most common form of lighting is 'three-point lighting' made up of the *key*, *fill* and *back* light.

*   *The key light* is the main source of illumination and is directed on the subject, from approximately 45 degrees above and to one side of the camera. It is a hard, direct light which produces sharply defined shadows.
*   *The fill light* is a soft or indirect light that 'fills in' the shadows formed by the key light.
*   Unsurprisingly, *the back light* shines from behind the subject, usually to differentiate it from the background. It can also give a halo effect around a subject's head; this is often used in glamour photography.

High-key lighting is where the scene is evenly, and brightly, lit. This is the most commonly used form as it allows more rapid shooting of a scene. In contrast, low-key lighting, which will have very little fill lighting, requires a careful set-up. Here, the contrast between light and dark is used for expressive purposes, such as the deep shadows of *film noir*, for example.

In most audio-visual texts, the colours in a scene will be very carefully chosen by the designer. The type of lighting used by the cinematographer will greatly affect the look of these colours. In addition, whereas lighting is often used simply to illuminate the action and setting, it can also be used in an expressionist fashion. For example, characters who have half of their faces obscured by shadow might suggest that the person has a hidden side.

The setting

The setting is self-explanatory; we would have different expectations, for example, of a tropical setting to one in the Arctic. Imagine people wearing swimsuits in the latter; *Cool Runnings* (1993) was advertised with the incongruous image of Jamaicans in the snow.

It is useful to split the image into *foreground* and *background*, or figure and ground. Usually the subject, being the most important part of the image, occupies the former and the setting forms the background. The setting itself is usually used to support the action, but can itself be the focus of a text, such as in documentaries on the natural world.

EXERCISE 1.5

Now add the above to the analysis of your advertisement from Exercise 1.3.

1.7 Making meaning

While it might seem obvious that meaning resides in a text, without an audience the meaning can never be communicated (just as Bishop Berkeley questioned whether it was necessary for someone to perceive trees in order for them to exist). In addition, if meaning wholly existed in the text, then the task of analysis would be only to unpack this message. Assuming a text had an unambiguous meaning, then *all* analysis of that text would be the same. As we shall see, meaning isn't necessarily clear in a text, and even if it was, not every member of an audience would agree on the same reading. We shall consider the way audiences can read text in the next section.

As the media, by its nature, is concerned with communication, there has to be socially agreed conventions that allow producers to ensure that audiences have a good chance of understanding what they are trying to say. So far we have considered only what the codes are – NVC, angle, distance and so on at the level of denotation. What codes usually *mean* depends upon a consensus, and this is the level of connotation (see also section 2.2).

Table 1.1 Examples of codes and their conventional meanings

Formal aspect	Conventional meaning
Angle	
High	Subservient position
Normal	Neutral
Low	Position of power
Distance	
Long shot	Sets a scene and/or places subjects into context
Medium shot	Places audience at a 'safe' distance, near enough to observe but not intrude
Close-up	Places audience in an intimate position and signifies an emotional moment
Composition	
Conventional (symmetrical/ rule of thirds)	Posed, calm composition
Unconventional (asymmetrical)	Documentary style, real life as it happens
Dynamic	Disturbance, conflict (see, for example, Figure 1.10)
Static	Calm
Depth of field	
Deep focus	Expressive, *mise en scène* very important
Selective focus	indicates what is important in scene
Soft focus	Nostalgia and/or romance
Lens type	
Telephoto	Voyeuristic
Standard	Normal
Wide angle	Drama
Film stock	
Fast (grainy look)	Documentary style, looks 'real'
Slow (high resolution)	Normal
Mobile frame	
Pan	To survey an area or follow a subject at a distance
Tracking	To follow a movement from close proximity
Tilt	To follow a movement up or down
Crane	To dramatically move toward or away from a subject
Handheld	Point-of-view shot
Zoom in (telephoto)	Allows us to see more detail from a distance
Zoom out (wide angle)	Places subject into context
Lighting	
High key	Optimistic
Low key	Sombre
Fill	Natural; a lack of fill creates extreme contrast between light and dark; often seen in *film noir*
Back	Glamour; creates a halo effect around the head

It is, to some extent, a false exercise to analyse codes on their own, because their meaning is usually determined by the other factors, such as the context in which they appear and the message being conveyed. We can, however, give some examples of what codes conventionally mean before considering the other parts of the communication. As these codes are socially constructed, they vary in different societies. We shall consider here conventional meaning in Western society (though that does not mean they don't have a similar meaning elsewhere) and, in section 1.9, we shall look at other cultures. This will also serve as a revision of points made so far; however, it must be emphasized that the presence of a high-angle shot will not *guarantee* that a subservient position is being represented.

EXERCISE 1.6

Analyse and compare Figures 1.7 and 1.8, using what you have learnt in the chapter. List the denotative elements first before considering connotation.

Figure 1.7 Rita Hayworth in *Gilda* (1946)

Figure 1.8   Housewife and child

A brief analysis of the two images is given on page 24. This is not the 'right answer' to Exercise 1.6 (there isn't one), but it does demonstrate that codes can be used to read the images.

Neither of these images has a clear message. In terms of denotation, Gilda, the character being played by Rita Hayworth in the eponymous film, is analysed first.

It should be no surprise if your list differs from mine. I hesitated over designating smoking as 'cool' as the social consensus about smoking is changing, particularly in the UK, where it has been banned in public buildings.

The most striking formal aspect of Figure 1.7 is the lighting. Hayworth is shot for glamour with an emphasis on the backlighting, which creates a halo effect in her hair and emphasizes her 'hour-glass' figure by clearly delineating the shape of her waist and hips.

Denotation	Connotation
Smoking with the cigarette held upwards	Slightly transgressive; cool
Has her head tilted to one side and her eyes appear to be looking at the audience	A sexy, assertive pose
Is wearing a black, strapless dress that hugs her figure	Sophisticated; sexy
Is loosely holding a fur wrap	Wealthy; owns a fur and doesn't mind it dragging on the floor; decadent
Is set against a black background	An abstract setting, highlighting the character's sexiness; there's nothing to distract us from her
Low-angle shot	She is in a position of power.
High key lighting (however, there is a clear shadow cast by her hand)	Glamorous, but also slightly sinister claw-like shadow

The low angle of the shot puts her in a position of dominance, as does her gaze, which is directly at us. The half-closed eyes are calculating, as is her pose, with head to one side: it is as if she is deciding what to do with us. Hayworth's glamorous image is also reinforced by make-up, particularly on her lips, which are half-parted in a seductive fashion. The lips are ready for the cigarette, held in an assertive position, the smoke from it caught by the key light, helping to create a 'smouldering' atmosphere.

The key light also creates the only clear shadow in the image, that of her hand holding the cigarette. Her long fingernails cast a rather vicious shadow on to her chest, suggesting that her assertiveness borders on aggression. The cat-like claws link with the fur she is holding in her other hand. The fur is a sign of luxury and decadence (particularly as she is trailing it along the floor), and she appears to have taken it from around her shoulders. Clearly, this is the image of a 'sexy' woman. However, the fur draws our attention to the elaborate ring (showing wealth) on her left hand, and thus to the fact she is married. While the image suggests that this woman is sexually available to men, the ring hints at transgression: any sexual relationship with her would be adulterous.

Gilda is given no context, and the background is black. She appears to be an abstraction of feminine sexuality, at once alluring and dangerous and is therefore a typical *femme fatale* of *film noir*.

Now to an analysis of Figure 1.8.

Denotation	Connotation
Woman and young boy baking	Mother and son
They are wearing 'everyday clothing'	They are ordinary people
Woman is smiling	The mother is enjoying cooking with her son
Kitchen setting	They are in their home
Back door open	It is a warm day
Deep focus	The context is as important as the subjects; they are in harmony with their setting

Figure 1.8 shows a housewife and mother. The lighting is naturalistic, signifying that it is a realist image; this could be a photograph taken by the woman's husband. The work of the housewife, and mother, is shown to be fun; she is smiling and can prepare an elaborate-looking meal and look after 'junior' at the same time. The open door, showing a back garden, suggests the weather is warm, which adds to the positive atmosphere that has been created.

The deep focus of the image allows us to see the scene in detail. The counter draws our eye towards the back wall and we see the paraphernalia of cooking. The woman's dress is plain and practical, as is her hairstyle. The proximity of mother and child suggests that they are working as a team, and while the woman is leaning across the child, her smile negates any possibility that he is getting in the way.

Could the woman in the kitchen be represented as Gilda was? Probably, but the worlds of domesticity and eroticism are usually represented as being very different and often inhabited by different types of people. This raises questions about the representation of women in particular, and gender in general – see Chapter 5. Imagine how our understanding of Gilda would change if she were to be placed in the kitchen setting.

Meaning is also conveyed by the medium in which the text is carried. Each medium has its own technology and a particular set of codes and conventions – its media language – to convey its message.

1.8 Medium and the message

Cinema projects the film image on to a screen and individuals (spectators) usually experience it as a member of an audience. In cinema, the image is also often the prime provider of information, even over-riding the dialogue. In *Citizen Kane* (USA, 1940), directed by Orson Welles, the scene where the young Kane is adopted takes place in his parents' hut, and we hear the conversation concerning the boy. Kane is playing outside in the snow, and Welles' use of deep focus places the boy at the centre of the *mise en scène* as the audience can see him, through a window, playing in the distance with his sled. The significance of this is revealed only at the end.

Going to the cinema is usually a social event (most people don't like going on their own), and there is an almost ceremonial aspect to the visit – including the buying of sugared water and saturated fats from which exhibitors actually make their profits.

During the film, an audience's reaction can greatly influence how the film is experienced. This is particularly the case in horror and comedy, where screaming and laughter, respectively, are particularly infectious behaviours. While these often enhance the experience, adverse audience reaction can result in a different way of understanding the meaning. For example, a contributor known as danleary25 described his experience of viewing *Appleseed* (*Appurushîdo*, Japan, 2004) on the Internet movie database (http://www.imdb.com/title/tt0401233/usercomments; accessed April 2007):

> Once the film started the reaction was good. Everyone (including myself) seemed stunned by the visuals, and if not impressed at least forgiving of the Matrix style slow-mo shots. But about forty minutes in people began laughing. Unfortunately the laughter was actually coming from the ridiculous nature of many clichéd and over dramatized moments. The first of which came when the character Hitomi, an emotionally engineered 'Bioriod', [*sic*] wonders what it would be like if she was able to love, leading a soft piano chord to swell onto the soundtrack. The entire audience actually burst into laughter. Sadly to say Appleseed has quite a few more moments that caused the same reaction.

The laughter was a result of what appeared, to Western eyes, to be 'corny' emotive scenes. It's highly likely that these would play differently in East Asia, where melodramatic, emotive texts are more conventional.

Television is an electronic medium that sends both sound and visual information. There has been an increasing emphasis on television as an interactive medium, allowing viewers to choose what to view from libraries of programmes, or to purchase goods and services. There has also been a development towards large, flat-screen televisions (though, to date, these have not offered improved picture quality over the cathode ray tube – CRT). Sound, neglected by the television industry for many years, is increasingly heard via multi-speaker systems, allowing audiences to experience the often-wonderfully designed soundscapes of films.

Television relies more heavily on words to convey information, as the image it beams into our homes is not as rich or as detailed as in the cinema. Although the arrival of high definition (HD) may change this, the institution of television is likely to continue to favour the script over the director for some time.

Radio is also electronically transmitted, usually in a broadcast form (analogue and digital), although it is also available on cable and via the internet. Radio can also be transmitted locally through induction. Most information is transmitted by sound (but digital radio allows for text to be displayed too). Different acoustics are used to create an outdoor or indoor settings. A reverberant acoustic could be used to signify a large hall, or swimming pool. Radio is often played in the background and so doesn't necessarily demand our complete attention.

Both television and radio are characterized by 'flow' rather than consisting of discrete texts; 24-hour broadcasts obviously have no beginning or end. In order to structure this incessant flow, segments are used; these can be the programmes themselves, often sub-divided in segments such as the title sequence, the station ident, trailers for future programmes and so on; see Williams (1974).

Print media are purely visual; they are usually distributed physically but can be transmitted electronically using email and facsimile (fax) machines via the telephone network. Print media include newspapers, magazines, books and posters; with the exception of the latter, these are usually experienced privately, because we read them silently (this was not always the case; early newspapers were often read to an illiterate audience, leading to discussion of current issues among a community).

The text most affected by the channel of communication is film. Film is seen at its best in the cinema, but most films are watched on television, whether they're broadcast or on DVD (digital video disc). The quality of the image on a standard television set is poor when compared with that in a cinema: the audiences are literally seeing different things; HD TV is an improvement, but still doesn't match cinema projection. Spectacular films lose the most on the small screen, and some films become almost meaningless; for example, director Peter Greenaway's films can be virtually unwatchable on TV.

As mentioned in section 1.5, the aspect ratio is important. For many years, the 4:3 format of television necessitated wide-screen films to be 'panned and scanned'. Here, a shot would be reframed by focusing on the main action, leaving out (usually) the sides of the original frame (Wikipedia has an excellent demonstration at http://en.wikipedia.org/wiki/Pan_%26_scan). The advent of DVD, and wide-screen television, has ameliorated this problem; DVD is also improving the quality of home video by approximately doubling the picture quality and so matching the usual broadcast standard.

Video is also important, because it gives the audience power to stop, pause, rewind, review or fast forward a text. This makes it an excellent resource for Media Studies students who are studying sequences, but has also contributed to 'moral panics' about 'video nasties': it is imagined that 'innocent' children will use it to 'analyse' particularly gory or pornographic bits of film.

Computer games are usually experienced, like television, in a domestic setting, though it's as likely that this is the bedroom as the living room. In addition, they are usually played on a TV set or a computer monitor; however, at this point, the similarity with television ends. The key difference of contact between the computer games and their audiences is the fact that games are *played* while most other media texts are *read*. Games are inherently interactive, so the users of this medium are probably the least passive consumers of any media texts.

While most of the media noted above are probably more likely to be consumed as a social activity (except possibly radio), gamers are often represented as solitary individuals. James Newman (2004) argues this is a myth relying on a 'moral panic' viewpoint about the medium that betrays a misunderstanding of the activity. Arcade games, for example, are often played in a group. Gamers also tend to form supportive social networks offering advice on how to play the games. And many games are designed for more than one player, of course; indeed, games intended for sole play can be played by more than one person by simply taking turns.

The *internet* has been cited as the reason for the large decline in the number of people watching television as well as causing a drop in the circulation of newspapers and certain magazine sectors, such as the 'lads' mags'. It seemed as though computers' ability to mediate sound, text and images (moving or otherwise) would simply replace these traditional media. However, fuelled primarily by the growth of broadband connections, which allows large packets of data to be accessed, the use of computers, and games consoles, have evolved from simply being an electronic form of Old Media (essentially the media in existence before computer games) into Web 2.0.

Essentially, Web 2.0 allows audiences to become producers and so find their own audiences. Key aspects of Web 2.0 are blogs, podcasts, social networking, tagging and wikis. While some of these (blogging and wikis are written texts; podcasts are radio, and so on) are similar to Old Media, social networking and tagging has fundamentally altered the way we can experience media texts.

Of course, in considering the internet, we need to redefine what we mean by a media text. Films are discrete texts (though they can be accompanied by a variety of ancillary texts – such as games or compact discs (CDs) – each text is separate), but television and radio texts are experienced as part of a broadcast

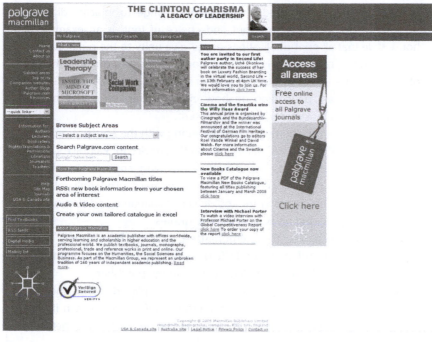

Figure 1.9 Palgrave's home page

'flow'. Hyperlinks allow the user to switch between pages as quickly as changing channels with a remote control, but with far more texts available. The conventional use of a *home page* gives a website a stability that is more apparent than real; it may be best to consider one website as a text with the same URL (uniform resource locator), but with different pages accessed by use of the forward-slash symbol (/).

Box 1.2   Analysis of www.palgrave.com

As would be expected from an academic publisher, the home page presents a lot of information in a straightforward fashion. Like magazines and newspapers, a six-column grid structures the page, with a very flexible attitude towards column width; the fifth column is noticeably wider. Traditionally, print publications had a pre-defined width necessitated by hot press printing technology, and while this is much more flexible now, the column grid is still used to lay pages out.

The colour is predominantly blue, which connotes academic 'coolness' as well as being a trustworthy colour (don't ask me why, but designers use it as such). The left-hand column and the bar along the top operate as a template for the rest of the site, though the colours change to indicate different sections. This consistency in layout and choice of font, is an example of house style that all print publications use to give unity to the publication.

A search engine is regularly found on home pages, as a guide to the rest of the site. The left-hand column acts as a contents page here, but the search engine can, depending on how effective it is, be a very helpful device when you looking for a particular item.

The language of the home page is in keeping with the academic emphasis. Despite the site being essentially a marketing device for Palgrave's publications, the hyperbole associated with advertising copy is absent; key words include 'subject', 'information' and 'interest'. The only obvious advertisement is the banner at the top, which is animated and shows three different images, including positive review quotes.

New media technologies are emphasized: RSS web-feed format, audio and video content, and the Second Life party for authors. This suggests that Palgrave is up-to-date and a modern, cutting-edge publisher.

Although the marketing aspect of the site is played down, the 'My Palgrave' invitation personalizes the publisher, as if we could own it, in a way that is common in marketing. The idea is that the relationship between publisher and consumer will be mutually beneficial.

The typeface used for 'palgrave macmillan' and the logo were analysed in *Media Institutions and Audiences*:

> The typeface is elegant with the 'classy' dropping of the upper case first letter. The word itself is unusual, clearly a name, possibly connoting seriousness, '... grave'. The logo is star-like, reaching out (to the reader?).
> (Lacey 2002: 3)

Overall, the page is an effective portal to the rest of the site. It offers plenty of information and markets its products unobtrusively.

1.9 Context and meaning

In simple terms, texts are intended, by the producer, to convey meaning to the audience. However, there can be no certainty that the individuals in the audience will read the text in the way it is intended; for example, an advertisement's message is usually about the effectiveness of the product or service being promoted, but anyone may disagree with, or misunderstand, the text.

Texts are, in most instances, very easy to understand; after all, most producers want to communicate clearly to the audience. So they use codes and conventions that are readily understood by the target audience. The exceptions to this are texts that want to make the audience work at creating meaning; Arthouse cinema occasionally seems to relish being obscure, sometimes to the point of suggesting that there may in fact be no message or meaning to impart. The ambiguity of the ending of *Hidden* (*Cache*, France, 2005) was clearly an important aspect of the film.

On other occasions, the message is not understood because the audience has no knowledge of a text's codes, possibly because he or she is not part of the target audience. These codes, of course, can be learnt; anybody can learn to appreciate, say, Cubist art, or opera.

In most cases, images are used to illustrate and reinforce the message, and, as we shall see in the next section, words are often used to anchor the image's meaning. An exception to this for many years in Britain was cigarette advertising, which was heavily reliant upon the image because it was illegal to use words to state anything positive about the product.

Clearly, in silent cinema, the image alone must carry virtually all the information about the narrative. The only other channels available are intertitles, which give written information on screen to the audience, and the accompanying music and sound effects.

While images are clearly the most important bearer of the message in photography and painting, the artefact's title is bound to influence an audience's reading of the text. Leonardo da Vinci's *Mona Lisa* could have been entitled 'Virtue' or 'Whore', thus creating, possibly, completely opposite messages.

In popular music, image and sound invariably come together. The music and lyrics carry most of the message, but it is important that the artist 'looks the part'. An artist looking like REM's Michael Stipe but singing a bland, romantic 'Europop' song, would be incongruous; whereas, say, Snoop Dogg's look suits his music.

So far, we have been considering how texts convey meaning in isolation. However, the context in which the text is read can easily have as much of an influence on our understanding as the text itself. The effect that context has on meaning can readily be seen by imagining how the meaning is altered in different situations. For example, earlier, you analysed an image of Rita Hayworth in a Media Studies context. If you put the same image in a different situation, say on a bedroom wall, it would communicate differently. One is less likely to respond to a poster on a wall by analysing its formal codes; desire might be a more likely response.

Similarly, your reading of the housewife would be very different if it were in your family album, which you were looking at in your home. Looking at a family album in class, however, would return it to an educational context.

Particular media are associated with specific social contexts. For example, the institutional context of cinema creates, in the audience, certain expectations: the dimming of the lights is a cue that the performance is about to begin; it is common for sweets to be eaten during the performance; and the back row used to be for snogging couples.

Much of our media experience takes place in the home, which may be a family setting (with competing voices) or a one-person household. In many households it is normal to 'talk over' the radio or even the television, but this would be frowned on in a cinema.

The people present when a text is being experienced can also alter the context in which it is being consumed, so watching a sexually explicit film can be embarrassing for adolescents and parents in each other's company, whereas enjoyment is the more likely emotion if each generation was watching the scene on their own.

Think of the different experiences you have when watching texts in an academic context compared to the home, where the emphasis is usually on entertainment. How do you feel when your academic knowledge of, say, the codes at work in images, starts to impinge on your 'normal' viewing habits (many students have 'complained' about not being able to watch films any more without thinking about them!)?

Regardless of who the audience is, the medium the text is conveyed by, or the context in which a text is consumed, meaning can only be communicated successfully if both producer and audience share an understanding of the codes and conventions deployed.

1.10 Codes and conventions

In our earlier consideration of form and content, we described the formal codes of image analysis. Codes are objects or symbols that have a consensual meaning; in addition, less tangible things, such as light and camera angles, qualify as codes because they too have a generally agreed meaning.

There are three types of code that concern us:

* *Technical*: considered in section1.5, for example, the meaning of low angle shot or low key lighting, and are connected to particular forms of media
* *Symbolic*: considered in section 1.2 in relation to non-verbal communication and are usually social in nature; that is, they exist outside of media texts in society as a whole

- *Written or spoken*: words and speech are coded as a particular language (and entirely social in nature).

Conventions are the practices by which codes are combined by a particular medium or type of text. For example, the conventions of Hollywood cinema necessitate a realist aesthetic and so use codes that create a coherent narrative space (see section 1.12), and characters very rarely directly address the camera. In contrast, TV news has the convention that the 'characters' – the anchor and reporters – should address the camera directly. Genres also have a set of conventions and are often defined by the way they combine their particular repertoire of elements. Close analysis of texts needs to consider the use of codes in the type of text being considered.

Earlier in the chapter we considered how we interpret the world around us. It is no surprise that the media uses the codes we use in everyday life to send and interpret messages. For example, someone who lowers their eyebrows is usually angry: the position of the eyebrows is understood as a (symbolic) code for anger. It makes little difference, in terms of your reading of the code, whether this person is with us or is being represented by an image (if the individual is really angry, then it's probably better that he or she is an image!). While Exercise 1.1, where you had to imagine your response to a bunch of lads, was described as a contradiction in terms (because you were asked to imagine the image as real), as far as coding is concerned 'lack of reality' makes little difference.

However, as we have seen in our consideration of technical codes, the media does not simply draw upon codes from 'real life'. In fact, the relationship between 'real life' and the media is not one-way; how could it be, as the media forms part of the 'real world'? Indeed, the influence of the media on the 'real world' is a source of much debate: our moral guardians seem to believe that by watching 'sex 'n' violence', particularly on television, the nation's youth will become corrupt; these issues are dealt with in *Media Institutions and Audiences* (Lacey 2002). Clearly, the media does have an influence on us – who would spend money on advertising if it did not? – but the relationship is complex and hard to quantify.

To consider coding specific to the media, in addition to the technical codes already considered, we must investigate to the use of:

- anchorage
- image choice, cropping and digital manipulation
- juxtaposition
- genre
- colour.

Anchorage

We are more than capable of interpreting images that stand on their own. However, it is unusual, in the media, to see images that are unsupported by any words. In newspapers, it is a convention that a caption be used with all images; in advertising, the words range from the pithy slogan to a detailed description of products or services, and in cinema and television, the only images we do not expect to 'speak' to us are those of silent cinema.

The function of these words is to reinforce the producer's intended meaning. Roland Barthes (1977) described this function as 'anchorage': that is, the meaning of the image is anchored by the caption. For example, an image of a person sipping from a cup appears very different with the captions: 'The tea was delightful' and 'The tea was poisoned' – same image, different anchorage, therefore a different meaning.

An image's meaning can often be ambiguous. For example, Figure 1.10, taken during the 'poll tax' riots in London in 1990, shows a policeman restraining a young man, and a female onlooker appears to be getting involved.

Figure 1.10   Poll tax riots in London

(Photograph: Richard Smith, Katz)

EXERCISE 1.7

Analyse the image and write a caption that summarizes – anchors – your interpretation.

It is a useful, and fun, exercise to write your own captions to newspaper photographs: can you make the image have the opposite meaning from that intended?

Box 1.3   Analysis of Figure 1.10

The codes of dress are very important in this image. Clearly, the policeman represents authority; the young man's appearance suggests he is a non-conformist, while the woman appears to be 'respectable'. The most obvious reading (the preferred reading – see section 3.3) of this image is, I think, that the woman is giving the young man 'a piece of her mind'. Indeed, this is how the photograph was used in the press. However, the woman actually wrote to a publication which used the image and explained that, in fact, she was more concerned about police brutality and was urging the young man to stay calm (he was upset because the police had manhandled his girlfriend).

The composition of this image is dynamic as there are strong lines running horizontally through the image created by the barrier and the building in the background. The young man's lurch forward cuts across these lines and so helps to convey the conflict represented by the image.

Our socially learned expectations suggested that the young man was a troublemaker, because of his appearance; however, the truth was (apparently) very different. The only way the erroneous impression, gained by our expectations, could be eradicated is through anchorage, a caption explaining what was actually happening. The fact that the original caption did not do this may mean the image was being used to distort the truth, or the picture editor did not know the true circumstances.

Image choice, cropping and digital manipulation

Anchorage, however, is not only provided by words. The choice of image itself is a factor in determining meaning. Picture editors of newspapers will often have numerous photographs of the same event, or dramatic moment, to choose from. Their choice will be determined by what appears to them to convey the desired meaning most effectively.

Photographs are often cropped, particularly in news publications. This consists of cutting an image both to fit the space available and to emphasize the image's subject. This can be done for several reasons: to make the composition more pleasing; to cut out extraneous detail; to allow it to fit the space. However, cropping can radically alter the meaning of an image. Take, for example, the following description of a photograph of a returning soldier being hugged by a loved one:

> Zealous cropping killed the story ... [in the original] we see the discarded crutch first and then the soldier on one leg, home from Vietnam. In the cropped version it is possible to see that he has only one leg – if you look. But a newspaper picture has to catch a glancing eye in fractions of a second, and without the crutch or a pointing headline the reader may not linger enough to appreciate that this is not just another welcome-home picture. (Evans 1997: 227)

The issue of fakery in photos is not new; the 'Cottingley fairies' photographs bamboozled many into believing fairies existed in Yorkshire in 1917. However, digital photography has probably raised awareness of the potential for deception as more people manipulate photographs with software on their own computers than ever messed about in a darkroom developing pictures. In addition, high-profile examples of such manipulation have helped to raise awareness of the potential for deceit in photographs.

In 1994, *Time* magazine's front cover of a mugshot of O. J. Simpson, who had been arrested on suspicion of his wife's murder, made the culprit seem much blacker than the same image on *Newsweek*; this might lead to the conclusion that *Time* was emphasizing Simpson's ethnicity. In 2006, a Reuters photographer was sacked after it transpired he'd added smoke to a photograph of Beirut after it had been attacked by Israel. Less dramatically, in 2003, *GQ* made Kate Winslet appear thinner on their cover image than she was in reality.

It is obviously difficult to know whether an image has been digitally altered or not. However, audiences are usually just as unaware of cropping or deceptive anchorage; while the camera may not in itself tell lies, images have always been used to do so.

EXERCISE 1.8

Cut out, or create, an image, and write as many different captions as you can for it; try to create opposite meanings using the same image.

Juxtaposition

Juxtaposition means 'being placed side-by-side'. It is obvious that any other information, written or otherwise, near an image is likely to influence the reading of that image. For example, an image of a craggy, handsome man juxtaposed with a mansion on the cover of a novel would suggest that it was a romantic story. The same man, however, juxtaposed with a gun and the mansion would probably suggest a murder mystery.

The juxtaposition of images can create very different meanings from the images on their own. 'Before and after' advertisements, such as those for slimming or muscle-building products, create a narrative simply by placing the images together: 'use this product and you will be transformed from this to this'. Clearly, if the 'before and after' images were analysed in isolation, the narrative would not be present. In newspapers, similar juxtaposed images – such as photographs of a building being demolished – also imply a narrative.

Collage takes juxtaposition to extremes by placing numerous, usually unrelated, images together within a frame. These same images could be placed together in alternative ways to form a different pattern, and these would then yield different meanings.

In cinema, the power of juxtaposition is demonstrated by the 'Kuleshov effect'. During the 1920s, a Soviet film-maker, Lev Kuleshov, is reputed to have filmed an actor with a neutral expression on his face and followed this shot with various other images, such as a baby and a bowl of soup. The audience was asked to determine the actor's emotion and, despite the fact that his expression was always the same, the audience assumed he was reacting to the objects inter-cut with himself; in the first instance they interpreted the actor's expression as affection, and in the second as hunger. In other words, they assumed that the actor and the objects occupied the same space and time.

We are moving here toward a consideration of images in sequence, which will be covered later in the chapter.

Genre

Genre provides producers and audiences with a clear set of expectations that are used to interpret the text. For example, we expect to be frightened by a horror text and will be surprised if it lacks at least some of the following elements: a large, old, decrepit house with a squeaky door (brilliantly spoofed in Tim Burton's *Edward Scissorhands* (1990) when Dianne Wiest's character opens such a door and shouts 'Avon calling'); thundery weather; a cellar; blood and gore; blood-curdling screams; horrible deaths; monsters; supernatural powers and so on. An image of, say, a young woman approaching an old house has a very different meaning in a romance when compared to a horror text. Genres are obviously not restricted by a medium: a horror text can appear on television, on the radio, in the cinema or in print, and audiences will use the same generic framework for each medium.

We understand the codes of a genre through our knowledge of other texts we have experienced from the same genre. Of course, there was a point in our life when we had never seen, say, a horror movie, and so our understanding of the text as being generic would be lacking at that time.

The genre (more accurately a format) of a magazine, for example, can determine how an image is read; numerous different types of magazines could, hypothetically, use copies of the same image on their front covers and generate different meanings. An image of a woman on the cover of *Cosmopolitan* is intended to attract women, while on the cover of *Esquire* – a men's magazine – the same image could obviously be used to attract men. The image in the context of *Cosmopolitan* usually means 'buy this magazine and you could look something like this', while *Esquire*'s message reads: 'buy this magazine, and you could get to see women who look like this'. This is not to say that *Cosmo* readers actually believe that a physical transformation will take place; it is probably more in the hope that something of the glamour purveyed by the publication will rub off on to the purchaser.

Although the convention of having glamorous people on the front cover of lifestyle magazines, such as those cited above, is one that is worldwide, the actual coding of 'glamour' can itself be culturally specific. For example, when *Maxim* launched a South Korean edition they found that attractive women had better be dressed in smart outfits rather than not be dressed at all. However, when accessing the website http://www.maximkorea.com in August 2007, this convention seemed to have changed, with an image of a woman in her underwear; in the November issue, however, the model was fully clothed once more.

Similarly, it is possible to imagine the same image being used on the cover of different types of books; the meaning generated would then depend on the book's genre. For example, Figure 1.11 could be entitled *The Return of Romance*, or *Castles of England*, or *Walking in the Sussex Downs*. Each title, specifying a genre for the book, anchors the image's meaning in a slightly different way. In practice, of course, the images used are usually different because each genre has its own iconography (see below).

Part of our understanding of what genre a text is comes from the anchoring provided by the title. The appearance of a woman on the front cover of the *Angling Times* would suggest she had caught a very large fish.

It is not only titles that anchor meaning; the kind of lettering, or font, used can do the same. For example, such fonts as those used here for the words

Figure 1.11 A building in the Sussex Downs

Romantic and **Science Fiction** give a clue to the content, and blood dripping off the title will invariably indicate a crime or horror novel.

Iconography is also an important code used by genres. It refers to objects we recognize as having specific meanings when associated with a text's genre. For example, a crucifix usually represents Christianity; in a horror film it is also a totem, or weapon, against evil. A ten-gallon hat and six-shooters are indelibly linked with the 'cowboy' genre; indeed, it is probably impossible to make a Western without them. While the root of iconography is real life (in this case, the 'Wild West' of nineteenth-century North America, for most people the understanding of these codes is derived from the media – mainly films (media representation of the original 'Wild West' is usually more mythical than historical, as we shall see in section 4.7).

EXERCISE 1.9

Choose a genre (for example, horror, war, science fiction, romance) and list as many objects that you associate with it as you can.

Iconography operates in stereotyping in a very similar fashion and is seen most powerfully in advertising. Any man on a horse herding cattle is likely to be a cowboy. This image is ubiquitous (in the West at least) because of the influence of American popular forms; however, for many, the music video for

Robbie Williams' *Feel* (2002) was highly incongruous, as a 'cheeky chappie' (Williams' persona) doesn't normally ride horses.

A question for UK readers: what does a middle-aged, white man, wearing a pin-stripe suit and bowler hat, and carrying an umbrella, do for a living? Answer: something to do with finance or, more specifically, the City of London. The fact that this form of dress was the norm decades ago, and is virtually obsolete now, is irrelevant to the stereotype as long as audiences understand the code. Some stereotypes, however, have little, if any, relationship to reality. The colour of a female's hair cannot possibly have an influence on her intelligence, and yet the 'dumb blonde' is a common stereotype – see section 4.4 Types and stereotypes. Genre is dealt with fully in *Narrative and Genre* (Lacey 2000).

Before we conclude this section on codes, there are a few more we need to consider that are specific to the media and not drawn from 'real life'.

'Silent' cinema developed a whole series of non-verbal codes to overcome the lack of sound (often limited to musical accompaniment but sometimes with sound effects). As a result, the gestures of silent film actors today often seem 'over the top': the heroine, flung to the floor by the villain (who twiddles his moustache), raises her arms in a mixture of pleading and prayer; cut to close-up of villain, eyes wide open, with obvious make-up, relishing his power. All this melodramatic exaggeration of gesture was necessary because of the lack of dialogue.

Since the arrival of sound, however, this style of acting has become redundant. Modern audiences, while understanding the codes of silent cinema, find them too obvious and prefer the subtler coding of contemporary texts. It could be argued, however, that this exaggerated form of gesture still exists, albeit in a different form, in the 'action' movie.

Opera and musicals also use codes generated by the medium; it is rare, for example, for people to burst into song in real life (unless they're in the bath, perhaps). To the uninitiated, the sound of Mimi faultlessly singing her final aria in Puccini's *La Bohème* – complete with the odd cough – before she dies of consumption is laughable; nevertheless, opera *aficionados* (who understand the code) are moved to tears.

Just as we learn 'real life', or social, codes through the process of socialization, codes specific to media representations are learnt through exposure to the media. Codes can only exist if there is a consensus between producers and audiences about their meaning. Producers use conventions of a medium and/or genre to combine codes in such a way as to entertain and/or inform the audience. For example, it is a convention of magazines and newspapers that text is formatted in columns, whereas the text of novels usually runs across the whole page. In Western culture it is the convention that we read from left to right, but in Arab cultures and East Asia, the convention is right to left.

The object of textual analysis is to ascertain what codes mean when combined with particular conventions. However, we must consider one other variable that may be present in the still image: colour.

Colour

As colour takes its cue from society, it is a social code. Red is associated with passion and violence; and blue with coolness and melancholy – in the West, at least. Even if, say, film directors do not consciously wish to make an expressive point with colour, they need to be careful that colours do not clash within the frame; a melange of green and orange, for example, may make an audience feel sick (but this could, of course, be an expressive point).

One way in which colour is used is to focus the audience's attention within the *mise en scène*. This is done with bright colours, which draw the eye more than pastel shades.

Colour is obviously linked with lighting. Film directors may suffuse their film with a particular coloured light; red in *Taxi Driver* (1976), directed by Martin Scorsese; and blue in *Blue Steel* (1990, Kathryn Bigelow). The effect of this is to link various themes in the film.

Director Vincente Minnelli has a reputation as a stylist, and a number of his films – for example, *Lust for Life* (1956) – use painters' styles as the basis for the use of colour. Another good example of the expressive use of colour occurs in Minnelli's film *Home From the Hill* (1959), which

> revolves around a conflict between a man and his wife. The husband's den … is painted a deep, blood red all over and is furnished in a 'masculine' way, with leather armchairs, rifles and hunting trophies. The rest of the house is the woman's domain – it is decorated in off-white, with chintzy patterns and in upper-class good taste; she wears pastel colours that blend in with the setting. The house is thus divided dramatically between the male and female parts, as is the family itself. (Dyer 1981: 1154–5)

EXERCISE 1.10

List as many associations as you can with different colours.

In Western society there is a tradition of associating the colours, or shades, white and black with good and evil, respectively, and this feeds into many stereotypes. It is arguable that this expressive use is racist, as the word black now has negative associations and vice versa. In contrast, in China, the colour of mourning is white.

Ironically, given that everyday life for most of us is 'in colour', it is usually the lack of colour – in the form of black-and-white photography – that is used to signify a certain type of realism. It could be the lack of glamour, or the apparent cheapness, of black-and-white images which suggests to the audience that what is shown is real – with 'warts and all'.

Conventions – newspapers, Japanese horror and Big Brother

Different media usually have different conventions, which they use to communicate their message by way of the socially agreed codes. We shall consider the conventions of newspapers, and how global television formats, which necessarily use the same conventions, can lead to very different texts, depending on the country in which they are produced.

Newspapers

The conventions that newspapers use to deliver news include:

- the masthead, on the front page, which includes the name of the newspaper, the date, price and lures (highlights of what's inside and/or special offers)
- headlines
- reporters' bylines
- text in columns
- illustrative photographs with captions.

While all newspapers follow these conventions, there are different types, or formats, of newspaper. In the UK at the time of writing, there are three sectors of national dailies (ignoring the specialist *Financial Times*): red-top, middle market and quality. Red-tops are aimed at a working-class audience; 'qualities' at the middle classes; and, inevitably, the middle market bestrides the two. The red-tops are far more likely to use sensationalist headlines and soft (trivial) news stories in their leads (the day's most important story). The type of language employed also forms part of a newspaper's conventions. The headlines in Exercise 1.11 came from a rare day of unanimity regarding what was the most important story.

EXERCISE 1.11

What type of newspaper do you think the following headlines (from their websites on 21 November 2007), are taken?

A. Cameron blasts Brown over benefits blunder
B. Govt bunglers lose 25m names
C. Brown apologises for data blunder

Although the headlines are similar, C, from the quality *The Guardian*, is less sensationalist than the other two. A and B, are possibly interchangeable; however, the use of the word 'bungler' is typical of red tops – it's from *The Sun*, and the alliterative headline in A is from the middle-market *Daily Express*. The *Express* takes a typical pro-Conservative angle with the story, while the left-leaning *Guardian* emphasizes the government's apology.

It's likely, as print and online editions of newspapers become fully integrated, that traditional headlines, which seek to grab attention and give a gist of the story, will be compromised by the need to be optimized for search engines. So the use of key words will prevail over verbal gymnastics such as this one in a reference to a song from the film *Mary Poppins* (US, 1964) – 'Super Cally Go Ballistic, Celtic Are Atrocious' from *The Sun* (when non-league Scottish football team Caledonian Thistle beat top side Celtic); or, when emphasizing the chances of a racehorse called April: 'April May March into August History', from *The Times*.

One convention that unites newspapers is that the opening paragraph of a story should include: who, what, when, where, why and how. This enables readers to get the gist of the story and read on, if they are interested, or move on to another story. Similarly, the least important part of the story, any background information, will be found at the end, so if sub-editors need to cut it in order for the piece to fit on the page, then no vital information will be lost (of course, there's no need to cut on the internet edition). Newspapers are designed to be browsed through and not read end to end.

British newspapers are reputed to be among the most unprincipled press in the world because they won't let the truth get in the way of the story. For example, the *Daily Express* front-page headline on 27 July 2005 was the inflammatory (and inaccurate): 'Bombers are all sponging asylum seekers'; coming soon after attempted bombings in London (see http://keywords.dsvr.co.uk/freepress/body.phtml?category=news&id=1171; accessed November 2007).

Sex, Lies and Democracy (Stephenson 1994) examines this, as it:

offers [an] unflattering view of the British press, seen through the eyes of foreign students encountering it for the first time when they come to London to study journalism at City University. 'Their reactions are invariably ones of disbelief, dismay and, occasionally disgust – in tabloid terms one might say Shock Horror. Their overwhelming view is that no press is as intrusive, offensive, quasi-pornographic, arrogant, inaccurate, salacious and unprincipled' (quoted in Evans 1997)

So while the codes and conventions of US tabloids (such as the *New York Post* – incidentally, this is owned by Rupert Murdoch's News Corporation, as is *The Sun*) are the same as Britain's, cultural differences mean that the newspapers operate in different ways, hence the view of British newspapers quoted above. Of course, conventions are often broken. The day after England's disastrous failure to qualify for the 2008 football European Championships, *The Sun*'s front page consisted solely of a picture of a deflated football in a gutter.

Codes of Japanese horror

Japanese horror (J-horror) has 'crossed over' into the Western world, both in the original versions, for a niche fan base, and in Hollywood remakes – which Americanize Japanese codes and then export them across the world. For example, the distinctive long hair of Sadako in the *Ring* trilogy has a cultural reference (code) in Japanese culture, whereas in the West it may simply add a distinctive, and unsettling flavour (since you can't see her face):

Many demonic women in Japanese theatre have long, black hair. Contemporary Japanese horror cinema's reiteration of this motif can be evidenced through the unkempt hair obscuring Sadako's face in *Ringu* or the spiralling tresses in *Uzamaki*. (Hand 2005: 26)

Western horror texts invariably stage a battle between good and evil, and the latter is embodied in the monster. In Japan, however, notions of good and evil are far less pronounced. The Buddhist/Shintoist religions encourage the belief that spirits are all around us and are not necessarily evil, though some may not be able to rest until they have been avenged. Similarly, the more 'rational' West requires a clearer narrative explanation for events, whereas in the *Ju-on* series (2000–):

Where there has been violence ... a ghost may return to the scene of the crime, seeking a means of 'satisfaction' or 'sleeping easy' ... all the people who enter the house are pursued to their deaths. The American series often have victims who are killed because they have 'sinned' in some way (e.g. teenagers having sex), but in *Ju-on* there is no 'justification' for their deaths. (Branston and Stafford 2006: 98a)

The injection of Japanese, and Korean, horror conventions has helped to reinvigorate the Hollywood genre staple. Of course, such influences work both ways. So Martin Scorsese influenced John Woo's Hong Kong films that, in turn, were recycled in Quentin Tarantino's playful pastiches such as the black suits in *Reservoir Dogs* (1992).

It's likely that the Internet, which is a global medium by default, will further encourage cross-cultural exchange. For example, there has been a dramatic increase in the number of Western fans of *anime* and *manga*, particularly in the United States. *Anime*, however, has been shown on Western television since the 1960s – for example, *Marine Boy* (1968–9). Early *anime* was essentially 'stripped' of its Japanese culture – a process most obvious in the Power Rangers series, which interpolated American-shot sequences into the Japanese action. More recently, as fans could access the originals – via the often pirated texts on the internet – there's been greater demand for the original material.

Big Brother

In recent years, the globalization of television has seen an increase in formats that enable local variations on a common set of conventions. Of these, *Big Brother (BB)*, first produced in the Netherlands in 1999, is among the most successful. The convention of placing together of a disparate group of mostly young people in a house isolated from the outside world to be voted out, one by one, by viewers, has, in many places, engaged a substantial young audience that is attractive to advertisers. In Africa, however, *Big Brother Africa (BBA)* had a greater meaning for audiences than in, say, UK, as it united a continent in a way that other texts failed to do:

> While certainly *BBA* did not unite Africans in an ideological sense under the rubric of a political party or project, *BBA* did unite Africans in a shared conversation that ranged from the trivialities of on-screen romances to discussions of premarital sex, AIDS, the role of women in African societies, racial, ethnic, and national stereotypes, and … common challenges of many African countries. (Dolby 2006)

While in the UK *BB* aspires to be no more than 'water-cooler' TV, a popular discussion point at work necessitating that people watch it or risk being left out of office gossip, in Africa, where ideas of nationhood are far more unstable after colonial rule, the programme offers a 'public sphere' to discuss crucial issues. So the same set of conventions – format – are likely to offer very different meanings in different cultures.

Before moving on to 'Images in sequence' it will be useful to once again revise and apply the tools of analysis described so far.

1.11 Analysing still texts

Print advertising

Despite the fact that the advertisement in Figure 1.12, for Nokia 232 mobile phones, appears to be relatively simple in construction, it yields a massive amount of information when subjected to analysis.

Frame   The frame is standard magazine shape, which immediately suggests it is a magazine advertisement; it could also appear at certain outdoor poster sites, such as those on bus shelters. This particular advertisement ran in thirteen magazines (listed later in this section) during the summer of 1995.

Angle and height   The shot was taken from a low angle; we are looking up at the woman. The height is about at her knee-level, thus putting her in a dominant position.

Distance   The frame encloses a medium–long shot of the subject, a woman, and the background of a marble bust on a pillar. The medium shot allows us to see most of the woman, with only her shins and feet 'cut off', so her face, dress and legs are all visible.

Cant   Unusually, the angle of this image in the advertisement is canted slightly to the right. This appears to suggest (I do not think we believe that the setting is actually sloping) that the woman is walking uphill.

The cant also creates three diagonal lines formed by the bust and pillar, the woman and the darker wall behind the woman emphasizing the 'rule of thirds' conventional composition. These lines give dynamism to the image and open up a space, in the bottom right-hand corner, for product details.

Mise en scène

The subject   The most important subject in the image is clearly the woman (despite the key element of the advertisement being the mobile phone). She

Figure 1.12   'An unforgettable little black number' – image analysis

is wearing a black dress and tights, long silver earrings, has an immaculate coiffure and is holding a mobile phone. Her gaze is directed at us, and she is smiling. She has one hand on a pillar.

Lighting   The key lighting, from about 45 degrees above her on the left, emphasizes her face, which stands out further because of the lack of fill lighting on the shadow cast by the key light. No backlighting appears to have been used, as her black dress makes her stand out from the setting. Fill light has been used on the shadow cast by the bust; if it had not been used, the woman would have been undifferentiated from the background, as the shadow cast would have merged with her dress.

Setting   While clearly a studio shot, the use of a classical bust and pillars suggests a museum setting. In this case, however, because there is no clear sign that the location is actually a museum, the setting is abstract.

The wall behind the woman is shaded, and the effect of this is to make the woman's face, which is brightly lit, stand out more than it would on a pale background.

Anchorage   The anchorage is provided, linguistically, by the copy: 'An unforgettable little black number' and 'It's not what you say, it's how you say it', and by the image of the product. The 'unforgettable ...' copy is a pun, because it is referring to both the woman's dress and the product. First, let us consider how it is applied to the image's subject.

The 'black number' is clearly referring to the woman's dress. 'Little' is slightly more ambiguous, as we are given no sense of scale and, because of the low angle, the woman could be very tall. However, this is a good example of anchorage, because the copy says 'little' so we assume that the woman is petite. 'Unforgettable' refers to the 'turn on' of the image: because the woman is (conventionally) beautiful and is wearing a '(sexy) little black number' ('sexy' is implied in the phrase), she is sexually attractive (to heterosexual males) and a model of sexual attractiveness (to heterosexual females). In other words, the woman is an object of desire and a model for appearance. The rhetoric of the anchorage is that, once seen, this woman is never forgotten (untrue, of course).

This copy also indicates that the target audience for the product is female, because being 'little' is something that men do not usually want to be associated with.

The meaning of the Nokia 232 is anchored in exactly the same way: it is a sexy, unforgettable, little, black number. The qualities of the image's subject are transferred to the product which the woman is holding in her hand.

Nokia's slogan ('It's not what you say, it's how you say it') emphasizes that lifestyle is a main selling point of the product and harks back to Marshall McLuhan's phrase 'the medium is the message'. The implication is that it is the product itself that is important: you can say exactly the same thing on numerous makes of mobile phones – or indeed via the conventional telephonic system – but only with a Nokia 232 will you become an 'unforgettable little black number'. As in many advertisements, what is offered here is more the lifestyle that purchasing the product will allow you to experience rather than the product alone. This 'explains' the low angle of the shot, which signifies that the woman is powerful: buy this product and you too will be powerful.

The final piece of linguistic anchorage is the Nokia logo, which emphasizes the social nature of the product ('connecting people') and the dynamism associated with it – the three arrows pointing forcefully upwards.

Image choice and cropping   Because this is a 'custom-made' photograph, it is not only the particular choice of image that is important (one of many that would have been taken with different poses and/or settings), but also the choice of content: the look of this particular model and the certain type of marble bust. We have already described how the model is beautiful; however, it is also likely that the choice of this woman was also influenced by the presence of the classical bust, because there is a similarity of facial shape; this is emphasized by the shortness of the model's hair (long, flowing locks would not have had the same effect). (Of course, it is possible that the model's face suggested the use of the bust; all we can state with certainty is the similarity.)

For 'custom-made' images, cropping is often not important, because the photographer would know what frame size was required, so the lower part of the woman's legs have not been cut off to facilitate the image fitting the standard magazine-sized frame. It is possible that this image was cropped along the diagonal line created by the shaded wall behind the woman, although care was obviously taken not to cut off her leg.

Juxtaposition   There are three items placed side-by-side within the advertisement – the Nokia 232, the woman, and the classical bust and pillars. We also need to consider the position of the copy.

When analysing juxtaposition it can be fruitful to follow the direction that your eyes, when looking at the image, appear to take naturally. In this case the key lighting and the beauty of the woman's face draws our gaze to the top of the image, where the copy 'unforgettable little black number' immediately anchors the advertisement's meaning. It also creates a slight puzzle, as it does not look like a 'fashion ad': what is the product? This is answered quickly by the observation of the mobile phone held to her ear directly between her face and the copy. Many advertisements, and magazine front covers, follow a pattern that assumes the audience will first look across the top, then diagonally down to the bottom left and finally, across the bottom to the right; a Z-shape. In keeping with that pattern, our eyes will finally rest on the product in the bottom corner.

The three diagonal lines drag our gaze downwards, taking in the classical bust and pillars, toward the bottom of the page where the product name and contact for further information (a freephone number) is situated. The juxta-position in this image creates the order in which the producer (Nokia) wishes the audience to read the advertisement.

Genre   Advertisements are usually without specific generic connotations; an exception would be car advertising, where exotic and extreme locations are the norm. The content of the advertisement, however, can refer to a genre as a short-cut to meaning (by using, for example, a 'Wild West' setting). As I have already mentioned, this advertisement could be classified, generically, as a 'lifestyle' advertisement, which enables us to understand the equation that buying a Nokia 232 will give us access to a better existence.

Convention   As an advertisement, it must follow clear conventions that serve to distinguish it from editorial matter (though 'advertorials' purposely blur this line). It is common to have the product's, or service's, logo in the bottom right-hand corner. The use of good-looking models and an ever-positive outlook are ubiquitous.

The way an advertisement is read is also influenced by the genre of the text (or institution, in the case of cinema and television) in which it is placed and its position within that text. I originally saw this advertisement in the June 1995 edition of *Esquire* magazine.

Esquire markets itself as 'the award-winning magazine for men'. It is a lifestyle magazine, which means that it is aimed at a middle-class, adult audi-ence who are probably 'thirtysomething'. The presence in a male-orientated magazine of a product aimed at women suggests it is attempting to get men to buy this for the 'woman in their life'. The lifestyle equation here becomes: 'buy this product and your woman will look like this'. It's unlikely that anyone would expect their female companion to be transformed into this beauty, but associations of power and attractiveness are transferable.

The magazine is printed on glossy, high-quality paper emphasizing the desirability of the product. Newspapers, even with colour printing, cannot hope to reproduce this effect on newsprint. However, many have weekly glossy magazines in order to pick up advertising such as this.

The advertisement's position was on page 32 of the magazine, a left-hand page facing editorial text; the influence of the editorial (entitled 'In Search of Yamashita's Gold') in reading this particular advertisement is probably insignificant. However, if the editorial covered, for example, the high cost of mobile phones or, alternatively, their benefits, then it is likely that it would have had some bearing on the reading.

This particular advertisement had a 2/3-month life, in 1995, with a frequency of one or two insertions in consecutive months in women's and men's monthly magazines. The actual schedule is reproduced below (courtesy of Nokia and its agency Greycom):

You magazine, 7 May
Company, June and July
Elle, June and July
She, June
New Woman, June and July
Vogue, June
Harpers & Queen, June and July
Vanity Fair, June
OK, June and July
Esquire, June and July/August
FHM, June and July
GQ, June
The Spectator, 3 June and 17 June.

It is usually very difficult to obtain such information as this, and it is unlikely that you will ever need to know an advertisement's schedule. I have included it simply as an example of an actual schedule.

This appears to have been a very full analysis but is, in fact, far from exhaustive. In Chapter 2 we shall return to the advertisement and consider it from a semiotic perspective, and in Chapter 3 we will analyse it from a variety of discourses.

1.12 Images in sequence

The images we have considered so far have all been still. While the principles of still image analysis can also be used on moving images – but they must usually be stopped in order to analyse them accurately – there are additional codes that are unique to images in sequence.

The relationship between still and moving images can be understood from an early age: the ubiquitous 'stick person' animated by flicking quickly through the pages of a book is a common trick learnt by young children. The rapid juxtaposition of images, each slightly different from the previous one, gives an illusion of movement. The same principle is used in cinema; a still image, or frame, is projected momentarily on to a screen, to be immediately followed by another, and so on. In silent cinema, the speed of projection was approximately 16 frames per second (fps); while sound cinema requires 24 fps. (Note that the figure for silent cinema is approximate, because early cameras were hand-cranked and the speed depended on the camera operator. The difference between the fps rate of silent and sound explains why, some-times, in silent film, people appear to walk too quickly: this is because 16 fps film is being projected at 24 fps.)

The first films exhibited in cinemas were short and straightforward portrayals of events from everyday life. However, once film is used for narra-tive purposes, it is necessary to structure images into a sequence.

A narrative is a sequence of events that are linked, usually by a cause–effect chain, in a given setting – or space – and within a specific time-frame. Unless these elements are constructed carefully, the audience may become disorien-tated: at an obvious level, we do not expect a novel's characters to change their names without reason; similarly, if the novel opens in a particular place, any change in setting must be described, or motivated, by the narrative. If the narrative is taking place on a Monday we do not expect the next day to be a Friday. Comics are an interesting combination of still and moving images; obviously, they don't literally move, though motion lines do connote move-ment; however, their juxtaposition with other frames does offer a temporal dimension (see Box 1.4).

Box 1.4   Comics

Comics have a long history, with antecedents including the *Bayeux Tapestry*; however, they are identified primarily as print publications in a magazine format. When published, as a collection of issues or as an origi-nal item, as a book, they are known as graphic novels. In the West, many people struggle to take them seriously as they are associated in the mind of the public with children's picture books; however, in Japan, for example, they are mainstream adult texts.

Scott McCloud (tentatively) defines comics as:

> Juxtaposed pictorial and other images in deliberate sequence, intended to convey information and/or produce an aesthetic response in the viewer. (McCloud 1994: 20)

McCloud's book, *Understanding Comics*, which is itself in comic form, runs brilliantly through the codes and conventions of comic books. Unsurprisingly, many of these are already familiar to us through our consideration of still images – the use of non-verbal communication, for example. He distin-guishes between realist images and the abstract, simple, line drawings that many comics use; a circle with two spots for eyes and a line for a nose is invariably recognized as a face.

He also shows there are six types of relationships between frames:

1. *moment-to-moment*: the second frame follows a 'moment' after the first, so it's likely that there's little difference between them
2. *action-to-action*: features a single subject but there's a distinct action shown, such as a footballer kicking a ball
3. *subject-to-subject*: the link between the frames has to be read actively by the audience: a runner breaks the finishing tape, followed by the click of a stopwatch in close-up, for example
4. *scene-to-scene*: significant changes in space and/or time. A detective may say, 'He can't outrun us for ever' followed by a house with the caption '10 years later' (in audio visual texts this is known as *montage*)
5. *aspect-to-aspect*: 'bypasses time for the most part and sets a wandering eye on different aspects of a place, idea or mood' (McCloud 1994: 72). An example would be a montage of the debris left in the aftermath of a party (this is analogous to Eisenstein's montage – see section 3.9)
6. *non-sequitur*: no link whatsoever.

McCloud suggests that No. 2 is used most commonly, followed by Nos 3 and 4. In these relationships, it is relatively easy to make the links between the frames, and so they are particularly useful for mainstream texts. One of the essential skills of the comic artist is to choose the correct moment to show – in a sense, which frame to freeze.

Comics often consist of a number of strips, whereas graphic novels are often one complete narrative. Comic strips, in particular, are character-driven: the *Beano*'s Dennis the Menace, Minnie the Minx and the Bash Street Kids, for example.

Linking together different shots in film is similar to linking together sentences in a novel. Unless the addressees understand the codes being used, they will not get the full message. Linking images in sequence, whether film or television, is primarily the product of editing – the juxtaposition of one shot with another.

Editing

The word edit often means 'to cut out'; in audio-visual texts it refers to the join between shots. The purpose of conventional editing is to make this join as smooth as possible; indeed, the objective is to make the join seem invisible. This can only happen if the audience is not confused by the edit; if they understand the link between the shots, narrative cause and effect is maintained.

The potential for audiences to be disorientated by the editing process was first exploited by a French pioneer of cinema, Georges Méliès. The story runs that while he was filming (horse-drawn) traffic, the film stuck inside the camera. Having fixed the problem he continued shooting. When the film was seen later, one vehicle 'miraculously' turned into another. Méliès used this 'trick' later to create illusions in his fantasy films.

Méliès' use of editing was intentionally disorientating; in narrative film, however, disorientation is usually the last thing a film-maker wants the audience to experience. The need for a narrative flow, to tell the story, led to the development of the continuity system of editing. This was perfected by film-makers in Hollywood and is one reason why this particular part of the USA has dominated film production in the Western world ever since.

One objective of continuity editing is to create a coherent cinematic space in which the action can take place. Early cinema placed the camera as if it where in a theatre's stalls, and the players acted in front of it. This was clearly very limiting, with no alternative camera positions or camera movement.

Once the camera moves, whether the movement is seen on screen or if it's done between cuts, it is essential that the audience know where it has moved to, or they become disorientated. To prevent confusion, the following rules are used – rules that form the codes of continuity editing. The fact that audiences understand these rules unconsciously, but cannot describe them (unless they've studied film or media), is a testimony to their effectiveness.

Continuity editing

The basic rules of continuity editing are as follows:

The 180-degree rule

The 180-degree rule was established as the best way of facilitating continuity of cinematic space within one scene. An imaginary 'axis of action' is formed through the subject(s) early in the scene, and this should not be crossed. This ensures that audiences have a clear idea where characters are, in relation to one another, in the scene. In Figure 1.13 the 'axis of action' runs through characters A and B, and so shots 1, 2 and 3 are all valid as they stay on 'this' side of the line.

If, however, the 180-degree line is crossed (as in shot 4), and the camera remains facing the characters, then everything would appear the other way

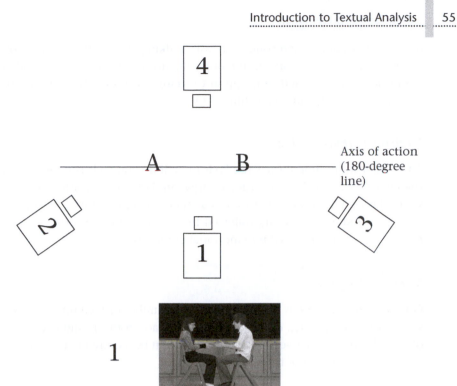

Establishing shot – the axis of action runs through the characters

Shot reverse shot: maintains characters' position in frame

Crossing the line: from the other side of the axis of action it appears that the characters reverse places.

Figure 1.13 Continuity editing

round. For example, someone who was walking from left to right would suddenly appear to be going in the opposite direction; two characters talking to one another would suddenly appear to change positions. The axis of action is usually created by an establishing shot.

Establishing (Master) shot

The 'establishing shot' creates the 'axis of action', and so it is necessary that the characters, and the space they occupy, are both seen clearly within this shot. This isn't always the first shot of a scene; though, if it isn't, it's likely to be the second and is usually followed by a conventional shot/reverse shot pattern with close-ups used for emotional emphasis.

Re-establishing shot

Once a scene's space has been established, a number of medium or close-up shots may follow, which could fragment the space from the audience's point of view. In this case a 're-establishing shot' might be required to re-anchor the audience's perception of the scene's space.

Shot/reverse-shot

Once the scene has been established, medium shots can show each end of the 180-degree axis, but they must always stay on the same side (camera positions 2 and 3 in Figure 1.13). The angle of these two shots from the axis of action must be the same. This technique is usually used in filming conversations between characters; for example, an over-the-shoulder shot could show one person talking, and a cut to over-the-shoulder of this person would show the other listening. This is a shot/reverse-shot pattern. As you can see in Figure 1.13, the shot/reverse-shot pattern maintains the characters' positions in the frame, despite having been taken from very different positions. This maintains continuity.

30-degree rule

Whenever a camera position is changed it must move by at least 30 degrees, in relation to the shot's subject(s), from its previous position in order to make a smooth transition between the two. Directors are usually careful to maintain a subject's position within the frame so that, despite the change of angle, the character stays in he same position in the frame. Anything less than a 30-degree angle tends to have a jarring effect as the position of the subject(s) is(are) very similar and so seems to 'jump' within the frame – known as a jump cut.

Eyeline match

When a character looks off-screen followed by another shot, the second shot shows what the character is looking at (this can also work the other way round).

Match on action

If a character starts to move in a particular direction it is possible to cut out part of the time taken to move from one place to another. Because of the 180-degree rule, and the consistency of the character's direction, audiences tend not to notice the missing space and time.

The cut

As stated at the beginning of this section, edit normally means 'to cut'. Unless the editing is done 'in camera' (which is what happened with most home videos before the advent of cheap editing software – the cut occurs where the camcorder was paused), editing requires film to be cut and then spliced to the next shot. Digital editing means, of course, that nothing is physically cut any more.

A cut simply describes an immediate transition between two shots. There are, however, four other main types of transition:

- *Fade-out*: where the scene simply fades to black, which means it has ended
- *Fade-in*: the scene appears from black; this usually signifies a beginning
- *Dissolve*: the second shot fades in and is superimposed over the first shot, which fades out (usually taking less than a second); this generally suggests the passage of time or is expressively linking the two scenes (for example, a dissolve from a shot of an evil character to a shot of a fire may suggest that the character will burn in hell)
- *Wipe*: the second shot flows horizontally across the first, as if it were a curtain being pulled across the frame, giving the effect of an abrupt conclusion to the scene.

As has been suggested in the above description, each of these edits has a meaning; these may vary, though, depending on the scene in which they are placed. The fades and dissolves usually indicate the passage of time (though a cut can also do this). A wipe can often imply that the second scene is happening at the same time as the first.

Most edits usually happen so quickly, in continuity editing, that the audience rarely notices them. Indeed some dissolves are so quick that it is unlikely that anyone other than a media student analysing a sequence will perceive them. One of the most outrageous dissolves I've stumbled across was from *Written on the Wind* (US, 1956) where a shot of a young boy, bouncing up and down on a mechanical horse, is 'placed' between the thighs of a woman. This isn't wholly, gratuitously outrageous, as the film is about hysterical masculinity.

Of course, in actual film-making, characters appearing in the same scene may, in reality, have been miles apart. This is particularly true when location shooting is mixed with studio work (which will probably be responsible for producing close-ups). Unless told otherwise – by an establishing shot – audiences assume that there is a spatial relationship between one shot and the next: the Kuleshov effect, discussed earlier. The overall effect of continuity editing is that it is not noticed; it appears, in fact, to be invisible.

EXERCISE 1.14

Using two minutes of any movie (the odds are that it will use continuity editing), count how many different shots there are. Show the sequence to friends, without telling them what they are looking for, and ask them how many shots there were. You are likely to get wildly differing responses.

The creation of coherent space for the narrative to be enacted is not the only function of editing. When analysing images in sequence, we must consider the effect that the juxtaposition of different images (which is what an edit produces) has on the creation of meaning. Four relationships between images should be considered at the edit: graphic, rhythmic, spatial and temporal.

- *Graphic relationships*: graphics refers to a shot's brightness, and the patterns of line, shape, volume, depth, movement and stillness. The focus of analysis is on whether the graphic properties of shots are edited to create either continuity or contrast. The 'rule of thirds' is a graphic relationship within one shot.
- *Rhythmic relationships*: these are created by the length of shot; how long a shot runs before the edit. If a sequence consists of shots of the same length, a rather monotonous rhythm will be created; conversely, a series of long shots followed by rapid editing is likely to create an exciting affect (often used for set pieces in action movies). Some documentaries use the

'long take'; that is, with very little editing, in order to create a sense of reality.

- *Spatial relationships*: as already discussed, continuity editing uses various rules – such as the 180-degree rule – to create coherent space.
- *Temporal relationships*: how on-screen time is constructed. It is unusual for on-screen time to match 'real time' (that is, 30 minutes on-screen takes 30 minutes of time to show). A text can take place across any length of time; from a few hours to the aeons of *2001: A Space Odyssey*. Editing is often used to cut out redundant actions: for example, a character may stand up to leave a room; an immediate cut shows the character exiting by a door – the character's movement towards the door is taken out. This is known as *an ellipsis*.

Intensified continuity

As with any set of conventions, we can expect them to evolve over time. The rules described above developed during the early years of film-making, particularly in Hollywood, and have set the template, with some exceptions, for audiovisual language in different places and media, such as television. There has been some debate about the extent to which the 'classical' continuity editing style has been, in recent years, superseded:

> Traditional editing regimes are said ... to have been undermined by the importation into feature films of the rapid cutting and 'shallow' imagery of advertising or MTV. (King 2002: 5)

Bordwell (2006) describes these 'new' techniques as consisting of the following:

- rapid editing
- reliance on close-ups to convey performance
- whiplash pans and jerky reframing
- using short single shots rather than two-shots for dialogue
- cutting while the camera is in motion
- using long (telephoto) lens to shoot close-ups from a distance and flatten perspective
- having the establishing shot in the middle of the scene.

However, as David Bordwell, with typical thoroughness, shows, the belief that these techniques are something new has been exaggerated. Continuity editing remains the system used in audio-visual texts in the Western world, but there are other systems, such as montage, which will be discussed in

Chapter 3. Bordwell explains how the influence of television, which traditionally 'prefers' the close-up to convey narrative information because of the screen size, new technology and economic constraints have led to the evolution of the classical style since the late 1950s:

> nearly all scenes in nearly all contemporary mass-market movies ... are staged, shot, and cut according to principles that crystallized in the 1910s and 1920s ... [however] [t]he new technical devices, encouraging heavy stylization and self-conscious virtuosity, have changed our experience of following the story. (Bordwell 2006: 180)

So while the camera appears to have been liberated, in terms of its movement and position, from the axis of action, in fact it still invariably sticks to the 180-degree rule. Bordwell contends that, used by intelligent directors (he cites James Cameron for *The Terminator* [1984] and Kathryn Bigelow for *Point Break* [1991]) these techniques can summon considerable story-telling power by generating 'keen moment-by-moment anticipation' (ibid.). However, at their worst (for example *Matrix: Revolutions*, 2003) scenes verge on visual chaos.

Bordwell suggests that sound bridges an important aspect of 'intensified continuity' as they bind together scenes that might consist of frenetic action. As noted at the beginning of this chapter, the bodily sense from which we gain the most detailed information is sight. This may be the reason that sound is often given little emphasis in analyses of audio-visual media texts. However, sound carries vitally important codes for the creation of the meaning of these texts (and it goes without saying that it is the carrier of meaning in radio).

1.13 Sound

There are four dimensions of sound that need to be analysed:

- *dialogue (or monologue)*: the most obvious dimension – what characters are saying on-screen
- *sound effects*: non-verbal sounds, created within the on-screen space, the source of which is clear to the audience
- *ambient sounds*: background sounds that add to the atmosphere of the scene
- *non-diegetic sounds*: not originating from on-screen space, for example, a voice-over or sound-track music.

EXERCISE 1.15

Record the audio of a movie sequence with which you are familiar. Make notes of sounds you hear for the first time. (The exercise is best done using a movie sequence because they tend to be much more carefully constructed than do television texts.)

Dialogue

Dialogue on the soundtrack is usually carefully mixed to make it very clear. It is either recorded at the same time as the scene is filmed or may be added later (*post-dubbed*). A more experimental use of speech in audio-visual texts is overlapping dialogue, where characters 'talk over' each other: Woody Allen uses this technique to give a heightened realism to scenes; for example, in the opening of *Husbands and Wives* (1992), the announcement that a married couple are splitting up leads to frantic questioning by the Woody Allen and Mia Farrow characters. Although more than one character is often talking at the same time, the mix ensures that the audience hears clearly the voice the director wants to be heard.

Sound effects

Sound effects are anything that is not spoken and has a clear source within the world represented, and the source is usually, but not always, observable within the frame. This includes the opening and shutting of doors, characters moving around the scene and so on; an off-screen knock at a door would also be considered as a sound effect.

These sounds can be post-dubbed. For example, the sound of fist fights is usually added later, often with particularly unconvincing results.

Ambient sounds

Ambient sounds form a background to a scene and, while they do originate in the narrative space, need not necessarily be identified specifically. For example, a country scene would probably include the ambient sounds of insects and birds. These are called *spot effects*.

A scene on a city street will probably be accompanied by the spot effects of traffic, though the audience will not necessarily see the traffic. If this scene is followed by one inside a building on this city street, then the ambient sounds will probably continue but at a lower volume; this helps to give continuity to the scenes.

Non-diegetic sounds

The most potent non-diegetic sound is music. There are few films that dispense completely with the expressive qualities of music. Even the gritty, realist BBC television drama *Cathy Come Home*, directed by Ken Loach and produced by Tony Garnett in 1968, used the song 'Stand By Me' early in the film.

Music is often used to cue drama and evoke emotion. The approach of danger in a thriller is usually signalled by 'sinister' music; while a romantic moment will often be accompanied by a lush orchestration of strings. So music not only adds to meanings generated by the image; it also creates meanings. The composer John Williams' use of percussion in *JFK* (US, 1991) created a very physical effect with its insistent, militaristic rhythms; this enabled the director, Oliver Stone, to create tension, even though the audience knew that President Kennedy was about to be shot in the Dallas motorcade.

Music is often used to evoke a period, so a medieval setting may be accompanied by medieval-sounding music (it does not have to be genuinely medieval, it simply needs to connote the era). Since the 1950s, when 'youth culture' was 'invented', the use of rock 'n' roll music, in particular, not only evokes an era but also produces nostalgia in an audience of the relevant generation.

Music is not always non-diegetic, however. In films like *Control* (UK–US–Australia–Japan, 2007), a biopic of Joy Division's Ian Curtis, the performance of music is on-screen and therefore must be considered to be a 'sound effect'.

An institutional dimension of music is its use in generating publicity for movies when the theme song is performed by a popular artist; each time the song is performed, or the accompanying pop video is broadcast, the movie is also being promoted.

As noted in the Introduction, the ubiquity of new media technologies has led to what some call a paradigm shift in the media. In section 3.5 we shall consider the degree to which these new technologies have changed the way that the media operate. However, it doesn't take long clicking through videos on YouTube to realise that the rules of media language apply just as much to these 'new' media texts as they did to the 'old' ones.

Semiotics

2.1 Introduction to semiotics

Chapter 1 introduced the analysis of images. This chapter considers the science of signs – or semiotics – which has proved a fruitful way of looking at texts of all kinds. One of the great strengths of a semiotic approach is that the reader is encouraged to look at familiar objects and ideas in a fashion that makes them appear strange; nothing is taken for granted. It is, because of this, conceptually difficult; however, the effort is repaid in the resulting analyses.

The 'study of signs' was founded, simultaneously and without knowledge of each other's work, by Ferdinand de Saussure in Switzerland and Charles Peirce in USA; they termed their creation semiology and semiotics, respectively (the root of the term is the Greek 'semeion', meaning 'sign'). Semiology and semiotics mean the same, though the latter term appears to have gained greater currency.

At the heart of semiotics is the study of language and how it is the dominant influence shaping the way we communicate. Semiotics is also a wonderful tool for analysing images. Although the terminology (signifier, signified, paradigm, syntagm, synchronic, diachronic etc.) may at first make the science appear obscure, semiotics is an important discipline in the study of media language.

2.2 Saussure

Ferdinand de Saussure's theories were collected, posthumously, in *Course in General Linguistics* (1916) from lecture notes compiled by his students. When Saussure described how signs are created he was referring not only to formal signs, such as those in the Highway Code, but to any system of communication. Language is, of course, the most fundamental system human beings use.

Signifier and signified

Saussure's revolutionary approach defined signs structurally. He stated that the sign is the sum of the signifier and signified: the signifier is the perception of the sign's physical form, which may be material, acoustic, visual, olfactory or a taste; and the signified is the mental concept we learn to associate with that object. The relationship between the sign and its referent (the actual object the sign is representing) is the signification.

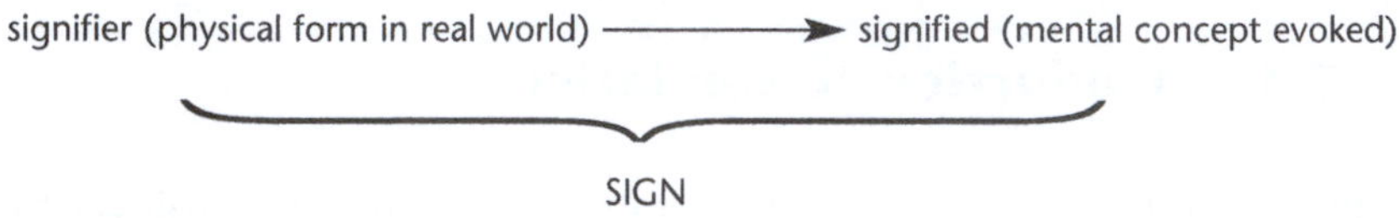

signifier (physical form in real world) ————————▶ signified (mental concept evoked)

SIGN

Figure 2.1   Signifier–signified creates the sign

If we perceive a furry animal with four legs, that barks (the signifier), this evokes the mental concept of a dog (the signified); the combination of 'sound-image' and concept creates the sign 'dog'. Similarly, when we see the letters d,o,g, placed together, the word is a signifier, and once again the mental concept of a dog is signified, and the combination of these elements results in the sign 'dog'. Although the signifier and signified are separated for the purposes of analysis, in terms of our perception they are inseparable, so are better considered to be vertically related:

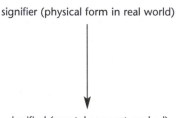

signifier (physical form in real world)

signified (mental concept evoked)

Figure 2.2   The vertical structure of the sign

The basic act of signification operates at the level of *denotation* (as described in section 1.2).

The level of denotation

Denotation is simply about identifying a sign; when we perceive something through any of our senses, the word or words (signs) we attach to the perception is the denotation. Denotations operate at the first-order level of signification.

The relationship between the signifier and signified is usually arbitrary. The fact that a furry animal that has four legs and barks is called 'dog' in English was selected from a multitude of other words (ignoring for a moment the ancestry of the English language); dogs could have been called cats or fardels. This explains why we have different languages throughout the world; if the signifier determined the signified, the word for the animal called a dog in English would be very similar, if not the same, in all languages (in fact there would probably be only one language).

Similarly, the word 'dog' can also signify 'to follow tenaciously', 'a mechanical device for gripping' and 'a worthless person'; thus a signifier can have many signifieds. It also follows that a signified can have many signs – for example, some synonyms for 'dog' are bitch, canine, cur, 'man's best friend' and so on.

Clearly, the arbitrary nature of signs means that they can have many meanings, or are polysemic. This does not mean that there is anarchy in the search for meaning; all languages have rules that structure meaning in a conventional fashion, and these will be described later in the chapter.

Not all signs are entirely arbitrary in nature. Some have a resemblance to what they represent; for example, a photograph is a sign that usually looks like its referent. The word 'buzz' sounds like what it describes, and, in English, pigs 'oink'. However, these signs are *not* what they represent – that would be impossible: they act as similes. For example, onomatopoeic words sound *like* what they represent, but this does not mean they sound the *same*; in Japanese, for example, pigs apparently make the sound '*buu buu*' (http://web-japan.org/trends00/honbun/tj991126.html; accessed November 2007). Signs that possess a resemblance to their referent are iconic, as defined by C. S. Peirce (see section 2.4).

Saussure's description of signs, which include both technical and symbolic codes described in 1.10, is important in Media Studies because it emphasizes that they are social constructs; they do not possess inherent meaning. Once this is understood, the task of analysis is to deconstruct not individual *signs*, but *sign systems* to show how meaning is created.

EXERCISE 2.1

Write down a description of your environment at the level of denotation as the first column in a table with two columns.

The level of connotation

Our understanding of signs rarely stops at the level of denotation. Once we perceive a sign, we often have particular associations with that sign that colour our understanding; for example, a person who dislikes dogs would have negative feelings about the sign 'dog', but if they were a cat lover they would feel positive about the sign 'cat'. These associations are a second-order system of signification, or *connotations* (as described in section 1.7). (It can be argued that even the first-order system of signification – denotation – is itself a connotation because we learn to *associate* a particular signified with a signifier.)

In the second-order system of signification, the individual has perceived (at the level of denotation) the original sign 'dog', which has then become another signifier that evokes an associated mental concept to create another sign consisting of 'dog' + 'associations'.

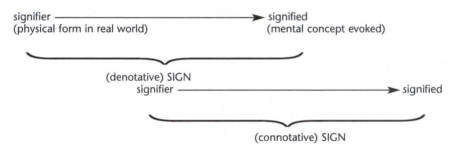

Figure 2.3   Denotation and connotation

Many connotations have reached the status of being a social consensus. For example, if the dog is a border collie (sheepdog), sitting down, tongue hanging out, with its head to one side (a denotative description), it is difficult to avoid the connotation that the beast is friendly. Some signs carry particularly powerful connotations; these are (Barthesian) myths (see section 2.4) – which should not be confused with 'untruths' or Greek myths.

EXERCISE 2.2

Add connotations to your denotative description from Exercise 2.1 in the second column of your table.

As noted in Chapter 1, when analysing texts, merely describing (denotation) is worthless – we must explain what the text means and how it creates this meaning. What a particular sign means is greatly influenced by context.

Meaning and context

Because of their arbitrary nature, meaning cannot exist in individual signs, but is derived from their context. For example, we can only understand the two different meanings of 'dog' in the following sentence because of the other signs (words):

(a) 'The dog barked loudly at the postman.'
(b) 'The man said he'd dog Noam for ever.'

If we read sentence (a) to say 'the follow tenaciously loudly at the postman', then it is clearly nonsense. So a sign's value – the particular meaning 'dog' represents in this case – is created by the difference between it and other signs in the same context.

This isn't, however, just a result of the sign 'dog' having more than one meaning; all signs only have value because they are different from other signs:

> If a sign gets its meaning from other signs, it works through a system of differences (from what it isn't), rather than identity (with itself). It means something not because it has some fixed identity, but because it is different from other signs. We could put that in a succinct but paradoxical form by saying that what a sign is is due to what it isn't. (Thwaites *et al.* 1994: 23)

This is obvious in relation to size. Scooby Doo, a Great Dane, would be described as big; however, if confronted by King Kong, he would suddenly become small.

One of the fundamental structures that help to anchor meaning is the *relationship* between *langue* and *parole*.

Langue **and** parole

Saussure distinguished between:

* *langue*: the rules of a sign system (which might be grammar), and
* *parole*: the articulation of signs (for example, speech or writing),

the sum of which is language:

$$\text{language} = langue + parole$$

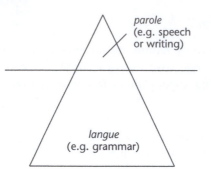

Figure 2.4 *Parole* and *langue*

While *langue* could be the rules of, say, English grammar, it does not mean *parole* always has to conform to the rules of standard English (what some people erroneously call 'proper' English). *Langue* is less rigid than the phrase ' set of rules' implies; it is more a guideline and is inferred from the *parole*. However, it is the rules of grammar that allow us to understand that 'the follow tenaciously loudly at the postman' is nonsense. Language systems are often likened to an iceberg: the parole is visible while the rules, the supporting structure, are hidden.

As the diagram suggests, the rules of any communication are hidden. However, these rules are necessary for the language to be intelligible. It should also be noted the *langue* itself does not guarantee meaning. Noam Chomsky's famous phrase 'Colorless green ideas sleep furiously' is grammatically correct but meaningless.

An example of how this would apply specifically to Media Studies are the codes and conventions of media language, discussed in the previous chapter. The codes are the equivalent of *langue*, and the conventions used to combine the codes is the *parole*. Unless a person has studied the media language, it is unlikely that they would be able to explain, say, the rules of continuity editing (*langue*); however, most people can make sense of the editing when watching films (*parole*) because they implicitly understand *langue*. Similarly, you can probably can write a sentence, but might have some difficulty if you were asked to parse it.

Synchrony and diachrony

As stated above, *langue* and *parole* are structures that help to give meaning to (arbitrary) signs. Saussure showed that meaning is also created via vertical and horizontal dimensions of sign systems: called *synchrony* and *diachrony*. These dimensions are obviously useful in the study of language. For example, if we were analysing the line from Shakespeare's *Romeo and Juliet*:

'that which we call a rose/By any other name would smell as sweet' (2:2, lines 43–4).

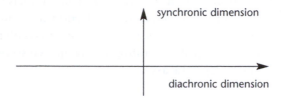

Figure 2.5   Synchronic and diachronic dimensions

The synchronic dimension could be a particular word, say 'rose'; while the diachronic dimension could be the whole sentence.

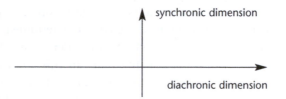

that which we call a rose/By any other name would smell as sweet'

Figure 2.6   The sentence as diachronic

Our understanding of the sentence would depend on us knowing, for example, what 'rose' means (synchronic) in the context of sentence (diachronic). When we study a still from a film, or a freeze-frame of a video, we are, in effect, looking at the synchronic dimension, and the sequence from which the still is taken is the diachronic dimension.

The relationship between the synchronic and diachronic dimensions is relative: we could argue that the letter 'o' is a synchronic dimension, while the whole word 'rose' is the diachronic; or that *Romeo and Juliet* is synchronic and the *oeuvre* of Shakespeare is diachronic. As noted earlier, the meaning of a sign is determined by its context, it has no meaning on its own. We understand that, in this (diachronic) context 'rose' does not refer to 'getting up' but to the category of objects called flowers. Incidentally, Shakespeare, in this line, is anticipating semiotics. It's certainly true that 'roses' could have been called 'farts' and still smell like roses.

Similarly, the synchronic and diachronic dimensions demonstrate that our analysis of individual signs or texts is determined by the perspective we bring to them. For example, if we focus on the letter 'o' in Shakespeare's line, we would probably be looking at it from a linguist's point of view. If we were considering the play *Romeo and Juliet* in comparison with Shakespeare's *oeuvre*, then we are likely to be engaged in theatrical or literary criticism.

Langue is organized along two axes, those of selection and combination; we selected the meaning of rose to be 'flower' because it was combined with the idea of smelling (you don't smell something getting up). Saussure called these the paradigmatic and syntagmatic axes.

Syntagm and paradigm

The syntagm is the horizontal, or sequential, arrangement, and the paradigm is the vertical set of associations (beware, this can be confusing, because the *synchronic* dimension is vertical). Paradigms consist of signs that can belong in the same category. For example, the paradigm 'audio-visual text' consists of film, television programmes, music videos and so on. The paradigmatic dimension to which a sign belongs is not fixed, but determined, in the main, by the syntagmatic arrangement – which in turn is determined by *langue*.

Take the sentence: 'The cat sat on the mat'. In this context, we might decide that the paradigm associated with the subject of the sentence, cat, is that it belongs to the category 'animal'. However the 'cat' could also belong to the paradigm 'the cat family', and so it's possible that the animal referred to was a tiger! However, the paradigm 'floor covering', to which 'mat' belongs, suggests that the cat is part of the 'domestic animal' paradigm in this sentence.

Once we've established that 'cat' belongs to the 'domestic animal' paradigm, we can then understand the most likely meaning of the sentence. Obviously, we don't have to think through these conceptual problems, because we've learnt language. There was, however, a point when we *did* have to think through these issues; a baby's facility for learning language (doing all this hard work) is astonishing.

We established earlier that meaning is created through difference; a sign's value – meaning – is determined by what it *isn't* rather than what it *is* (as it is arbitrary in nature). So the specific meaning of cat, in the 'domestic animal' paradigm, is determined by other signs that belong in that paradigm but are *not* cats:

'The cat   sat on the mat.'
    dog
    tortoise
    hamster
    parrot
and so on.

We understand that the referent the sign 'cat' refers to is a cat because it is *not* a dog, tortoise, hamster or any other domestic animal; as was stated above, it is the qualities that distinguish one sign from another that give the sign meaning.

In summary: to form a syntagm, the paradigmatic dimension must combine with other paradigms, which it does according to the rules of *langue*. The syntagm then anchors the meaning of individual signs (from the paradigms) by creating a context; in other words, it helps us to choose the appropriate paradigm of a sign. Paradigms, by their very nature, expand the possible meanings of a sign; the syntagm prevents confusion by limiting the number of meanings. This is the way that signs have meanings despite their arbitrary nature, and the same sign can have many different meanings that are determined by context.

A classic example (from Barthes) from everyday life of these dimensions is a three-course menu that offers a choice of starter, main dish and dessert. Diners are asked to choose from three paradigms which have a conventional order (the *langue*), and their syntagmatic choice gives them a three-course meal.

These dimensions are particularly useful in image analysis. For example, the use of a cat in an advertisement for double-glazing relies, for its meaning, on the paradigm 'domestic animal' combined with the syntagm, which places the cat next to the double-glazed window. This communicates that the product is effective in eliminating draughts, because cats like comfort.

Placing a dog in the same position would not have the same effect, even though it too can belong to the 'domestic animal' paradigm. The syntagm 'dog and window' has different associations, such as waiting for its master to return home, or wanting to go for a walk.

This replacement of one sign by another is called a commutation test and illustrates how powerful paradigms and syntagms can be in image analysis or indeed other types of analysis (for example, replace the gender of a character in a novel). By substituting objects for other signs in the same paradigm, and decoding the new meaning, we can isolate what contribution the original sign is making to the meaning of the image.

Look again at Figure 1.8 on page 23; let us consider what insight we might gain using commutation test. We can simply describe the image, at the level of denotation, as showing:

A woman preparing a lot of food in a kitchen with the help of a boy.

In preparing for a commutation test, it is useful to suggest different signs of paradigms that are present in the image. For example:

A | woman | preparing a lot of food in a kitchen with the help of a | boy |.
   | man | | girl |.

By simply replacing two signs, we have three additional possible combinations:

1. A man preparing a lot of food in a kitchen with the help of a boy.
2. A woman preparing a lot of food in a kitchen with the help of a girl.
3. A man preparing a lot of food in a kitchen with the help of a girl.

If we exchanged 'woman' for 'man', as part of the human paradigm, what interpretation could we make of the image? I would then read the image to suggest that the adult was an expert, possibly a chef. The woman, according to my analysis in the first chapter, was a housewife. Why the difference? Clearly it is more unusual to see a man cooking in a domestic situation than a woman and so, in my interpretation, I had to consider why he should be engaged in preparing food, whereas it *seems* a natural activity for women. These assumptions, of course, reflect the norms of Western society; it is interesting that the commutation test reveals that there is more likely to be a connotation of expertise associated with a man.

Often, when the gender of a person is changed, the effect is ridiculous; imagine a man taking Rita Hayworth's pose as shown in Figure 1.7. However, because all we have done is to change one sign of one paradigm, we can be sure that any alterations to the meaning of the image is caused by gender and our assumptions about gender.

EXERCISE 2.3

Analyse Figure 1.8 using combinations (b) and (c).

EXERCISE 2.4

Do a commutation test on an advertisement (don't restrict yourself only to switching gender).

The contribution of semiotics to Media Studies is sometimes derided because of its obscure jargon; the commutation test, however, demonstrates semiotics at its most powerful. It is a particularly effective way of unmasking myths that (as we shall see in section 2.5), signify themselves as being natural.

In addition to Saussure, two other people have made seminal contributions to the science of signs: C. S. Peirce and Roland Barthes.

2.3 C. S. Peirce

C. S. Peirce created a tripartite categorization of signs: iconic, index and symbol.

Iconic

An iconic sign bears a resemblance to what it represents and can be an image, images or graphical. A photograph is iconic: we may recognize a photograph of a particular pet, but we know that the photograph is not the *actual* pet. Similarly, a recording of a dog barking is aurally iconic.

An iconic sign does not necessarily have to *physically* resemble the thing to which it refers: maps, for example, are graphical iconic signs. However, in order to be able to read, say, Ordnance Survey maps, we need to understand the codes used, such as contour lines.

Index

An index sign has a direct relationship, or causal link, to the thing it represents. For example, a thermometer is an index of temperature. A picture of someone sweating while lying on a beach is an index of heat.

Shots of the Houses of Parliament are often used in films to establish that the setting is London. Obviously, the image of Parliament is iconic, but it is simultaneously an index in that it represents more than itself. The relationship, of course, is that Parliament is situated in London. Similarly, the Eiffel tower is an index of Paris; the Opera House of Sydney; the Kremlin, Moscow; and the Statue of Liberty, the USA.

Indexes, or indices, can be specific to individuals; for example, the presence of a car is an index of the car's owner.

Symbolic

Language is the most obvious symbolic sign because, as Saussure stated, its relationship with what it represents is arbitrary. Indeed, any arbitrary sign must be symbolic, since it can only be a sign of something because there is a consensus about what it means. Formal signs are usually symbols – for example, those used in the Highway Code.

Peirce's categories are useful in distinguishing between different types of signs and their functionality.

EXERCISE 2.5

Using any advertisement that includes images, find examples of Peirce's categories.

2.4 Barthes

Roland Barthes' crucial contribution to semiotics was his definition and exploration of myths. Barthes was not concerned with archetypes, untruths or Greek myths and legends, but how signs take on the values of the dominant value system – or ideology (see 3.6) – of a particular society and make these values seem natural. For example, a flower with red petals, green leaves and a thorny stem signifies the mental concept *rose*; this is at the first level of signification or denotative level. As we have seen, the level of denotation gives the basic meaning of the sign. However, the sign 'rose' can, in turn, signify the mental concept of romance, particularly if it is red and placed in the context of St. Valentine's Day.

EXERCISE 2.6

List any connotations of romance you can think of.

Romance is a myth that defines heterosexual love as tender and caring; traditionally, the female is likely to be passive, and the male active, in establishing the relationship. Romance can also include unproblematic sexual relations and affluent lifestyles.

So, how does this 'flower with red petals, green leaves and a thorny stem' take on the meaning of romance?

We have already seen how the original denotative sign can become the signifier of a second-order system of signification, creating a connotation. Barthes showed that Saussure's sign can become a signifier to create, not only a connotation, but a myth.

Because it is virtually impossible to understand 'a red rose on Valentine's Day' as meaning anything other than romance, it appears that a signifying system, which is a connotation, is acting as a denotation. Myths are connotations that appear to be denotations. This 'trick' allows myths, in texts, to infuse the meaning of the communication without appearing to do so; they efface their own existence. Like continuity editing, myths position the audience in a specific relationship with a sign and simultaneously disguise themselves. So

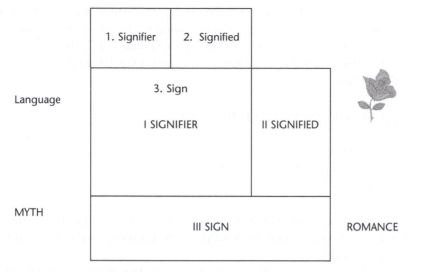

Figure 2.7 Barthes's myths

Source: Adapted from Barthes 1973: 115.

your idea of romance is likely to have been heterosexual (gay romances are rarely represented) and, if you had included an 'ideal wedding' in your connotations, then that is likely to cost a lot of money, hence the myth is at the service of capitalism, which needs to stimulate demand.

As we did with image analysis, it is necessary to deconstruct the meaning of myths in order to understand how they work. For example, Barthes, writing about the advertising of the soap powder *Omo* in the 1950s, showed how the imagery draws upon myths:

> Powders ... are separating agents: their ideal role is to liberate the object from its circumstantial imperfection: dirt is 'forced out' ... dirt is a diminutive enemy, stunted and black, which takes to its heels from the fine immaculate linen at the sole threat of the judgement of *Omo*.
>
> *Omo* cleans in depth ... [assumes] that linen is deep, which no one had previously thought ... foam ... signifies luxury ... its abundant ... almost infinite proliferation allows one to suppose there is in the substance from which it issues a vigorous germ, a healthy and powerful essence ... Foam can even be the sign of a certain spirituality ... a large surface of effects out of a small volume of causes. (Barthes 1973: 36–7)

Even though Barthes was writing about advertising from over 50 years ago, the myths employed are still in use. The representation of dirt as 'black and stunted' draws on the myth that to be black and/or stunted is both negative and something to be got rid off (thus drawing on fascist ideology, which is racist and unforgiving of 'imperfection'). A Garnier ad, published in the edition of *More!* considered in Chapter 4, drew on similar myths, having the following copy:

New *pure* extra-strong daily purifying pads.

- Reduces shine
- Targets impurities
- Purifies pores.

They are myths because they seem to be a natural way to represent germs; so natural, in fact, that you might be surprised to learn that germs aren't in fact 'black and stunted'.

Masculinity is also a myth, as gender is a social creation. To be defined as masculine in Western society, the male needs to be strong (muscularity), physically skilful, rugged and adept in the use of technology. Take, for example, the way that cars aimed at men are represented in advertising: they are almost always fast and usually have the following aspects of masculinity: they are powerful (speed); they corner beautifully, and, obviously, they are (advanced) technological creations.

In order to deconstruct this particular use of the myth we could use a commutation test (substitute the car for a bicycle?). Alternatively, it is possible to use an oppositional way of reading the text; for example, a feminist reading of the car could emphasize that the car's speed signifies men's lack sexual staying power. This sort of reading helps in the deconstruction of myths because it emphasizes that the association, in this case, of speed and masculinity is not natural but a social construct. In order to make such a radical reading, it is necessary to use ideas, or discourses, that are alternative to the consensus; this will be considered further in the next chapter.

The identification of myths, because they appear natural, can be difficult. As we shall investigate below, even nature is a myth: while clearly nature, in its unmediated form, is natural, society's idea of the character of nature is clearly a social construct. This is particularly evident in any documentary text that talks about 'mother nature': this can lead to many deterministic assumptions about nature and draws on the myth of femininity as nurturing.

Myths are a potent way of making meanings in society. Other areas that Barthes (1973) investigates include: wrestling; holiday writing; soap-powders and detergents; margarine; Einstein; and striptease.

Using the same images as in the previous two exercises, try to decide what objects are myths and then attempt to make an alternative reading of them.

2.5 Binary oppositions

We have established that signs do not possess intrinsic meaning but are defined by their relationship to other signs: signs are defined by what they are not. Some of the most powerful creators of a sign's meaning are binary oppositions. Here, signs are contrasted with opposite meanings. For example: town and country; man and woman; child and adult; public and private; civilization and savagery. Binary oppositions, like all signs systems, are not natural descriptions but cultural creations.

Write down what you associate with 'town' and 'country'.

Binary oppositions are often structurally related to each other, and function to order meanings. For example, town and country are characterized by the following oppositions:

town	country
artificial	natural
commercial	non-commercial
dangerous	safe
exciting	boring
over-crowded	deserted
polluted	clean
sophisticated	backward

These lists consist of connotations of both town and country. Taken together, they form myths of urban and country life.

EXERCISE 2.9

Think about your experience of towns, or cities, and the countryside that contradict this 'town and country' dichotomy. For example, in towns, there are often parks that can be characterized as natural, and the countryside is covered in excrement.

It is possible to find contradictions for all the oppositions, which are also known as *antinomies*. For example, the countryside is polluted by artificial fertilizers; has exciting areas for activities such as rock-climbing; is commercially exploited by farming and so on.

Binary oppositions articulate power relationships. For example, the idea that country folk are not as sophisticated as city dwellers could be used to legitimize governments spending less money on the rural population. Similarly, the 'inferiority' of women, from a traditionalist perspective, can lead to the female sex getting paid less for the same work (see also Chapter 5).

The media often use binary oppositions to determine the framework of their representations. For example, a news report about Africa will draw upon a first world versus developing world opposition that 'assumes' the latter to be underdeveloped, poverty-stricken and riven by wars, regardless of whether that is the case in this particular story.

People or objects that fall in between opposites form an ambiguous category. Representations of this 'in-between' category often classify its inhabitants as abnormal. Transsexuals, in terms of the signification of gender, are neither men nor women, and so are defined as deviant. While it is true to say that transsexuals, statistically, are deviant, the connotations of 'deviance' suggest moral corruption and sickness. The representation of adolescents is similarly contentious: they are, obviously, neither adult or child, and as a result are often represented as being a 'problem'.

A text that uses binary oppositions usually assigns a positive value to one side against the other; by stating that one side is good it follows that the other is bad. For example, 'them' and 'us' categories are often used in a nationalistic context to affirm a nation's identity, or a racist discourse serves simultaneously to denigrate the 'other' and elevate the 'same' (us). These oppositions are so powerful that diverse groups can be subsumed under one category: white versus black (to include Afro-Caribbean and Hispanic).

The final part of this chapter is an analysis of an advertisement for the Nokia 232 mobile phone. This analysis is an attempt to apply both our semiotic knowledge and the tools of analysis described in Chapter 1. It is not meant to be an example of how to present analysis of images; it is far too exhaustive for that. What follows is meant to be an example of how to approach the analysis of an image.

2.6 Semiotic analysis: Nokia 232

Peirce's tripartite categorization sheds some new light on the analysis in Chapter 1. Clearly, the images are iconic, and the words and logo are symbolic; these we have already analysed. However, the index category yields the information that the classical bust and pillars may represent either ancient Rome or Greece, while the reading in Chapter 1 only suggested that the setting was a museum.

The word Nokia is an interesting symbol because it is meaningless in the English language; what is signified, however, is 'a Japanese company' (unless, of course, you know that it's actually Finnish). The connotations of 'a Japanese company' are that its products will be reliable and good value for money. Image is far more important than fact in the creation of brands; a few years ago, a British-based manufacturer of electronic goods, Dixons, launched the Matsui range to benefit from this connotation. And not all Chablis wine is produced in France.

Let us consider Saussure's *paradigmatic* and *syntagmatic* dimensions and Barthes' myths.

Paradigm

The paradigm 'humanoid object' for the woman in the image could include:

man
child
old woman
gorilla
robot, and so on.

Other potential paradigms are: fashion models; race; clothing as signs. A commutation test using the 'humanoid object' paradigm might lead to the following analysis:

As already suggested in Chapter 1, men's relationship to size would suggest that they would not find 'little' a turn on. If a man were used, the word 'compact' would be more appropriate, as it would have connotations of 'executive portability'; that is, the modern executive is very busy and has to carry a lot of equipment; a compact mobile phone would allow him to keep in touch with important business contacts without being over-burdened.

What meaning would we get from the advertisement which featured a *man* wearing 'an unforgettable little black number'? It would probably be laughable – whether intentionally, as in parody, or unintentionally as a result of incompetent advertising. Because of this, the construction of the advertisement is gender-specific: it only works with a female holding the phone. Whether this is sexist or not depends on your viewpoint.

The use of a *child* would suggest that the product was a toy; it would also mean, however, that the sexual element of the image would be disturbing.

An *old woman* would again fail the 'sexy' test, not because old women cannot be sexy (see the 80-plus-year-old Lauren Bacall, for example) but because the convention is that old people are not sexually attractive. In any case, youth is important for this particular product as it aims to be trendy.

The *gorilla*, again, would be laughable. The incongruity of the image would be enough to draw an audience's attention, as it did in the Cadbury's drumming gorilla advertisement, but it is unlikely that they would find the gorilla more attractive than the woman.

The *robot* would also attract attention, and a robot connotes high technology and the future, so both of these connotations would be appropriate for a product that is high-tech and trendy. The lifestyle theme of the advertisement, however, would be lost. Selling the product on its technological advancement is usually a specifically male address.

The value of this paradigmatic analysis is that it shows the meanings created by the image's specific elements: the use of a young, beautiful woman is crucial to the preferred reading of this advertisement. By noting how different parts of the paradigm change the advertisement's meaning, we can understand how different parts of the paradigm contribute to the advertisement's meaning; we can isolate the actual contribution of, in this case, the beautiful woman.

EXERCISE 2.9

Using different paradigms, analyse the different meanings the advertisement can generate.

The syntagmatic dimension takes us back to how juxtaposition influences meaning, which we considered in Chapter 1. There we suggested that the positioning of the image's elements led the eye through the advertisement to a preferred meaning. We should also consider the combination of elements; for example, how the black dress contrasts with the white bust and pillars. These opposite 'colours', and the way the bust's head is tilted away from the woman, links her with the bust – the similarity of their features has already been noted. The syntagm of the woman and the classical sculpture generates the meaning that the image, as a whole, is 'classy'. This, of course, includes the product.

Myths

Barthes' myths are part of the second-order system of signification; that is, we are analysing the connotations of images. We have already described the woman as being conventionally beautiful, and the 'unforgettable little black number' as having sexual associations; clearly, these are connotations because notions of beauty and sexiness are socially constructed (for example, the supermodels of the twenty-first century would not be suitable material for Botticelli nudes, and Marilyn Monroe – the sex symbol of the 1950s – was probably too ample in build for today's scrawny standards). What, then, is the myth of female sexuality?

The woman is not only sexy because she is beautiful; the clothes she is wearing also have connotations of being fashionable – they are stylish and show off her (sexy) legs. What is considered to be sexy depends on a person's gender and sexual orientation; in Western culture, sexy suggests a woman is displaying herself for the male gaze and is therefore available. A sexy man is less likely to be on display in the same way, though it is arguable that men have been represented more frequently as sex objects in recent years.

The immaculate coiffure not only links the woman with the bust; it also emphasizes her attractiveness, as does the make-up on her hands and face.

Although being defined sexually can often oppress women – that is, if it is defined that their only function in society is being sex objects for males – post-feminist advertising often suggests that a woman's status as a sex object can work to her advantage. For example, a Triumph bra ad stated that it is 'The bra for the women's movement'. In doing so it implies that the product can give women power by associating it with the feminist 'women's movement'. However, this isn't social power but

> represents ... the idea that women can gain control through the commodification of their appearance ... by acquiring a particular look. (Gill 2007: 89–90)

Although it suggests that being sexy is powerful, it is, in reality, actually reinforcing the idea that women are simply sex objects.

The gaze of the woman in the Nokia advert – directly at the audience – is powerful. It is not a hostile gaze, as direct eye contact sometimes can be, but (her smile signifies) an inviting one: 'Look at me, aren't I powerful?' Her power is emphasized by the dynamism of the image; she is moving (the position of her legs signify a step) 'uphill' and her earrings are swaying with the movement: this woman is going places and talking (to the lover who bought the phone?) at the same time.

Considering the myth of the bust and pillars is, fortunately, more straightforward. These are classical figures and have connotations of:

purity
beauty
wealth
intellect
tradition
long-lastingness
technology.

These connotations are inevitably a product of my knowledge of what is 'classical' and do not necessarily have to be accurate. As in genre, associations only have to have a social consensus; they do not have to be rooted in reality.

As already stated, the syntagmatic structure of the image links the classical elements with the woman. Thus the connotation of 'classical purity' is that the woman is pure. This, in turn, relates to a (one hopes, old-fashioned) myth of femininity that women should be pure (that is, virgins) and set on a (classical?) pedestal. This purity is constructed as an object of desire and therefore the Nokia 232 is also desirable. The relationship between the beauty of the woman and the sexual power this may create has already been discussed.

The connotation of someone owning such a marble bust is that they are wealthy and have good taste. The association of wealth, aesthetic judgement and intellect ('only "brainy" people are interested in such ancient artefacts') adds to the power of the woman. The ancient provenance of the artefacts suggests tradition. The myth of tradition is a great favourite with advertisers. Its use exploits the nostalgic feeling that things were better in 'the good old days'. The association with the product (with which, as we have already stated, the woman is closely identified) is twofold: the product is well-made and is reliable (as things used to be).

Of course, cutting-edge technology (which the Nokia 232 implies it is, with its emphasis on size) contradicts the idea of tradition. This apparent contradiction does not make the myth incoherent; it is the power of myths that such contradictions can be glossed over: products can be both at the cutting edge of technology *and* traditional. The bust and pillar represent a stunning technological achievement of an ancient time: Nokia 232 is also stunning (and will also be superseded by another product as technology is developed).

CHAPTER

Advanced Textual Analysis

3

3.1 Introduction

We learnt in Chapter 1 how we use media language to understand texts. In this chapter we shall see how we can use media texts to understand society. Media Studies is sometimes thought of as being similar to English Literature, because it analyses texts closely. The apparent lack of discrimination in the selection of these texts (soap operas are as likely to be studied as classic films or television programmes) has often been used to criticize the academic validity of the subject. However, because Media Studies does not have a preordained canon of what texts are worthy of study, it is so effective in enabling us to better understand society. Media Studies does not only deal in the present, it can also teach us, as can Literature, about the past.

By analysing the conventions used to represent reality in the past we can better understand our predecessors' world-view, and often, because the past is a precursor to the present, better understand modern media conventions. Part of this understanding is derived from authorial intent or, more usefully, a text's dominant reading (these may not be the same thing).

We often find that texts are polysemic – that is, they can have several meanings – and how we, as individuals, read these 'open' texts is determined by our understanding of the world – our 'world-view'. It is in analysing 'world-views' that we are confronted by the concept of ideology, one of the defining theories of Media Studies. Arising from ideology are the concepts of hegemony and discourse.

The final part of this chapter will consider alternatives to mainstream conventions. These are often defined in opposition to the mainstream and so serve to challenge our expectations about how we make sense of the world.

The first two chapters have shown that there are a large number of variables in image analysis. Our understanding of these variables is, in the main, derived from socialization. From the moment we begin to interact with the world we are socialized into the codes of language, both verbal and non-verbal, and into society's conventions of behaviour. The primary socialization starts at a very young age and usually takes place in the home; while secondary socialization is the more formal education we receive in schools.

Language is often used and understood in an unconscious fashion that is a testimony to the human brain's sophistication: we are usually unaware of the large amount of information our brain is processing at any one moment. The objective of Media Studies analysis is, in part, to allow us to become aware of the unconscious reading we are making of, in the first instance, media texts, but also – and this is a consequence of the first step – how we also unconsciously read our social environment. We do this by pulling apart, or deconstructing, texts and considering how institutional factors influence meaning.

This deconstruction is not, however, an objective, mechanical exercise because we can never categorically state what any communication means to any one individual. Everyone's way of seeing is a product of her or his values and beliefs, and so any analysis will be made from a specific point of view. However, because our values and beliefs are obviously influenced by the society of which we are a member, it is unlikely that this viewpoint is unique.

In this third and final chapter on textual analysis, we shall consider more advanced techniques that allow us to link the individual components in a comprehensive manner. The tools described in the first two chapters lead us to look very closely at texts as if we are pressing our nose against a subject and looking at each component individually. In this way it is easy to see the separate parts, but makes looking at the whole problematic. In this chapter we attempt to 'pull together' the disparate elements into a coherent whole.

Before we continue it will be useful to understand why Media Studies does not discriminate against texts that lack cachet (that is, texts that are trashy and worthless); all texts should yield interesting information from a Media Studies perspective.

3.2 High culture verses low culture

Raymond Williams (1976) states that culture is one of the most difficult words, in the English language to define. Terry Eagleton (1983) traced how English Literature came to embody the values of high culture as a response to an ideological crisis in late Victorian England:

> As religion progressively ceases to provide the social 'cement', affect values and basic mythologies by which a socially turbulent class society can be welded together, 'English' is constructed as a subject to carry this ideological burden. (23–4)

In other words, the subject of English was studied for the first time, rather than Classics, as a way of defining common – 'universal', as they came to be called – values by which we should aspire to live:

> It would communicate to them the moral riches of bourgeois civilization, impress upon them a reverence for middle-class achievements, and, since reading is an essentially solitary, contemplative activity, curb in them any disruptive tendency to collective political action. It would give them a pride in their national language and literature. (Ibid.: 25)

We shall consider the values of bourgeois ideology later in the chapter (section 3.7). Reading hasn't always been a 'solitary activity', however; in the early nineteenth century, radical newspapers, which campaigned on behalf of the increasingly exploited working classes, were often read out loud to people who were illiterate:

> The impact of the radical press was further reinforced by the discussions that followed the reading aloud of articles from newspapers in taverns, workshops, homes, and public meetings ... this social pattern of consumption ... resulted in political newspapers having a much greater agitational effect than those of today. (Curran and Seaton 1991: 35)

Getting the news in a social situation, where it can be discussed and exchanged, is far more likely to encourage communal action. It was this threat to bourgeois values that Matthew Arnold and others were worried about and hoped that the study of English would ameliorate:

> Arnold believed that the franchise [vote] had given power to men as yet uneducated for power. A working class which has lost 'the strong feudal habits of subordination and deference' is a very dangerous working class. It is the function of education to restore a sense of subordination and deference to the class. (Storey 2001: 20)

EXERCISE 3.1

List up to ten 'great' works of English literature or 'great' novelists (apologies here if you're not English – in that case, choose from your own nation's 'great' literature); note how many you have read.

Does your (English) list include works by Jane Austen, Emily Brontë, Charles Dickens, Thomas Hardy, D. H. Lawrence and William Shakespeare? Given that you're not likely to have read more than a small percentage of novels and plays, how do you know these are great? These authors, and others, constitute the canon of English Literature; if you're not familiar with the English canon, does your culture have a canon of great literature?

The English canon (why not British?) was invented by, among others, F. R. Leavis, an Oxford University professor in the 1920s. His purpose was to cement Arnold's intent of giving moral heft to the study of literature, in particular, emphasizing the close reading of texts. Anything outside the canon would be deemed to be second-rate at best. And anything that didn't offer skilfully written expositions of bourgeois values – and most (all?) genre fiction was condemned for failing to do this – would not be worthy of study. In fact, it would be defined as low culture, because it was consumed by the masses.

In common-sense terms, culture is often synonymous with art; literature is culture, as is opera and 'classical' music. However, artefacts such as block-buster novels, soap operas and popular music are often excluded from this definition. Art is defined, in a common-sense discourse, as a collection of arte-facts that demonstrates 'universal truths'; for example, in English Literature, the novels of Jane Austen are deemed to speak the 'truth' to all cultures in all times. However, an examination of these 'truth'-bearing artefacts reveals that what the definition really means is that elite, middle-class, art is good and mass (popular) art is bad. The canon offers a 'cultural coherence based on authoritarian and hierarchical principles' (Storey 2001: 26).

'Common sense' is simply a way of describing something ideological as if it were natural; it is a 'sense' that is 'common' only because we have been socialized into its values. Media Studies is not concerned primarily with whether artefacts are 'good' or 'bad', 'high art' or 'pop(ular) culture', it is interested in what we can learn from them.

The fact that we can 'legitimately' study popular culture has its origins in Richard Hoggart's *The Uses of Literacy*, first published in 1957, as he 'shifted the debate in Britain from a stark opposition between elitist minority culture and lowly mass culture towards a series engagement with the value and values of majority cultural experience' (McGuigan 1992: 49).

Popular texts are particularly interesting to study, as they have much to teach us about how societies create meaning about the world and other cultures. As Raymond Williams insisted, 'culture [is] the "lived experience" of "ordinary" men and women, made in their daily interaction with the texts and practices of everyday life' (Storey 2001: 47).

The subject does more than simply analyse texts closely; for example, a study of the ownership of large media corporations can demonstrate how they have an enormous influence upon our lives. News Corporation (run at the time of writing by Rupert Murdoch) controls 20th Century Fox (film and television), HarperCollins publishers, Star TV in the Far East, four national newspapers in Britain, and British Sky Broadcasting (BSkyB) (with concomitant influence on association and rugby football) – among others. In 1998, when BSkyB wanted to take over Manchester United, two daily newspapers supported the attempt; the rest were opposed. Did the fact that the two newspapers that supported the deal, *The Sun* and *The Times*, were owned by News Corp. influence their reporting, and were all 'anti' newspapers against the deal because they were in competition with News Corp.? (You bet!). In 2008, it was reported that the editor of the *Far Eastern Economic Review* refused to publish a review of Murdoch's dealings in China (http://www.iht.com/articles/2008/02/28/technology/murdoch.php; accessed February 2008) – News Corp. owns the magazine.

One thing you may be familiar with from your study of Literature is the quest to find out what meaning the author intended.

3.3 Audience readings

There is a belief, particularly in the more traditional study of English Literature, that the task of analysis is to work out the author's intentions. It can, however, be very difficult to be sure of authorial intent; even if the author has written explicitly about her or his own work, who is to say that theirs is the true reading? Film director Alfred Hitchcock, for example, was notorious for stating that his films were 'merely thrillers' when they clearly articulate complex ideas about guilt and morality. As we saw in Chapter 1, there are numerous variables at work in texts, and if we assume that the author's view is the 'correct' one, we might as well dispense with analysis.

Certainly, authorial intent is of interest, but it must not be allowed to dominate the process of deconstructing texts. Searching only for authorial intention assumes that meaning does not change through time, so that the text will always mean what the author meant. This is related to the idea that great works of art, whether literature, painting or music (as long as they are not 'popular'), express universal values that speak to all peoples in all times. This approach to criticism is antithetical to Media Studies.

F.R. Leavis and his followers developed this view to an extent by focusing upon what the text said rather than on the author. However, Leavis's approach tended to ignore the text's historical background, as he believed that the close reading of extracts, even out of their textual context, would allow the text's essential message to be decoded; Media Studies is more concerned with what and why texts mean what they do to particular audiences.

In Media Studies, knowledge of authorial intent is, in fact, less important than knowledge of the author's (or, in the case of broadcasting and cinema, for example, the institution's) cultural background. If we understand the culture in which the text was created, whether it is from the past, from our own society, or from a culture that possesses values different from our own, we have a better chance of understanding the text's codes. Ultimately the meaning that any text possesses is determined by who is reading it.

While authorial intent can at times be difficult to ascertain, the producer's intention is often contained within the text, either explicitly or implicitly. It is clear that an advertisement's function is to sell a product, a service or a company image, and the way in which advertisers would prefer the audience to read the text is usually obvious. Texts that have a clear, dominant meaning are 'closed' texts; Barthes (1990) called these 'readerly' texts. Because a text is closed, however, does not mean that alternative readings are not possible.

Other texts are more open; for example, some film directors, such as Wong Kar Wai and David Lynch, relish offering ambiguity. Barthes described these as 'writerly' texts, and he praised them because 'the goal of literary work ... is to make the reader no longer a consumer, but a producer of a text' (Barthes 1990: 4).

Some texts, such as instrumental music, are almost completely free from linguistic anchorage (though most music has a title), giving greater latitude to the audience's reading. While instrumental music does not have linguistic anchorage, though, it still possesses codes that are conventional; for example, minor keys can create sad feelings in listeners.

Texts, then, are closed, open, or – most likely – somewhere in between the two. Stuart Hall (Hall *et al.* 1980), with members of the Centre of Contemporary Cultural Studies in Birmingham, described three possible reader positions that are created by an individual's social position and class:

1. The *dominant* hegemonic position, in which the reader understands the message conveyed by a text; such a reader would believe that the Nokia 232 (see page **47**) is a desirable object, because it would make the owner appear to be more sexually attractive and powerful (hegemony is consider in section 3.7).
2. The *negotiated* position, in which the reader understands the dominant position but may not believe that it applies to them; the Nokia 232 could be acknowledged as desirable but inappropriate to them (readers may recognize that they do not need a mobile phone, or that while the product might make others sexually powerful, it would not work for them).

Similarly, the dominant position is understood but only partially accepted as accurate (the woman looks good, but I wouldn't want to buy a Nokia).

3. The *oppositional* position, which, while understanding the dominant coding, rejects the values it is putting forward. Here, the Nokia 232 advertisement's message would be rejected, possibly on the grounds that it is perpetuating sexist stereotypes (this reading would be using feminist discourse).

O'Sullivan *et al.* (1994) added a fourth position, which they termed an *aberrant* reading. Here, the dominant meaning is not understood, and the text is read in a deviant fashion ('Why is the number the woman is calling black?').

Finding the dominant reading of open, or writerly, texts can be difficult. However mainstream, commercial texts usually have a specific purpose or an explicit 'moral to their tale', and the dominant position is clear; though we don't have to agree with it.

EXERCISE 3.1

Choose any text – an advertisement, a song, a film (or extract), a novel, short story, and so on, and create three different readings using Hall's categories.

It should be noted that a dominant reading does not necessarily concur with authorial intent. The creators may be attempting to convey a particular message that is not apparent in the text itself; for example, the films of Ed Wood have many fans who enjoy watching his 'they are so bad they are good' movies, while he took himself seriously. So this begs the question of where the dominant reading is situated: in the producer's intentions, in the text itself, or as a result of audience's readings?

It should be clear that the notion we might have had when reading Chapter 1, that textual analysis was a relatively straightforward exercise in deconstructing meaning, is far too simplistic:

> The meaning of a text will be constructed differently according to the discourses (knowledge, prejudices, resistances) brought to bear on the text by the reader: the crucial factor in the encounter of audience/subject and text will be the range of discourses at the disposal of the audience. (Morley 1992: 87)

Bennett and Woollacott (1987) elaborated this to formulate the social contexts involved in the creating the range of discourses available to the audience:

> Reading formation ... is the product of definite social and ideological rela-
> tions of reading composed, in the main, of those apparatuses – schools, the
> press, critical reviews, fanzines – within and between which the socially
> dominant forms for the superintendence of meaning are both constructed
> and contested. (64–5, quoted in Tulloch 1995: 127)

Tulloch goes on to distinguish between 'situational' and 'intertextual'
contexts. The former refers to the situation in which the readings take place;
the latter concerns the extent to which an audience is familiar with a text's
historical context.

Situational contexts

It's highly likely, given that you're reading this book, that you are, at least
some of the time, reading texts in an academic situation. While most
people don't care what a preferred reading is (and indeed, will argue vocif-
erously for what they think is right!), in the 'situation' of Media Studies we
must consider texts with an academic discourse that attempts to analyse
dispassionately.

Frantz Fanon, writing in the 1960s when 'negro' was a commonly used
term for black people, described how the situation can lead to a radically
different reading of a film:

> Attend showings of a Tarzan film in the Antilles [West Indies] and in
> Europe. In the Antilles, the young negro identifies himself de facto with
> Tarzan against the Negroes. This is much more difficult for him in a
> European theatre, for the rest of the audience, which is white, automati-
> cally identifies him with the savages on the screen. (Quoted in Shohat and
> Stam 1996: 155)

Tarzan films were popular in the 1930s and are now considered racist in their
representations of white superiority, but Fanon does demonstrate how a spectator's view can shift depending on their situation. Tulloch demonstrates how
fans (in his book on *Doctor Who*) can refer to earlier episodes and series in
their reading of individual episodes, whereas the casual viewer is less likely to
have such extensive knowledge and so will read the episode differently; we
shall consider intertextuality in the next section.

A similar duality of readings is apparent in the reception of *Lost in
Translation* (US, 2003), starring Bill Murray and Scarlett Johansson. Murray
plays a clapped-out movie star in Tokyo making an advert for Suntory
whiskey where he meets the much-younger disaffected wife of a rock star. It's

a wistful film that avoids the clichés of romantic comedy but does get much of its humour through the clash of cultures and the 'funny' way that Japanese people speak English:

> Camps are generally divided between those who feel the film makes a mockery of the Japanese people, and those who defend the authenticity with which Coppola portrays the experience of dislocated foreigners bumbling in Tokyo. One group calls for fair representation; the other believes that political correctness shouldn't snuff out the rich humor and romance of an honestly wrought film. (Paik, 2004)

Paik goes on to argue that, because the Japanese characters are all stereotypes, that they are not presented as fully rounded humans, that the film typifies the idea that 'Americans have made the peculiarly imperialist combination of ignorance and arrogance a national identity' (ibid.). Paul Julien Smith, however, suggests, 'In fact the cruellest and crudest satire is against Los Angeles' (Smith 2004: 15a).

As Shohat and Stam suggest, 'Perception itself is embedded in history' (1996: 163), so Paik's and Smith's views are not mutually exclusive but a product of their cultural backgrounds. Shohat and Stam call for a 'multi-cultural audiovisual pedagogy' (ibid.) as an essential tool for understanding texts in a globalized media economy. This means being sensitive to other's cultural contexts rather than assuming one's own context is the default position.

We know that signs can generate more than one reading – they are polysemic – which means that audiences are no longer under the yoke of the tyrannous text where Leavis and his followers would have liked us to be placed. What we must avoid, though, is total anarchy: while, theoretically, texts can mean anything readers wish them to mean, in practice they tend to have a limited ranged of meanings that are socially agreed. And so we are at liberty to make any reading of a text *if it can be justified* by that text. In other words, as long as we can demonstrate in our analysis that the combination of signs the text consists of could mean what we say, then we are justified in our reading. This variety of readings is a result of communication being a 'dialogue'.

Dialogic communication

Numerous readings of texts are possible because of the arbitrary nature of signs, so what signs mean in a particular context is determined by a large number of factors. In his investigation of *parole* and *langue* (the speech act and underlying rule system), Saussure concluded that because speech was wholly individual it was not a suitable object for study. However, a contemporary of Saussure's, the Russian Valentin Volosinov, pointed out that speech is not an individual act, but a social phenomenon. Volosinov concluded that a sign's meaning was created, not by *langue*, but in the dialogic interaction created by social intercourse (that is, speaking to someone), and this also increases the possibility of polysemy.

Volosinov argued that all communication is structured as a dialogue. All artefacts are created for an audience; even writing a diary assumes, at least, the audience of oneself at a future date. Once a producer has an audience in mind, this fact must inevitably influence the signs used to communicate the message. For example, if you are discussing a film with someone who hasn't seen it, you are likely to have to offer plot detail for the conversation to make sense. However, if you are explaining the meaning of a text to a fellow media student, you can assume a lot more knowledge and an understanding of terminology (jargon) than you could if talking to a layperson. Similarly, this chapter is written under the assumption that the audience has understood the ideas in the first two chapters; if you haven't read and/or understood them, then you might not make sense of at least some of this chapter.

This dialogical conception explains the power of genres, as both the makers and audiences have a common set of expectations that offers a very clear context for an exchange of meaning between producers and audiences. Those who are not familiar with the genre are likely to make different readings from those who are.

Volosinov described signs as being multi-accentual, as they are not fixed in their meaning because that is determined by their interaction with other signs; this creates the possibility of polysemy. However, as we saw in Chapter 1, in practice, anchorage usually suggests a text's preferred meaning.

It is not only society as a whole that influences how we read texts; *who* we are is also an important variable (which, of course, is also influenced by society). If we are the type of person who accepts things at face value, we are more likely to accept a text's preferred, dominant, reading. However if we are a 'questioning' or sceptical type of person, we are more likely to make oppositional readings. The form these oppositional readings take will be determined both by our knowledge and by our ability to use different discourses from those into which the text invites us (see section 3.8).

Mikhail Bakhtin, a contemporary of Volosinov, developed the idea of the dialogic to acknowledge this complexity. He suggested that 'meaning is [best] understood as something still in the process of creation, something still bending toward the future as opposed to that which is already completed' (Quoted in Holquist 2002: 24). To Bakhtin, the notion that meaning is fixed, so that texts can offer universal messages, is anathema. He focuses on the complex processes involved in reading texts:

> Every community comes to film from what Bakhtin would call a distinct 'dialogical angle' each brings its own cultural orientation and political aspirations to bear on the film. The textually constructed reader/spectator does not necessarily coincide with the sociohistorical reader/spectator. Subcultural groups can read popular forms to their own advantage, even without the 'authorization' of the text or its producers. (Stam 1992: 43)

So while the producers of *Lost in Translation* didn't intend to make a racist film, Paik's (2004) 'dialogical angle', his own cultural orientation, read the film as representing Japanese negatively. While Paik was commenting contemporaneously, we can obviously read texts from the past, and, given our different cultural (and political) orientation, it is highly likely that we shall understand their preferred reading differently from the way it was understood at the time.

For example, Ming the Merciless, the villain in the *Flash Gordon* serial (1936), is now clearly a racist stereotype of a fiendish and merciless Asian dictator. In episode one, for example, Flash launches himself at Ming when the latter dares to reach for the virginal (and white) Dale Arden. No doubt many Asians would have been insulted by the racist depiction at the time; however, the popularity of the serial suggests the mass audience were not concerned and may not have recognized it as such because the manifestation of the bad guy as Asian (despite being from the planet Mongo) reflected the socio-political geography of the time.

We can watch the 1936 *Flash* knowing that Ming is a racist stereotype and recognize that this was a product of its less enlightened time. The 2007 remake of *Flash* cast John Ralston, a Caucasian Canadian, in the role: 'According to Mark Stern, Executive Vice President of the Sci Fi Channel, the decision was made to sidestep Ming's Asiatic stereotype: "Ming was consciously or not an Asian dictator in that really kind of cliché, ridiculous way"' (Brownlee 2007). Brownlee went on to suggest that this was an example of 'political correctness gone mad', which suggests that he isn't sensitive to racist representations. The Sci Fi Channel couldn't countenance an Asiatic Ming in 2007 because its racism would be obvious to the majority of the audience. This certainly doesn't mean that the original *Flash* should now be banned because it was racist. In fact, experiencing such racist representations reminds audiences of what different values were held in the past. During the end credits of *Bamboozled* (US, 2000), Spike Lee includes a montage of racist representations, made by Hollywood, of African-Americans that are so extreme that they couldn't be viewed as entertainment now – other than by racists.

There have been occasions when media texts have been censored because of, what we now see as, unpalatable representations. In 2006, Time Warner excised the image of a cat smoking a cigar in *Tom and Jerry* (*Tennis Chumps*, US, 1949) after a parent complained. George Orwell described, in *Nineteen Eighty-Four* (1949), how a repressive government rewrites history as it pleases. If we retrospectively edit out all racist representations, then it might appear that racism never existed. The parent's complaint about smoking was presumably on the basis that her child, seeing a cat smoking, would want to follow suit(!). The person's viewpoint was peculiar, because that episode also featured the racist stereotype of a picaninny; this, apparently, wasn't seen as offensive.

It is no surprise that people of different nations and cultures may make divergent readings of texts. It is also likely that any sub-cultural group to which we belong will also influence our understanding of texts. Marilyn Manson is a figure of hate for some (who bizarrely attribute the Columbine Massacre of 1999 to him), but is a figurehead for Goths. Sub-cultural groups, however, can do more than simply offer a situational context for the reading of texts: they can also appropriate texts for their own purposes.

Sub-cultural Groups

The sub-cultural group that Media Studies is specifically interested in are fans, members of the audience who interact with texts in an active fashion. This can lead to texts being read in ways that the original producers certainly did not intend; such as the homoerotic slash K/S fiction centred on Kirk and Spock in the 1960s' *Star Trek*. Henry Jenkins (1992) dubbed these fans to be textual poachers: 'not so much under the influence of the media they saturate themselves in [but] unorthodox *users* of the media, shaping or recasting it to suit their needs' (Gelder 2007: 141). This is similar to the poaching Dick Hebdige described as *bricolage*, where groups co-opt signifying systems of, for example, clothing to suit their purposes. The punks of the 1970s borrowed 'Objects ... from the most sordid of contexts ... lavatory chains were draped in graceful arcs across chests encased in plastic bin-liners. Safety pins were ... worn as gruesome ornaments through the cheek, ear or lip' (Hebdige 1979: 107). Of course, thirty years after this was published, facial piercing is (almost) part of the mainstream. However, it has been argued (Gelder 2007) that Jenkins' textual poachers conception of fandom is more romantic than realistic in its depiction of the white middle class as oppressed rebels.

The 'textual poacher' is also evident among the amateur manga producers (*dojinshi*) of Japan. Fan fiction in the West has circulated primarily underground, in fanzines and then on the internet; but these Japanese poachers have a far higher profile. Being 'underground' has the virtue of steering clear of corporate lawyers ready to sue for breaches of copyright; in Japan, the law is flouted more openly – for example, at the Super Comic City market:

> The dojinshi markets amply confirm [that the] copyright regime can be inadequate, and even detrimental, in a read/write culture. Amateur manga remixers aren't merely replicating someone else's work. They're creating something original. And in doing so may be helping ... the commercial interests of the copyright holders. (Pink 2007: 222b)

Japanese corporations are not so ready as their Western counterparts to sue their fans. While fans can appropriate textual meaning through recreating (remixing, mashing) texts (sometimes radically), most readings are a result of audiences simply try to understand the text they are consuming. Much of our understanding is in fact derived from other texts; hence intertextuality is essential to the process of reading.

We should be wary of assuming that multiple readings of texts mean that the media, regardless of what politicians or business wants are inherently democratic because audiences are free to put their own interpretation on the texts. This can only be the case if audiences have an alternative framework of understanding:

> In the case of the Persian Gulf war [1990–1], for example, the majority of American viewers, including many people of color, lacked any alternative grid to help them interpret events, specifically a view rooted in an understanding of the legacy of colonialism and its particular complexities in the Middle East. Primed by orientalist discourse and by the sheer inertia of the imperializing imaginary, they gave credence to whatever views the administration chose to present. (Shohat and Stam 1996: 164)

Hence the importance of education; as we shall see in our consideration of television news, the 'bias against understanding' inherent in many news organizations compromises audiences' ability to fully understand what is being reported.

3.4 Intertextuality

Returning to our *Flash Gordon* example: it was noted that the 2007 version of *Flash* substituted the racist stereotype of Ming. Anyone new to *Flash*, of course, would think nothing of the change; everyone else, through intertextuality (that is, having another text in mind when reading), would understand the character differently. If the *Flash* newbie then went on to see the original version, their understanding of the character Ming would also be likely to change.

Intertextuality operates most obviously in genre; we can only recognize what genre a text belongs to by knowing other, similar, texts. It does not, however, refer to allusions in texts to other texts, such as those that fill *The Simpsons*. Bakhtin had a broader view of intertextuality (a term coined by Julia Kristeva when translating Bakhtin's work), as he believed that language was also intertextual:

> Since all signs must be original uses of signifiers but [also] refer back to existing practices to which they respond. In this sense all communication is both original but derivative. In any one person's voice and actions the works and signs of others are always presupposed. (Page 2000: 25)

We can conclude from this that texts do not possess intrinsic meaning, because meaning is created via the interaction of texts and members of the audience, so texts never have just one meaning because there are always dialogic meanings.

Conceptualizing meaning as such an unstable property is a difficult concept, because we spend the early years of our formal education being taught that meaning, whether it be in Maths, Science or English, as being a fixed quality. Exams usually assess knowledge and do not encourage learners to think 'outside the box'. We are presented with the world as a place with fixed meanings that are readily explainable (see 3.6 Ideology):

> Bakhtinian semiotics situates the process of using signs within a historical moment and specific social practices where the participants generate meanings. The sign has a specific meaning in a specific content of use, but it is open to multiaccentuality, and can be used in other contexts. (Ibid.: 30)

Thus any reading we make of a text is likely to be constructed by our social upbringing and the context of the reading. For example, in the context of Media Studies, our reading might be determined by our need to demonstrate our understanding of the key concepts. It is important to appreciate that readings of texts are at least as much determined by the (intertextual) context of the audience as the text itself. For example, the Islamic Human Rights Commission read the character Behrani (Ben Kingsley) in *House of Sand and Fog* (US, 2003) as follows:

This stereotype of the Muslim man as a 'wife-beater' is reinforced on several occasions. Whilst he isn't the kind of 'Muslim' who backed the Revolution, he is nonetheless Muslim enough to be domineering and violent towards his wife. (Ameli *et al.* 2007: 47)

My own reading of Behrani was that he is a flawed character who yearned for the privilege that was lost during the Iranian Revolution of 1979 (the report describes this as the 'Islamic Revolution'). His violence toward his wife was a manifestation of his frustration of no longer being the important man he was (in America he works as a cleaner) and not a symptom of being a 'domineering Muslim husband'.

Does this mean that Ameli *et al.* are wrong? Of course not. Their reading is informed by being members of a group – Muslims – who are routinely represented negatively in the Western media, so it's no surprise that they should see the representation of Behrani as being symptomatic of that.

The advent of the internet has made it much easier to access different readings of media texts, but it is important to maintain an open mind and remember that all understanding is dialogic.

3.5 New media technologies

New media technologies (NMT) is the term given to developments based on the digitization of media texts. The extent to which they remain 'new' is debatable; however, the term does serve to emphasize that they are different from 'old media' technologies, such as radio and television. The extent to which the development of new media technologies has led to an evolution in the way we read and use the media is debatable. Lev Manovich suggests that 'The human–computer interface has become a key semiotic code of the information society ... so the old dichotomies *content – form* and *content – medium* can be rewritten as *content – interface*' (2001: 66).

On the other hand, we still use the reading skills we apply to other media texts when consuming texts on the World Wide Web (WWW). However, we should be aware that the web pages themselves, as texts, arguably display a higher degree of instability than did old media texts: 'In the WWW it is impossible to know exactly what a reader will see on her or his screen, due to different factors, such as the kind of monitor, the operating system, the browser s/he is using' (Cantoni and Tardini 2006: 75). Arguably, this instability is also present in the consumption of old media texts; for example, seeing a film on a 'state-of-the-art' TV compared to an old portable. However, it is endemic on the internet.

The use of hypertext – on, for example, the Web – as was noted in Chapter 1, does raise the question of textual boundaries. In Chapter 1 we simplified the issue by considering a website as constituting a text. However, while we are likely to watch only one film at a time, or read one book, we rarely stick to one website (and we can consume television by browsing through several programmes in one sitting). Hyperlinks facilitate this movement from website to website: 'Hypertexts' capability of connecting more texts into a meta-text renders it more similar to a *literature* than a single work' (ibid.: 95).

The digitization of texts frees them from the form in which they were originally produced. Multimedia texts – originally CD-ROMs – allow all media forms to be combined within one text; so encyclopaedias are no longer limited to the printed word, and online encyclopaedias can be updated constantly.

Digitization has also facilitated *convergence*, so mobile phones have also become MP3 players, cameras and web browsers, and the miniaturization of devices means that multimedia technology has become *portabl*, while wireless connections have enabled net, and email, access anywhere in the home and in many other places.

As noted above, *interactivity* is a key feature of digital media. This is more than audiences choosing what texts to read. The growth in broadband has increasingly allowed audiences to become producers themselves who can find substantial audiences on the Web. This shift has been dubbed Web 2.0. Tim O'Reilly used the dichotomy listed in Table 3.1 to distinguish between Webs 1.0 and 2.0.

Table 3.1   Tim O'Reilly's Webs 1.0 and 2.0 comparison

Web 1.0	Web 2.0
Doubleclick	Google AdSense
Ofoto	Flickr
Akamai	BitTorrent
mp3.com	Napster
Britannica Online	Wikipedia
personal websites	blogging
evite	upcoming.org and EVDB
domain name speculation	search engine optimization
page views	cost per click
screen scraping	web services
publishing	participation
content management systems	wikis
directories (taxonomies)	tagging ('folksonomy')
stickiness	syndication

Source: O'Reilly 2005.

Most of the items in the table can be subsumed under: blogging, mashups, podcasts, RSS (really simple syndication) feeds, social networking, tagging and wikis. Audiences not only produce media texts but also find an audience for them on their web pages (either designed by themselves or using the templates of MySpace, Bebo, Facebook and so on), blogs or podcasts.

Mashups combine texts to produce something new; these are a feature of music that 'mashes' a track with (an)other(s). They can also be used for political purposes: 'One notable mapshup is the Tunisian prisons map [http://www.kitab.nl/tunisianprisonersmap; accessed April 2008] project which mashed together maps and information from political activists to highlight human rights issues' (Gillmore 2008: 46b).

RSS and tagging (also known as folksonomy) are both ways of accessing, and sharing, information. RSS feeds allow the user to find out quickly if there's anything interesting on selected websites; tagging allows users to link, and to find links, between disparate material under the same heading. These can be shown as tag clouds showing which words have been tagged most frequently by using a larger font. For example, a tag cloud for this book might look like:

Barthes BBC binary opposition **bourgeois ideology** Brecht dialogic **horror genre** manga **masculinity** masquerade McRobbie **patriarchy** Vertov

Wikis, exemplified by Wikipedia, epitomize the communal nature of the Web, where thousands of individuals work together without commercial gain for the benefit of humankind. While allowing anyone to edit entries does result in vandalism and misinformation, it is essentially an accurate, up-to-date, resource. Of course, the essentially liberal, factual tone of Wikipedia doesn't offer a world-view that everyone agrees with; see for example http://www.conservapedia.com, which at least has the virtue of highlighting its reactionary nature in its title; its logo, literally, wraps itself in the American flag.

It was suggested above that hypertexts make web pages more like a literature than an individual text. The fact that literature has traditionally been thought of as consisting of a canon (see section 3.2) at least had the advantage of limiting the number of texts to be considered. The democratic 'instinct' of the Web negates this, hence the importance of search engines in giving structure to the morass. However, in a sense, the search engine has become the new Leavis, in limiting what we read on the internet. The most successful search engine, at the time of writing, is Google, which uses what

James Surowiecki calls 'the wisdom of crowds' to determine the order in which search results are presented:

> PageRank capitalizes on the uniquely democratic characteristic of the web by using its vast link structure as an organizational tool. In essence, Google interprets a link from page A to page B as a vote [and] assesses a page's importance by the votes it receives ... it also analyzes the page that casts the vote. Votes cast by pages that are themselves 'important' weigh more heavily and help to make other pages 'important'. (2005: 16)

So the most popular Web pages are used to designate the most important results for your research. This democratic bent of the internet works against the hierarchical nature of old media, where only an Establishment elite has access to the means of media production. Unsurprisingly, the Establishment's world-view, or ideology, predominated; the internet might be the beginning of the end for old media power, but that doesn't mean it will be the end of their ideological influence.

3.6 Ideology

In Chapter 2 we found that *all* meaning, because of the arbitrary nature of the sign, is socially constructed. As society is not a random collection of ideas, morals and viewpoints, it isn't surprising that the principles underpinning how a society makes meaning, across a range of texts, should be the same, or at least similar. These principles are constructed by ideology that 'refers to a systematic framework of social understanding, motivated by a will to power, or a desire to be accepted as the "right" way of thinking, which has wide ... support within a particular society or social group' (Macdonald 2003: 28). There is, arguably, a dominant ideology that informs the status quo; however, there are also competing ideologies, which may be relics from the past, or new ways of understanding the world emerging to challenge the status quo. Raymond Williams (1977) described two types of ideologies that compete with the dominant: residual and emergent.

A *residual* ideology belongs to a past dominant ideology, one that has been superseded. Religion clearly belongs to a feudal era and yet still exists in the modern world (and in some places is obviously still dominant). In Britain, the monarchy is still extant, representing a former feudal power structure.

An *emergent* ideology is a new cultural development that may eventually supplant the dominant ideology, just as capitalism supplanted feudalism.

During the 1960s, the 'women's movement' was an emergent ideology that attempted to gain power from the patriarchal bourgeois system. From a perspective of forty years later, this clearly hasn't happened, and feminism has a fairly low profile in Western society. However, the feminist movements have made real gains, such as the Suffragettes' campaign for the vote and the UK's Sex Discrimination Act of 1975. Feminism is an example of an emergent ideology that forced the dominant ideology to adapt, but not change fundamentally, as patriarchy is still a powerful force. As a Cambridge University study concluded: 'British women are working in lower paid and lower status jobs than their male counterparts because they still shoulder the responsibility for housework and childcare' (Ward 2007: 2).

The patriarchal view that prefers to see women as sex objects rather then economic competitors is evidenced by the flourishing UK men's magazine weekly market publications *Nuts* and *Zoo Weekly* (see section 4.8).

It is possible that 'green' issues may form an emergent ideology. As it becomes increasingly obvious that technological progress, part of the bedrock of bourgeois ideology, has compromised the environment, the dominant ideology has to respond to these developments. One way in which this is detectable is in the existence of 'environment-friendly' products, and large corporations using advertising to suggest how ecological efficient they are; BSkyB, for example, was the first media company to declare itself 'carbon neutral' (http://phx.corporate-ir.net/phoenix.zhtml?c=104016& p=irol-newsArticle_print&ID=832905; accessed March 2008).

Box 3.1   Bourgeois ideology

Bourgeois ideology has dominated our understanding of the world, in the West, since the late seventeenth and early eighteenth centuries. At that time it challenged the 'feudal world' (see also section 3.10), where the social class into which you were born was almost certainly the one in which you remained until you died. The new, progressive bourgeois ideology offered the prospect of social mobility. The engine of this social mobility was money, as the growth in commerce, fired by the Industrial Revolution, made wealth generation, and hence the gaining of status, possible for those other than the aristocracy; so emerged the middle class.

Once the middle class, or the bourgeoisie, had gained power (at the expense of feudal rulers such as Louis XVI, who lost his head) they became reactionary as they defended the new status quo. Karl Marx and Frederick Engels:

associated ideology and class, asserting that the ideas of the ruling class were the ruling ideas. Ideological illusions were an instrument in the hands of the rulers, through the state, and were employed to exercise control and domination; indeed, to 'manufacture history' according to their interests. (Freeden 2003: 6)

Key to Marx and Engels' formulation was that bourgeois ideology was illusory and could be shown to be such if the working classes (proletariat) could gain class consciousness and see they were being exploited by the bourgeoisie. The idea that ideology is intrinsically false has been superseded by the recognition that, because our understanding of the world is socially constructed, ideology inevitably shapes the way we see that world.

In keeping with the idea that meaning is created through oppositions (see section 2.5), we can conceive of the values of bourgeois ideology as follows:

Table 3.2 Bourgeois ideology and its opposite

Bourgeois ideology	The opposite
Consumerism	Socialism
Freedom	Constraint
Free market economy	Managed economy
Individual	Community
Nuclear family	Extended family
Patriarchy	Matriarchy
Progress	Regress

Bourgeois ideology emphasizes the importance of the individual over the community hence the nuclear family (dad, mum and the kids) is the central social unit, rather than the extended family (which would include uncles, aunts, cousins and so on). The head of the family unit is the father who, traditionally, has been the breadwinner, emphasizing the patriarchal nature of the ideology.

Many people would argue that consumerism lies at the heart of Western society; and some believe this is a bad thing. Capitalism, the economic system of bourgeois ideology, necessitates people buying products and services even if they don't need them; for businesses, the emphasis is always on growth: that is, more sales than the previous year. On the other hand, socialism's dictum, derived from Marx, is 'from each according to his ability, to each according to his need (or needs)'. In other words, people contribute what they can and take what they need (the male gender used here suggests the early socialists were also patriarchal too).

We are used to believing in progress, that things, such as technology, get better each year. However, it is certainly arguable that technological progress has in fact blighted humanity, from the atomic bombs used in the Second World War, to the ecological disasters such as Bhopal in 1984, and global warming. Reality often contradicts ideology, and so ideology works, often through the media, to disguise such inconsistencies.

The belief in (individual) freedom is regarded as self-evidently important in Western culture. Since the 1980s, the monetarist economic tenet of the free market economy has held sway, replacing the mixed economy that saw both the public and private sectors providing products and services (for example, basic utilities such as electricity and water used to be state-run in Britain). It should be of no surprise that the emphasis on the private sector should have seen the decline of public transport and the increase in car ownership; in cars we can inhabit our own *private* space and do not have to share a *communal* vehicle.

Bourgeois ideology is not, however, simply a monolithic set of ideas that the above characterization implies. For example, while a right-wing version of the ideology believes that:

- the 'free market' should be at the heart of the economic system
- public ownership is an inefficient way of managing utilities
- the welfare state is something that encourages laziness
- criminality is a moral, rather than economic, choice.

A liberal version of the same ideology suggests that:

- it is right for the state to intervene in certain economic matters
- that public ownership is good for public utilities
- that the welfare state acts as a safety net and prevents poverty
- that crime is a product of social conditions, such as high unemployment.

The crucial point for Media Studies students is that ideology does not act as a 'window on the world', but *shapes* our view of the world. Bourgeois ideology, in fact, characterizes itself as natural, and this is one of the reasons it has been successful. It has inculcated itself into our lives so successfully that it is difficult to perceive it. Even the rules of continuity editing (see section 1.12) reflect bourgeois values by presenting texts as if they were showing us the world and not a re-presentation of the world (we shall investigate alternative media language in section 3.9). As Barthes suggests, 'The reluctance to declare its codes characterizes bourgeois society and the mass culture issuing from it: both demand signs which do not look like signs' (Barthes 1973: 116).

It was suggested, in Chapter 1, that the function of media analysis is to deconstruct a text to show how meaning is created. We can develop this further to state that ideological analysis of texts must show the ideological workings of the text. In some cases, such as advertising, this can be straightforward; however, many texts 'conceal' their values in order to convey an argument without appearing to do so. They suggest rhetorically that they are offering a 'window on the world', whereas the reality they are showing is ideologically constructed.

Box 3.2   Ideology and genre

In an essay on horror film, Robin Wood suggested how we might read the genre ideologically. He conceived the Other as central to horror:

> 'the Other': that which bourgeois ideology cannot recognize or accept but must deal with (as Barthes suggest in *Mythologies*) in one of two ways: either by rejecting and if possible annihilating it, or by rendering it safe and assimilating it, converting it as far as possible into a replica of itself [that is, bourgeois ideology]. (Wood 1985: 199)

He characterized 'the Other' of bourgeois ideology as being: women; the proletariat; other cultures; ethnic groups; alternative ideologies or political systems; deviations from ideological sexual norms; children. The monsters of horror films dramatize the 'return of the repressed'; that is, they represent what does not belong in (bourgeois) society. This is why horror is the stuff of nightmares and is inhabited by bogeymen. A few examples of Wood's ideas follow.

Barbara Creed (1993) described the 'monstrous-feminine' as locating the abject – the completely wretched – within women. She considers films such *The Exorcist* (1973), *Carrie* (1976) and *The Brood* (1979) as examples where women are represented as the monstrous Other. In a patriarchal society, women are defined as second-class and threaten, by claiming equality, male 'superiority'; the narrative of horror dramatizes this threat and invariably expunges it.

In the *Texas Chainsaw Massacre* (1974, 2003) the redundant workers (proletariat) of a slaughterhouse keep their 'body and soul' together through using passers-by as meat (a theme also evident in H. G. Wells' *The Time Machine*, 1895). This is similar to *The Woman of the Dunes* (*Suna no onna*, Japan, 1964) where a community cast adrift in sand dunes capture an entomologist to supply labour and sexual favours for a widow. This fear of the working class is probably most accentuated in the Southern Gothic, where backwoodsmen loom, and leer, menacingly out of the undergrowth in films such as *Deliverance* (1974). In Marxist terms, the proletariat are exploited by the bourgeoisie and so inevitably threaten the status quo should they gain class consciousness and revolt.

Monogamous heterosexuality is the bourgeois ideal:

> As Tudor [1989] has shown, from the 1970s on, 'madness' as a kind of transcendent evil is redefined as 'psychosis', secular in origin, and almost always having its root in 'perverse' sexuality. While this approach also involves issues of race and class, it is the various forms of repressed sexual energy, particularly within the site of the nuclear family, that has received the most critical attention. (Grant 1996: 40)

In *Fatal Attraction* (1987) a woman's seductiveness, and sexual appetite, are represented as monstrous as this leads to the central character's family being threatened. Wood cites *Shivers* (1975) as a film predicated on the horror of sexual liberation, where 'the release of sexuality is linked inseparably with the spreading of venereal disease' (Wood 1985: 216).

It should be clear by now that bourgeois ideology does not have a privileged relationship with the 'truth', or 'reality', but is merely sets of values that structure our understanding of the world. It is arguable that it is impossible to 'know' the real world, that there are only 'ways of seeing' the world using different ideologies. This conventionalist position posits that there are an infinite number of ways of observing reality. Reality, in this view, is merely the product of the framework, or paradigm, used to observe the world, and no paradigm, or ideology, can give an unadulterated picture of what the world is truly like.

Box 3.3   Ideology and narrative

Narratives also have an ideological function. Many mainstream texts dramatize the (patriarchal) Oedipal narrative where:

> The hero proves his worthiness to take up his place as a man, by accomplishing a series of directed tests: a process which will often culminate,

in self-contained narratives, with his integration into the cultural order through marriage ... it provides the most familiar structure for such male-orientated Hollywood genres as the Western and the adventure film. (Krutnik 1991: 87–8)

The TV series *Heroes* is, in part, driven by Oedipal conflict. In episode 1, Mohinder states 'I need to finish what [my father] started.' Hiro spends most of series one in paternal conflict until his father teaches him Samurai sword-craft. However, there is a conspicuous, once you think about it, absence of matriarchal narratives (when I 'Googled' 'matriarchal narratives' the search engine asked me, 'Did you mean: patriarchal narratives?'), but they do, arguably, crop up in unlikely places. Sarah Harwood suggests that *Jurassic Park* (1993) dramatizes the limits of patriarchal power: 'The film ... stresses the imperviousness of the dinosaurs to man-made interference and destruc-tion, an imperiousness based on a matriarchal ability to mutate and evade scientific regulation and the controls of patriarchy' (Harwood 1997: 189).

This resolution, where patriarchy is subverted rather than vindicated is unusual:

> The therapeutic function of mainstream Hollywood cinema would be to give play to fantasies of deviancy, disruption, and otherness, before channelling them in such a way as to affirm a single final goal: the estab-lishment and maintenance of a nuclear family, under conditions of bour-geois ideology, capitalism, and patriarchy. (Elsaesser and Buckland 2002: 223)

So difference is dramatized so that it can be rejected in favour of conform-ity. Elsaesser and Buckland illustrate this point with reference to *Die Hard* (1988); at the start, John McClane's wife has left him to develop her own career, but patriarchal ideology 'insists':

> She has to be stripped of all her (traditionally male) professional attrib-utes: she starts off in control ... But when directly confronting Gruber, she 'reverts' to female demands: a sofa for her pregnant colleague ... She is then taken hostage ... as wife of John McClane ... in another scene, she is shown ... acting as ... maid or midwife. In the end, she gets John back, but is properly reduced to the role of mother and nurturer. (ibid.: 75)

We can only speculate the degree to which the popularity of *Die Hard* was related to this ideological 'argument'; most in the audience certainly wouldn't have noticed it at a conscious level. However, the prevalence of the Oedipal narrative suggests that it is an important part of the appeal of mainstream texts; the film *10,000 BC* (US, 2008) would have us believe that seeking to emulate one's father preoccupied our ancestors too.

Of course, the audiences for all these texts are unlikely to be delving into ideological analysis, and most will consider them to be harmless entertainment. Analysis of the ideological underpinnings of texts does allow us to unmask the ideological basis of society, so we can see how the power structures of bourgeois capitalism operate and so better understand our world.

It should be noted that patriarchy is not limited to bourgeois ideology. For example, *Kikiru and the Sorceress* (France, 1998), based on West African folk tales, dramatizes how a (very precocious) baby becomes a man with the aid of his father's (phallic) dagger and wins the sorceress as his bride.

Ideology and reality

The fact that there are alternative perspectives on the world demonstrates that while ideology has a profound influence on our way of seeing, it does not have a monopoly on meaning. However, ideology is not subverted simply by an analysis of connotations; it is very resistant to a deconstruction of its ideas because the language we use to deconstruct it is itself a product of the ideology. Attempts to circumvent this have often led to obscure jargon (see Box 3.7). Ideology structures language, and language structures the way we communicate about reality.

Thoughtful Media Studies students often find that their 'naïve' view of the world has been compromised because once it is realized that meaning is a social construct, and not a product of objects, then it is obvious that reality is being mediated by systems of signs: we know a tree is a tree and not a 'plang' because the society in which we grew up tells us that it is a tree (or 'arbre', 'albero', 'Baum' and so on). Once it is understood that, in turn, society is not a neutral grouping of individuals but rather a system of competing power relationships, then it becomes clear that the language – whether it be linguistic or media – has a political purpose which may, or may not, be to our benefit.

Of course, the description of society given above is itself is an ideological construct. It is an example of an oppositional way of seeing our society; a society marked by conflict, not consensus. For example, 'common sense' is an idea that signifies itself to be sensible and natural. However, from an oppositional view, 'common sense' is 'bourgeois sense' because it is a product of people being 'told', through socialization, what to think. Human beings do not, genetically, possess 'common sense', so it is a social construct. As 'common sense' is consensual it must articulate the values of the dominant ideology. And the power of ideology lies in its ability to present itself as 'natural', as 'common sense'.

This oppositional ideological analysis, however, should not imply that there is a conspiracy to keep the majority in the dark and so make them readily exploitable. There is no individual who is independent of ideology and so can pronounce upon it except, possibly, God, if s/he exists. While individuals who wield power in Western society, whether elected or through their institutional positions, are usually financially richer than most of their fellows, they are, to an extent, merely fulfilling a role within the power structure. So the people who run the world's multinational media companies are, to that extent, merely fulfilling executive roles; it doesn't matter *who* they are, what matters is *what* they *do*, and that is defined by the institutional values of the organization, which, invariably, revolve around the need to be profitable.

Ideology and institution

Virtually all media corporations (the British Broadcasting Corporation – BBC – is one exception) need to make money. In Britain and the USA, and elsewhere, publicly limited companies must act in the interests of their shareholders, and this is defined as generating profit. This need to make money explains why most media texts inhabit the mainstream, as they are then more likely to gain a sufficiently large audience to offer shareholders a return on their investment. The profit prerogative means that minority views, and alternative modes of representation (see section 3.8) are marginalized; in a way they are the Other of media texts. So individuals who believe that, say, arthouse cinema or classical music isn't for them, are validating mainstream, profit-driven media.

The modes of production of media texts are determined less by the individuals in the organizations than by the:

> dynamics underlying the industrial strategies in the sector ... Regulation policy ... aesthetic ideologies, professional codes and histories of class, gender and ethnic relationships ... all affect the production processes and outcomes within media organisations. (Goldsmiths Media Group 2000: 21)

This point will be investigated more thoroughly in section 4.5 Who does the re-presenting? Suffice to say here that when the Director-General of the BBC said, in 2001, that the Corporation was 'hideously white', he was acknowledging the fact that having 98 per cent of managers of the same ethnicity was bound to have a limiting affect on how the institution served its audience. In 2008, the actor-comedian Lenny Henry made a similar comment.

It isn't only people from ethnic minorities who find their 'difference' is a barrier to success. Disabled people are also under-represented both in media organizations and in media texts. In 2007, Channel 4, as public service broadcasters should, initiated a scheme to help redress this imbalance:

> Channel 4 is looking for deaf or disabled people to form a new filmmaking team called The Shooting Party.
>
> The team behind the scheme are looking for people with strong ideas, bags of energy and the confidence to make an original 3–5 minute film – a documentary, drama, music video or any other kind of short – to be broadcast on Channel 4. (http://www.channel4.com/blogs/page/fourdocs?entry=the_shooting_party; accessed April 2008)

The drive for profit structures how mainstream texts operate. For example, many lifestyle magazines depend on advertising for their profitability. Most of the advertising carried by magazines such as *More* are for cosmetics (eight out of thirteen display advertisements in the edition of 1 January 2008). It is arguable that lifestyle magazines simultaneously generate and solve problems; for example, the existence of numerous 'dieting' articles suggests that there is a problem among readers with being 'overweight'. Whether this is in the readers' interests is debatable.

When media theorists began examining the women's magazine industry, it was 'understood as a monolithic meaning-producer, circulating magazines that contain "messages" and "signs" about the nature of femininity that serve to promoted and legitimate dominant interests' (Gough-Yates 2003: 7).

And these interests were seen, from the feminist perspective, as being detrimental to women, because patriarchal notions of femininity infused them. This model of ideology, however, was one that failed to respond to changes in society. Janice Winship (1987) demonstrated how the magazines would adapt their message to encompass changes in society. For example, 'The ideological work ... was accomplished through ... characterization of gender inequality as an issue to be resolved by the *individual* acting in their everyday lives rather than as a deep-rooted problem that demanded wide-ranging social transformation' (ibid.: 10).

So the magazines acknowledged the problem of gender inequality but posited a bourgeois solution, which emphasized individual rather than collective action. This is an example of hegemony, where ideology operates to gain consent for the unequal distribution of power.

Box 3.4   Religion and ideology

Bourgeois ideology is only one, albeit the dominant one, of a number of ideologies that exist in Western society. Religion is, of course, another ideological construct; however, most of those who have faith believe it is 'real' and not just a particular way of viewing and understanding the world. As we shall see in the history of images later in the chapter, the dominant way of seeing the world in feudal times was as an unchanging and unchangeable place: religion had all the answers.

The dominance of the religious world-view diminished, in the Western world, with the arrival of capitalism. It had survived for centuries by denying the possibility of change and claiming there was no alternative to the status quo – clearly an effective way of preserving a dominant status. When it became clear that religion's explanation of the world was partial, then religion either had to adapt or lose its pre-eminence. An ideology that is built on inflexible premises will find it very difficult to adapt to changes in the material world.

One example of how a new view of reality was dealt with by the Church (the institution of Christian ideology) was the case of Galileo Galilei. By using a telescope, invented in the Netherlands, Galileo showed conclusively that the Earth was not at the centre of the universe. By demonstrating that the moons of Jupiter revolved around their mother planet, and not around Earth, he shattered one of the central tenets of religion (Nicolas Copernicus had realized this 100 years earlier, but the time was not ready then for his ideas).

The Church's response to Galileo's 'blasphemy' was to force him to recant the truth or to die. This was a very weak response, as it attempted to hold on to a past way of seeing, rather than adapt to a new perspective. Because it could not adapt, religion become an inappropriate system of thought. However, it might have been successful in suppressing the 'new truth' were it not for the fact that the currents of the time were conducive to change; this is considered further with a history of realism in section 5.1. In recent years, religion seems to have been making inroads at the expense of bourgeois ideology. For example, Intelligent Design is taught in some places alongside Darwinism as an explanation of evolution, despite the fact that it has no scientific basis. The argument that Darwinism is 'just' a theory and so should be considered alongside the 'theory' of Intelligent Design is spurious, as Darwin's theory is based on scientific evidence whereas Intelligent Design has no such basis: science is proof without certainty whereas religion is certainty without proof.

3.7 Hegemony

As has been demonstrated, we do not have unadulterated access to reality, and our perception is influenced by the dominant ideological system. Both ideology and discourse (see section 3.8) are expressions of a society's power structures. Because there is an imbalance in the distribution of power in Western society (favouring the white, middle classes), clearly there must be groups who are subordinate (for example, the working classes and black people).

Exercising power is not necessarily a straightforward operation, as George Orwell described when he was a police officer in Burma, which was then part of the British Empire. He was 'forced' to shoot an elephant against his will, despite the fact that, as a policeman, he clearly wielded power. However, unless he used this power in an expected fashion then he would be at risk of losing it:

> Here I was, the white man with his gun, standing in front of the untamed native crowd seemingly the leading actor of the piece; but in reality I was only an absurd puppet pushed to and fro by the will of those yellow faces behind. I perceived in this moment that when the white man turns tyrant it is his own freedom that he destroys. (Orwell 1971: 267)

Although Orwell was an anti-imperialist, we can detect Orwell's colonial characterization of the 'untamed native crowd', suggesting they were uncivilized, with their undifferentiated 'yellow faces'.

Antonio Gramsci, imprisoned for many years by Italian fascists, theorized, in the 1920s and 1930s, that the dominant classes do not wholly wield power through coercion; in fact, their most powerful method is by gaining the consent of the masses. If the working classes did not feel oppressed they were far more likely to offer their consent that the ruling classes should be in power. Gramsci described Western society as a hegemonic alliance between the rulers and their subordinates in which the right of the dominant class to rule is accepted by all.

In democracies political consent is gained through the ballot box. However, in many countries there are only two political parties – occasionally three – to choose from. Despite this apparent choice it is extremely rare for any party to offer a genuinely radical alternative to the consensus. Voters are then left only with a choice of consensus parties that, some would argue, is in fact no choice at all. Gramsci emphasized that there was no one identifiable group that held power; rather there exists an alliance that forms the ruling bloc, an alliance dominated by white, male, middle-class individuals.

In Media Studies the concept of hegemony is useful in showing how, through images and texts, this consent to a dominant ideological position is won. For example, the position of women in Western society is generally subordinate, even though legally in most countries they have equal rights. This subordination is, in part, created through the representation of gender in which men are seen to be powerful and dynamic, and women weak and passive (we shall consider the representation of gender in Chapter 5). While, clearly, many do not agree with the way genders are conventionally represented, the predominance of such patriarchal representations are a powerful socializing agent. The subordination of women is an aspect of patriarchal, bourgeois ideology, and hegemony naturalizes this ideological representation.

The export of media texts – films, music, TV programmes – can also be seen as a way in which certain values are transported around the world. These values tend to be American, partly as a result of the economic power of US entertainment industries. However, the degree to which media texts are part of 'cultural imperialism' is debatable; see Box 3.5.

Box 3.5   Globalization or glocalization? – *Yo soy Betty la fea (I Am Ugly Betty)*

American television has been exported successfully around the world, *Baywatch* (1989–2001) has even played in Iran, but movement of programmes into the USA and Britain, the 'reverse flow', of non-English-language fare has been extremely limited. This is an example of cultural imperialism, as defined by Herbert Schiller in 1969: 'the export of US television programmes, equipment and advertising was part of a concerted effort by the American government, military and industry to subjugate the world for ideological and profitable ends' (quoted in Steemers 2004: 2).

More recently, this one-way notion of cultural flow has been superseded, to take into account such programmes as the Colombian telenovela *Yo soy Betty la fea* (1999–2001) that has been exported around the world. Telenovelas – television novels – have been a staple of Latin-American television since the 1950s. Over the last forty years, starting in Portugal in the 1970s, European countries have fallen under the spell of the melodramatic form that, while being analogous to soap opera, usually has a limited run of six months or so.

Just as Hollywood will remake virtually any popular foreign-language film, American television picked up *Yo soy Betty la fea* and gave it a US makeover:

Besides setting the show in the United States (at a fashion magazine rather than a design shop), producers turned it from a soap opera with daily cliffhangers into a weekly comedy [series] with plots that begin and end in each episode. (http://www.miamiherald.com/news/miami_dade/story/312084.html; accessed November 2007)

Yo soy Betty has been particularly successful as an export that is readily adapted for national audiences. Hugh O'Donnell (2007) states that, in addition to the US version, Germany, Greece, India, Israel, Mexico, the Netherlands, Russia, Spain and Turkey have all produced local variants of the Colombian original. The adaptation of the original material for the local market is an example of what Arjun Appadurai (1990) calls the Mediascape: 'The image-centred landscapes offering interpretations of the narratives of human lives within the global system. Such narratives involve imagination and fantasy as much as hard reporting' (Quoted in Holton 1992: 234). Appadurai's point is that globalization cannot be viewed simply as a situation where the economic powerhouses dictate cultural consumption. The adaptation to local markets of *Yo soy Betty* is part of the process of indigenization by media producers; audiences, of course, indigenize even Hollywood films through their readings: 'This overlapping of globalising, regionalising and localising forces is defined by Robertson [1995] as "glocalisation" – or the global production of the local and the localisation of the global in a process involving both homogenising and heterogenising forces' (Steemers 2004: 10).

So American television offers an 'Ugly Betty' that will articulate the values of its own society, just as European versions will do the same. However, while American television programmes and films will play in their original versions around the world, the market for foreign-language product in America (and Britain) is severely limited, so cultural exchange is heavily loaded towards American media.

Although this is less obvious than it used to be, an example of hegemonic representation was evident in American crime television series or films. In many texts, criminals were from ethnic minority groups and usually working-class. The representation suggests that these groups are naturally degenerate and this reinforces their subordinate position. If representations of working-class, ethnic minority groups focused on, say, poor educational opportunities or bad housing then it is possible that more would be done to alleviate such situations. As it is, because such groups appear to be degenerate, their deprived social situation is seen as being justifiable.

Another example is how national lotteries and game shows have supported the unequal distribution of wealth by offering the possibility of anyone (player) of joining the 'have-a-lots': '[These programmes] have been highly successful examples of the way ideologies around "the big windfall" can become deeply entrenched into group consciousness' (Casey *et al.* 2002: 119).

Hegemony is an extremely powerful tool of social control, because the distribution of power in society is often accepted as natural – as, in fact, 'common sense' (which, as we know, is not a natural construct). 'Common sense' should, in fact, be called 'hegemonic sense'. So the dominant classes do not merely control the coercive forces of society, such as the police, army and judiciary, but they also exercise cultural leadership. The values of the dominant classes become the norm through the codes and conventions of representation used by mainstream media. It is through the media that the meanings we use to make sense of our lives are often structured.

However, no hegemony can be complete. Emerging ideologies may 'attack' the established order. These alternative discourses can also be seen in the media. As mentioned earlier, the developing awareness of 'green' issues is a potential threat to the dominant ideology, particularly if the argument that economic growth should be sacrificed in order to conserve resources gains currency. If green politics is to take root it will have to combat a deeply entrenched consumer ethic in Western society, as the front page of *More*'s strapline puts it: Life > Shopping > Celebs. In many ways celebrities embody consumerism: they are used to sell products and validate an extravagant lifestyle.

The argument that texts such as women's magazines do not simply reflect reality but actively form our world leads us to a consideration of discourse.

3.8 Discourse

Discourse, like culture, is a multi-discursive concept. 'Multi-discursive' is a term coined by O'Sullivan *et al.* (1994) to describe concepts that have very different meanings depending on the context in which they are used. Myra Macdonald's definition is particularly useful, and distinguishes between discourse and ideology:

Both refer to systematic frameworks for understanding that are socially formed ... the emphasis in my working definition of discourse is on the *communication* of these, while ideology conjures up more abstract ways of thinking. (Macdonald 2003: 28)

In this definition, discourse is the way in which ideological power is communicated and used:

> Discourse is the means by which institutions wield their power through a process of definition and exclusions, intelligibility and legitimacy. (Storey 2002: 78)

In addition to this:

> Discourses do not simply offer 'neutral' descriptions of social reality – they actively work to constitute it. (Casey *et al.* 2002: 64)

The work of Michel Foucault has been particularly influential in explaining how discourse is linked to the coercive use of power:

> For Foucault, power is not the property of, say, a ruling class; power is a strategic terrain, the site of an unequal *relationship* between the powerful and the powerless. (Storey, 2001, p. 78)

So discourse is used to define, and exclude, what constitutes a discipline, such as medicine, and the terms of debate, such as in politics. Discourse is both a 'way of speaking' as well as a 'way of seeing'; therefore, definitions of, say, femininity are – in Western society at least – defined by patriarchy, so that both representations of women, and readings of women, are structured by patriarchal discourse – see Chapter 4.

Edward Said drew on Foucault in his seminal book *Orientalism* (first published 1978) describing the discourse the West, rooted in British and French colonialism, used to describe the East: 'Orientalism can be discussed and analysed as a corporate institution for dealing with the Orient – dealing with it by making statements about it, authorising views of it, describing it, by teaching it, ruling over it: in short, Orientalism as a Western site for dominating, restructuring, and having authority over the Orient' (Said 2003: 3).

In 2007, the Orientalist discourse proved very potent in the newspaper reporting of the capture, by Iranians, of fifteen Royal Navy personnel. Iran's hostility towards Britain may be puzzling to those who are ignorant of Britain's colonial role in the Middle East (itself a Eurocentric creation which situates Europe as the fixed point and Iran, with its neighbours, halfway between it and the Far East of China and Japan). Understanding Britain's, often duplicitous, relationship with the area explains much of the hostility that Iran, and other nations, have towards the UK.

Derek Bryce (2007–8) analysed how this discourse structured the reporting of the crisis through its narrative use of 'the myth of the captive' and the 'Oriental despot'. The 'captive' narrative has a long history: the Puritans evoked it in seventeenth-century New England: 'the New England Indian captivity narrative functioned as a myth ... In it a single individual, usually a woman, stands passively under the strokes of evil, awaiting rescue by the grace of God' (Slotkin 1973: 94). (The 'rescue' – its representation turned out to be bogus – of Jessica Lynch, during the Iraq War, similarly fed upon the captive narrative – see Faludi, 2007).

Bryce quotes from the *Daily Mail* of 31 March 2007:

Leading Seaman Faye Turney, paraded like a trophy by her gloating Iranian captors ... we see ... a terrified young mother, her blonde hair covered with a Muslim scarf ... hands shaking with fear. (Bryce 2007–8: 19c)

The emphasis is on Turney's femininity, her blondeness signifying her white ethnicity that, in a racist discourse, is constructed as 'pure'. Iran's president, Mahmoud Ahmadinejad, was represented as a typical Oriental despot (as in *Flash Gordon's* Emperor Ming, considered earlier in the chapter) in *The Sun* (5 April 2007):

Ahmadinejad bragged to the world that he ordered their release as an Easter gift to the British people.

Then he insisted on taunting the group one by one is a sickening line-up at his palace in Tehran. (Quoted in Bryce 2007–8: 21a)

Orientalist discourse is used to emphasize the Otherness of the East, thus reinforcing Western values as normal and civilized and simultaneously denigrating, in this case Iran, and celebrating, in this case British values.

It isn't necessarily only the Western media that use Orientalist discourse to articulate representations of the East. The film *Hero* (*Ying xiong*, Hong Kong–China, 2003), directed by Zhang Yimou, arguably renders its vision in Orientalist terms, particularly in the fight scene set on a lake with a pagoda. However, as Choong (2004) suggests, its use of Orientalist tropes – such as the despot – is far from straightforward.

Foucault took the view that our understanding of the world is wholly shaped by discourses and so, in effect: 'discourse [analysis] abandon[s] the representation of reality and plump[s] conclusively for the construction of reality' (Freedan 2003: 106).

We have already noted, in section 3.3 Audience readings, the meaning we get from a text depends on which discourses we bring to it. These are usually unconscious in that we simply make a reading based on our understanding;

however, we can also do this consciously by bringing different discourses to bear on the same text; see Box 3.6.

Box 3.6   Nokia 232 discourses

Middle-class values
As the earlier analysis has already made clear, this is a lifestyle advertisement: buy the product; enjoy the lifestyle. This dominant reading is structured by the middle-class values that celebrate culture, wealth and the importance of image. Unless we understand the connotations of the copy ('unforgettable ...'), the classical pillars, or the woman's looks, then we will not enter this discourse and thereby fail to make a dominant reading.

Marketing
From a commercial discourse point of view, this advertisement forms part of the 'marketing mix'. This mix consists of the product, price, distribution of the product and publicity. Clearly, advertising is part of publicity. Individuals who may use a commercial discourse are those with knowledge of marketing or are also involved in selling the product advertised.

Feminist
The discourse of feminism emphasizes the inequality between the sexes in society. Here, the emphasis would be on the portrayal of the woman as a sex object. This discourse would create an oppositional reading.

Psychoanalysis
In brief, Freud suggested that the root of most human behaviour was motivated by the libido, or sexual desire. In analysing texts from a psychoanalytical perspective, the emphasis is on sex symbols. Unsurprisingly, advertising often yields much to this approach, as the industry uses sex to sell anything. In the Nokia 232 advertisement, the pillar becomes a phallic symbol (representing a penis), and thus her hand placed on the object becomes significant.

The walk, which in another reading suggested dynamism, now emphasizes the model's legs and the fact that they are apart. The woman's gaze becomes one of sexual desire. The 'lifestyle' advertising equation 'buy this product and get a woman like this' becomes explicitly sexual.

As a science, psychoanalysis has many critics, but as a discourse for analysing media texts it is immensely useful in bringing to the surface what may be latent.

EXERCISE 3.3

Using any advertisement, write as many discourses as you can that would be appropriate in reading the text. What discourse does the advertisement invite you into (probably determined by 'metalanguage' and 'form')?

We have seen that our understanding of the world is a result of ideological processes; in discourse, as in myths, we can observe ideology in action. Discourses operate at the level of individuals, in a social context, and are subject to historical change. For example, it is a tenet of contemporary, bourgeois ideology that education is good for you, and the discourses of education are subjects such as English, Maths, Chemistry, Media Studies and so on. Before an educated workforce was required, education was not deemed to be important for the masses, but by the end of the nineteenth century, education was deemed to be intrinsically good: that is, the purpose of education was simply to become educated. In recent years, in Britain at least, this liberal-humanist view has been replaced by the view that the purpose of education is to service the needs of business.

Discourse is most obvious at a social level, particularly in a formal context. All institutions possess specific discourses that are expressed by different priorities. For example, the institutions of the law, medicine, politics and law enforcement have different discourses that involve different ways of looking at the world and different use of language to describe them.

It is not only institutions that use discourses, however; every human activity involves a certain prioritization of ideas, and often a particular language, formal or informal, to go with it. For example, we are all members of a particular social class, and our 'class discourse' may influence our behaviour. For example, for many years, the myth of the working class (usually defined by occupation) suggested that its members were hedonistic, deferential and instinctive, whereas middle-class people deferred gratification, were assertive and intellectual.

Gender is also a product of discourse. While the sex of individuals is obviously a biological variable, gender is a purely social construct. There is clearly nothing biological in the male's supposed preference for the colour blue, a delight in cars and aversion to child-minding (after you have done Exercise 3.4, see section 5.2 Representations of gender).

EXERCISE 3.4

List the differences between the genders and then tick those you believe are a result of socialization and not a 'natural' difference.

Discourse is central to our lives; it helps us to make sense of information. Each individual has access to numerous discourses, any one of which may be dominant at a given time. The number of discourses we have is determined by socialization and education: the more knowledge an individual has, the more discourses s/he can enter.

While media texts may invite us into a particular discourse, which will result in our decoding the dominant reading, the audience is free to choose whether or not to use the offered discourse. The same text can always be read using different discourses: for example, a photograph of a naked human being could be looked at anatomically (discourse of biology); lustfully (sexuality); as a photograph (decoding lighting, focal length and so on); or anthropologically (what race is the human?). While each discourse is using the same denotative image, the decoding of it is likely to be very different.

Discourse is not just a way of describing the world; it is at the centre of subjectivity. In fact, the whole notion of individuality is an ideological construct and is expressed within the discourse of subjectivity. In a common-sense view, subjectivity is unproblematic; it is simply the way an individual consciousness perceives the world. However, as Louis Althusser suggested:

In the ordinary use of the term, subject in fact means: (1) a free subjectivity, a centre of initiatives, author of and responsible for its actions; (2) a subjected being, who submits to a higher authority, and is therefore stripped of all freedom except that of freely accepting his submission. (1971: 183–2)

As the notion of a free individual is one of the central tenets of the dominant bourgeois ideology, Althusser's view immediately casts doubt on this freedom. Before this is dismissed as simply a 'play on words' – the punning of 'subjective' and 'subject to' – it must be remembered that language is an ideological construct. Language and discourse existed before the individual was born, and will exist after that individual's death. As socialized beings, we take on this ideological baggage and (largely) accept it as 'reality', whereas, in fact, our individual subjectivity is a discourse.

We have already investigated how bourgeois ideology effaces itself as an ideology; it does this most powerfully within the consciousness of the 'Western' individual:

> The individual is interpellated ['placed' in a position by ideology] as a (free) subject in order that he shall submit freely to the commandments of the Subject, i.e. in order that he shall make the gestures and actions of his subjection 'all by himself'. (Althusser 1971: 82)

Because we believe in the freedom of individual consciousness (presumably Althusser believes women are similarly subjected to ideology), we do not realize that we are reproducing the values of bourgeois ideology in the way we think. Media texts often attempt to 'interpellate' their target audience by their mode of address: 'they invite the reader/viewer to participate, and seek to engage her or him in specific practices of reading and viewing' (Tolson 1998: 53).

Advertising, in particular, is keen to align the audience with its view. 'Before' and 'after' adverts invite us to place ourselves in the position of the model and so imagine how the product would transform us. Tolson analyses an ad that hails the audience with a heading that asks 'Is that really me?'.

Similarly, adverts often address audiences using the imperative form, attempting to command the audience to buy their product:

> The imperative is not only used to evoke a sense of authoritativeness, but also friendly advice, recommendation ... The following verb forms occurred in a considerable number of the [sample of] 112 ads:

Be ...
Bring ...
Come ...
Do ...
Drink ...
Eat ...
Explore ...
Find ...
Give ...
Go ...
Have a ...
Imagine ...
Join ...
Keep ...
Let ...

Look ...
Make ...
Open ...
See ...
Stay ...
Take ...
Try ...

(Danesi 2006: 77–8)

Lev Manovich likened this to the way hyperlinks function on web pages. He argued that hyperlinking 'objectifies the process of association, often taken to be central to human thinking' (Manovich 2001: 61). In other words, by clicking on links we are following a pre-programmed set of associations and so 'we are asked to mistake the structure of somebody's else [sic] mind for our own' (ibid.).

Problems with Althusser's theory arise when we wonder how is it that certain people, such as Althusser, are capable of transcending their own subjectivity to understand the operations of ideology. Nevertheless, while we are not automatons at the service of the bourgeois ideology, Althusser's theory serves the useful purpose of shaking our conventional view and, it is hoped, help us to analyse texts with a greater awareness of the ideological position that we, as individuals, inhabit. There are alternative discourses of subjectivity, for example, Donna Haraway's (1991) 'cyborg manifesto' that celebrates the fluid, postmodern self.

Discourse in texts

It is important to be aware of the discourses that are used by media texts in any analysis: that of the producer; that of individual reading the text; and the discursive context.

Most (all?) texts invite the reader into its own discourse. Occasionally, if the text is specialist and we do not understand its language (discourse), we cannot enter. Usually, we understand, from its metalingual, formal and contextual functions, the objectives a particular text might have, whether to entertain (film), inform (news), persuade (advertising) or educate (text book). It is possible for texts to utilize more than one discourse: propaganda, for example, often intends to persuade in the guise of informing the audience; an entertaining film may contain a message for the viewer (for example, 'social problem' films, such as *Maria, Full of Grace* (US–Columbia, 2004); or a text book may appear to be educational, while providing information that is partisan).

The other discourse – or collection of discourses – we should be aware of is our own. You should by now be using the discourse of Media Studies to read all texts. Genre is the most obvious example of discourse in a media text. We usually recognize a text's genre immediately – often during the title sequence – and use this to read what follows. Some people, however, deem genre texts to be simplistic and 'merely entertaining', and so fail to appreciate the subtleties within the text. This can lead to problems for horror texts, and video games, when those who don't understand the generic nature of, for example, the slasher films, simply define the text as 'sick' and warranting censorship. For example, a number of horror films were banned in the 1980s in Britain and branded 'video nasties' for their ultra-violent and apparently 'immoral' content. However, many of these films in reality represent violence as disturbing and not entertaining. For example, *I Spit on Your Grave* (1978), a female rape revenge film:

> Like many disturbing films in disreputable genres ... it is so because of the manner in which it foregrounds and intensifies many of the elements that [some] find acceptable in more muted versions of other films in the genre. (Lehman 1993: 104)

In other words, the violence is not made palatable, and therefore entertaining. Andrew Holmes suggested that you could draw:

> favourable comparisons [between *I Spit On Your Grave* and] Oscar-winning *The Accused*, which seemed to skirt the issue by shifting its moral centre away from Jodie Foster's problematic trailer trash to district attorney Kelly McGillis and by prosecuting not the perpetrators of the rape but those who cheered them on. (Holmes 2002)

However, when we consider the attempts to ban or censor films, or video games, we are usually dealing with reactionary ideological views. For example, the UK newspaper *Daily Mail*'s belief in family values often leads it to call for censorship of texts that don't fit into this discourse; see also *Media Institutions and Audiences*: 149–53).

The task of the Media Studies student is to recognize the discourses present in media texts, and the ideological values that are operating within them. Often these will be the values of the dominant ideology; however, as already stated, we shouldn't consider this to be an uncontested world-view. For example, while Hollywood is essentially a capitalist institution that is primarily interested in profit and so can be expected to operate in the (ideological) mainstream, this isn't always the case. For example, Hollywood has produced some films that are, arguably, critical of capitalism, such as *Fight Club* (1999).

Obviously, the discourse of patriotism isn't limited to media texts, and it's possible that the Hollywood films were symptomatic of a change in American attitudes towards foreign policy after the failure to find weapons of mass destruction in Iraq and the increasing 'body count' there. Similarly, when analysing historical texts it is helpful to understand the discourses that were circulating at the time, such as the fact that racist discourses were more readily acceptable in the 1930s, as in *Flash Gordon*, noted earlier. In her analysis of British television crime fiction, in the 1990s, Charlotte Brunsdon suggests that there are 'three relevant discursive contexts for the production and consumption of the programmes' (Brunsdon 1998: 225). These are:

1. the increasingly punitive law-and-order rhetoric
2. privatization and private enterprise
3. 'Equal Opportunities'.

The identification of discourses that are circulating at the time help us to understand the text's social context and so better understand its intended meaning. For example, the Equal Opportunities discourse isn't simply about the Sex Discrimination Act of 1975 but also its impact pon policing and the criminal justice system. Brunsdon cites high-profile cases of female police officers successfully filing cases against the police for sexual discrimination. This issue then circulated in the crime series such as *Prime Suspect* (first broadcast in 1991), *Rockliffe's Babies* (1987–8) and *Between the Lines* (1992–4).

It could be, of course, that the dominant ideology is hardly present within the text. Alternative modes of representation may be used to 'make strange' our view of the world in an attempt to allow us to see the world from a perspective other than the one that has attained a consensus in society. See Box 3.7.

Box 3.7   Discourse and language

The language used in discourses is particularly important. Take, for example, dictionary definitions of 'jargon':

1. the language, esp. the vocabulary, peculiar to a particular trade, profession, or group; medical jargon
2. unintelligible or meaningless talk or writing; gibberish. (http://dictionary.reference.com/browse/jargon; accessed March 2008)

For members of the profession, who can access the discourse, jargon is a form of communication; for those outside the profession, the language used serves to exclude them further.

Media Studies has its own jargon that, at its worst (Althusser's 'interpellation', cited above, is one example) is elitist in that it serves to exclude the uninitiated. However, if the language of analysis is to escape the clutches of the dominant ideology, which inevitably shapes it, then language that can work outside the common-sense discourse is required. The danger is that it appears that academia is speaking to one very select audience: itself. *Screen*, a magazine of film theory first published the late 1970s, was arguably guilty of such preaching to the converted. For example:

> A discursive formation, that is, exists as a component of an ideological formation itself based in particular conditions of production (ideological state apparatuses) and the terms of the discursive formation/ideological formation relation are those of subject and interpellation. (*Screen*, vol. 18, no. 4, Autumn 1977/78, reprinted in Heath 1981: 102)

It is certainly unfair to quote material out of context (Stephen Heath's work is excellent); however, it is clear that unless you understand the concepts used, little communication will take place. It would be wrong, however, to criticize jargon *per se*; at best, it facilitates communication. For example, 'interpellation' means 'the way an individual is placed, by society, into a discourse': one word used instead of eleven. However, its use supposes a familiarity with the work of Althusser.

The consideration of discourse leads us directly to representation. Because discourse articulates an ideological position, it is giving us a particular and partial view of the world. Similarly, representation is the mediation of the world by a media text. What is emphasized and what is omitted in representation is determined by discourse, which is structured by ideology.

Roger Fowler listed a number of ways in which everyday language can be inscribed with patriarchy. For example:

- the use of marked expressions containing extra morphemes or words used to refer to females, implying deviance or irregularity ... 'actress', 'poetess', 'lady doctor' ... marked forms for men are almost non-existent, occurring only in contexts where the role is perceived as deviant: 'male nurse'
- the use of diminutive and juvenile forms to refer to or address women ... 'sweetie', 'girl'
- titles and address forms: the choice between 'Mrs' and 'Miss' forcing a woman to declare her marital status (sexual availability) ...

- there is said to be an asymmetry as between men and women in the terminology available to describe certain experiences, e.g. sexual intercourse: 'penetrate' but not 'enclose'. (Fowler 1991: 96)

In recent years there have been attempts to subvert man-made language with the use of 'chairperson', for example, and, particularly during the 1970s, many women insisted on being titled Ms, and thus not indicate their marital status. The latter title, however, does seem to have gone out of fashion.

3.9 Alternative texts

Texts can work against the dominant ideological view by operating outside formal conventions (which will be considered in this section), or by following mainstream formal conventions but subverting the norm in content.

In Chapter 1 we considered how images in sequence are usually structured so that the audience can readily understand the space in which the narrative is taking place; this is the system of continuity editing. The rhetoric of this system is that it conceals its own construction, so what we see appears natural; in fact, we tend not to see the joins between the images.

An alternative to this system could, of course, be to ignore all the rules completely, but this would not be an alternative system; it would be anarchy. In the continuity system, the expressive possibilities of editing are usually subordinated to the narrative flow. However, occasionally, the graphical relationships between shots are the structuring element. This is true, for example, both in Busby Berkeley's Warner Bros. movies of the 1930s *and* in Leni Riefenstahl's Nazi propaganda piece *The Triumph of the Will* (1934), despite the fact that they are, arguably, airing opposite ideological positions: fascism and the New Deal (see Box 4.3 *Triumph des Willens I, 42nd Street* and The New Deal).

Montage editing, which is non-classical in structure, also foregrounds the graphical relationships, and this will be considered in the next section. It should be noted that pre-Renaissance and non-Western systems of constructing texts may appear alternative to Western audiences now but are nevertheless conventional, so these systems appear natural to audiences who were (or are) used to these conventions.

The rhythm of editing can also be used to expressive effect. The famous shower sequence in *Psycho* (US, 1960) consists of seventy camera set-ups for

45 seconds of film. Audience disorientation is complete, even though we are aware that the location is the shower, as the frenzied attack is recreated in the 'violence' of the editing.

Because the creation of narrative space is the priority of classical editing, playing upon audience expectation of continuity by subverting it can create spatial discontinuity. In Dziga Vertov's *Man with a Movie Camera* (*Chelovek s kino-apparatom*, USSR, 1929), a man's throw of a javelin is immediately followed by a shot of a goalkeeper diving to save ... a football; our expectation is, of course, that the goalie is about to be pierced by a javelin. In *Un Chien Andalou* (France, 1928), a surrealist masterpiece created by Luis Bunuel and Salvador Dali, a character opens the door of a first floor flat and steps out on to a beach. The surreal quality of this is again created solely by their not fulfilling the audience's expectation of continuity editing.

Repeating the same event more than once can create temporal discontinuity. In *Blue Steel* (US, 1990), the robber shot by the film's female hero is seen to smash through a supermarket window three times, each shot from a different position; this breaks the temporal continuity evident in most texts. On the other hand, the use of a non-realist 'slow-motion action replay', often part of the presentation of sporting events on television, has become a conventional device.

Two non-classical devices that came to prominence in the French new wave (*nouvelle vague*) were the jump cut and the non-diegetic insert. A jump cut, used to great effect by Jean-Luc Godard in his first film *Breathless* (*A bout de souffle*, France, 1960), breaks the conventions of graphical, temporal and spatial continuity. The two shots that make the cut are of the same subject, but there is little difference between them. Because the difference in the camera's position is small (less than the 30-degree rule) it is experienced more as a 'jump' than as a smooth transition. The jump cut, however, is now comfortably part of the mainstream, as noted in Chapter 1.

A non-diegetic insert is the use of images that are not part of the narrative space. For example, in *Tirez sur le pianiste* (1960), when a gangster swears on his mother's life that he is telling the truth, a non-diegetic insert shows an old woman suddenly keeling over.

While it is unlikely that alternative modes of representation alone can motivate political change, they can suggest alternative ways of viewing, and discussing, the world, and this *might* lead to political action.

These non-classical systems are often used in avant-garde films, whose object is often simply to disorientate the audience by suggesting the possibility of other ways of seeing. There is also alternative (defined stylistically rather than institutionally) cinema that may use some, or all, of these alternative devices. During the 1920s, Soviet cinema made a number of attempts to theorize alternatives to the bourgeois camera style that predominated. One of the more dominant theories was that of montage.

Montage

It is, of course, no coincidence that alternative modes of representation should have originated in the Soviet Union, which was opposed to bourgeois capitalism (in 1950s Japan, Ozu Yausjiro also worked outside Hollywood norms). Foremost amongt the theorists was Sergei Eisenstein, who used editing, rather than narrative, to structure his films.

Eisenstein's implicitly modernist project utilized montage, which he likened to the Japanese ideogram. His belief was that a montage of images would create a dramatic collision within the audience's perception to create a meaning based on conflict, thus representing a Marxist view of society rather than the consensus, bourgeois view. The dramatic collision would often be created by bizarre juxtapositions of shots, forcing the viewer to consider what these might mean.

In 'A Dialectical Approach to Film Form', Eisenstein describes a sequence from *October*:

> Kornilov's march on Petrograd was under the banner of 'In the Name of God and Country.' Here we attempted to reveal the religious significance of this episode in a rationalistic way. A number of religious images, from a magnificent Baroque Christ to an Eskimo idol, are cut together. The conflict in this case was between the concept and the symbolization of God ... a chain of images attempted to achieve a purely intellectual resolution, resulting from a conflict between a preconception and a gradual discrediting of it in purposeful steps. (Eisenstein 1979: 117, 122)

It is likely that many find the film sequence under discussion difficult to understand; this is because narrative has been subordinated to image and so is a signifying system that we, in the West, do not find familiar. Eisenstein's cinema is in many ways the antithesis of Hollywood, and until we get used to Eisenstein's convention we shall have difficulty in reading his films.

To make matters worse for Western audiences, Eisenstein's films do not have characters with which to identify. This absence is deliberate, because identification with individual, usually heroic, characters is a bourgeois notion. It is usual in Western texts for the main character to serve as the main motivator of the action, as well as to act as a locus for audience identification.

While Eisenstein attempted to create a film form that reflected Marxist ideology with its emphasis on conflict and the dialectical construction of meaning, it is pertinent to point out that his films were not particularly popular in the Soviet Union at the time. Conventional narrative film was still the box office favourite, with films such as *Chapayev* (USSR, 1934), in which it is very difficult not to identify with the charismatic hero of the title.

It was not until the French new wave cinema of the 1960s that there was a more-or-less coherent theoretical agenda set out for Western alternative modes of representation. The politicized new wave of the late 1960s, which was a response to the French student revolt of May 1968, was based largely on the writings of Eisenstein and other Soviet theorists. The cinema of the politicized 'new wave' became known as *counter cinema*. See Box 3.8.

Box 3.8   May 1968 and theories of representation

The events of May 1968 in Paris, France, had far-reaching implications, originally for film theory, and later for media and cultural studies. The origin of the student and worker uprising in that month was the March 22 Movement, which organized the occupation of university buildings after the arrest of some anti-Vietnam War student protestors.

The confrontation between students and university authorities escalated on 3 May after police were brought in to arrest 'trouble-makers'. Students gathered in the Latin Quarter to protest against the arrests and were met by police using truncheons and tear gas.

The students received much support from the general public and their lecturers' union, who were also concerned about the authoritarianism of the university establishment. Despite being violently routed by the riot police on 10 May (the 'Night of the Barricades'), the students achieved a moral victory. Liberal public opinion was scandalized that young people could be beaten simply for protesting. By 13 May, the labour unions had joined the protest, uniting, for a short time, students and workers; up to half a million people took part in a demonstration. In addition, there were large-scale demonstrations all over France.

In fact, it seemed that the whole of France was involved in anti-government protests that spread throughout May. The arts, in particular, became extremely politicized in a way that had not happened in Europe since the Soviet revolution of 1917.

By 24 May, approximately 10 million workers were on strike and the de Gaulle government was on the verge of collapse. A day later, journalists from the state-controlled broadcaster, ORTF, joined the strike:

The pro-Government bias of the television and radio networks during the first few weeks of May was, in a sense, too obvious to be of very much use to the government. The huge discrepancy between what was actually going on in the streets and factories and workplaces and what was allowed to appear on television, was too apparent. The lesson of May, from the point of view of the government, must therefore be that in a relatively 'advanced' society, based on the principles of mass education and mass literacy, what is almost more important than the control of the mass media is the creation of public confidence in those media, and the skilful negotiation of the susceptibilities – and the code of ethics – of professional journalists. (Harvey 1980: 8–9)

After negotiations between government and unions failed to gain popular support, de Gaulle called a general election; what was potentially a revolutionary situation was negated by a non-revolutionary political device, and on 30 June the government was returned to power with a large majority. During June, most of the strikes were called off, though there were many violent situations and some protesters were killed.

Despite the fact that the political status quo returned in France, the legacy of the politicization of the arts – film in particular – is still with us. Gone were the old certainties of representation that had, largely, held sway since the Renaissance; in their place was a radical agenda that attempted to make sense of the ideological world.

Ironically, it was *Cahiers du cinéma*, the magazine that Andre Bazin had founded, that led the mockery of his own traditional view of realism:

The real nature of 'Cahiers" and 'Cinéthique's' objections to the 'impression of reality' or the 'depicting of reality' in the cinema is that this impression is offered from the point of view of the ruling class – in other words, that it is an instance of dominant ideology. It is objected to on the grounds that it 'presents the existing abnormal relations of production as natural and right', that it 'is never anything other than a method of permitting the audience to live an imaginary life within a nonexistent reality'; that it registers 'the vague, unformulated, untheorised, unthought-out world of the dominant ideology'. What the cinema offers is not the marvellous, refreshing reality of Bazinian aesthetics, but an impression or an account of social reality which is supportive of existing social relations, and which assists in the reproduction of those relations. (Harvey 1980: 108)

While early film theorists such as Kracauer and Bazin assumed an unproblematic relationship between film and reality, post-1968 aesthetics, politicized by Marxist philosophy, were ideologically-based. When, in the 1970s, the *Cahiers* articles were translated into English and published in *Screen*, the revolutionary fervour entered the Anglo-Saxon academy and has had an immense impact on the study of media.

Counter cinema

Foremost among these 'new wave' filmmakers was Jean-Luc Godard, who started his directing career, typically for new wave directors, with an affectionate pastiche of a Hollywood genre in *Breathless*. He formed the Dziga Vertov group, which attempted to make political films in a collective (non-bourgeois) manner. Peter Wollen (1972) used one of these films, *Wind from the East* (*Vent d'est*, France, 1972), to categorize the basis of counter cinema, contrasted with what he called 'old cinema' (see Table 3.3).

Table 3.3   Wollen's counter cinema

Old cinema	Counter cinema
Narrative transitivity	Narrative intransitivity
Identification	Estrangement
Transparency	Foregrounding
Single diegesis	Multiple diegesis
Closure	Aperture
Pleasure	Un-pleasure
Fiction	Reality

Source: Wollen 1985: 501.

Although the focus here is on cinema, the principles of counter cinema apply to any media text.

Narrative transitivity versus intransitivity

Transitivity is the narrative structure that is at the heart of most Western narratives. Conventional narrative consists of an opening situation (the thesis) that is disrupted (antithesis) and ultimately resolved (synthesis). For example, in *Jurassic Park* (US, 1993) the situation is a theme park inhabited by dinosaurs; the disruption is caused by the escape from their confines, thus threatening the protagonists; the disruption is resolved by the characters' escape to safety and the likely closure of the park. The resolved situation is usually very like the opening one except that the characters have been transformed, for the better, by their experiences. Heterosexual love is usually consummated as a by-product of the narrative, though this consummation wasn't required in *Jurassic Park* as the main adult protagonists were already married.

The narrative disruption in television series, which have a new narrative each week in the same setting and characters, is usually resolved by everything returning to the original situation, so that it can start again from exactly the same position in the next episode.

In conventional narrative, everything that happens within the world created by the narrative, the diegesis, contributes in some way to the development of the narrative; nothing is redundant. In *Groundhog Day* (US, 1993) the apparently meaningless conversation that Bill Murray has when leaving his bedroom is given significance later when he relives the experience.

Narrative *in*transitivity, you will not be surprised to learn, is the opposite of this. Counter cinema interrupts narrative flow with digressions and irrelevances that serve to prevent the audience getting 'caught up' within the narrative development. As Wollen says, counter cinema 'is within the modern(ist) tradition established by Brecht and Artaud, [who were] in their different ways, suspicious of the power of the arts – and the cinema, above all – to "capture" its audience without apparently making it think, or changing it' (1985: 502).

The picaresque narrative is favoured, as in Godard's *Pierrot le fou* (France, 1965); it is preferably a journey were characters have no idea where they are going: 'The basic story ... does not have any recognizable sequence, but is more like a series of intermittent flashes' (ibid.).

The narrative thrust, if it can be called that, is to alienate the audience.

Identification versus estrangement

Most texts offer the audience characters with which they can identify, and, in cinema, they are very often played by the stars of the film. Counter cinema attempts to prevent this by using distancing techniques such as introducing real people into the diegesis. While Godard, for example, did use film stars, he represented them as 'real stars' rather than 'stars playing characters'. In this way, the audience is made conscious of the constructed nature of the text. In *Tout va bien* (France, 1972), we are reminded right from the beginning that Jane Fonda is a film star playing a role in a film.

Again, this is a Brechtian technique meant to distance the audience from the text and so prevent any emotional involvement, so that audiences *think* about what they are watching.

Transparency versus foregrounding

The conventional system of continuity editing strives to hide its operation; counter cinema foregrounds the technique by simply ignoring the 180-degree rule. Once the convention is subverted it becomes noticeable, and so it is foregrounded.

The camera style of bourgeois cinema also signifies transparency. Taking its cue from Renaissance perspective (described at the end of this chapter), cinema creates an illusion of depth and allows the audience, by taking different views of objects, to gain a sense of perspective.

However, as Brian Henderson (1976) demonstrates, counter cinema attempts to employ a 'non-bourgeois camera style'. It can do this by denying the audience a rich and beautiful image and by flattening perspective within the frame, and thus emphasize its two-dimensional nature.

In an early film, *Le Mépris* (France, 1963), Godard used the 'film within a film' device to foreground the fact audiences were watching a film. Wollen contrasts this with the *avant-garde* device of scratching film, which simply draws attention to the medium; Godard, on the other hand, wants to problematize representation. For example, Camille, played by the 'sex kitten' of the time, Brigitte Bardot, lies naked on a bed and asks her lover if he loves different parts of her body. Godard is attempting to highlight the way in which women like Bardot are conventionally represented, that is, reducing her to a series of body parts.

Single versus multiple diegesis

The narrative world of conventional cinema is a unified place with consistent rules. These usually reflect those of the 'real world' but can also create fantasy worlds so long as they abide by their own stated rules.

In counter cinema, the sanctity of the narrative diegesis can be broken at will. Characters from different narrative worlds coincide in the text; Wollen cites Godard's *Weekend*, where 'characters from different epochs and from fiction are interpolated into the main narrative: Saint-Just, Balsamo, Emily Bronte' (Wollen 1985: 505).

A Cock and Bull Story (UK, 2005), based on Laurence Sterne's eighteenth-century novel, *The Life and Opinions of Tristram Shandy, Gentleman*, breaks its diegesis on a number of occasions. For example, the film is set in both the eighteenth century and 2004, when the film was shot. When the voice-over talks about Pavlov's dogs, archive footage of the experiment is inserted. The film is as much about the filming of the film as it is an adaptation of the novel; however, the film crew are also played by actors. But when Steve Coogan, the

star, is interviewed by Tony Wilson, it is in fact Tony Wilson doing the interview, which, the voice-over tells us, will be available as a DVD extra. Unlike
Wollen's counter cinema, however, *A Cock and Bull Story* isn't trying to make
a political point.

Closure versus aperture

The meaning of conventional cinema is contained wholly within the text.
Counter cinema, however, can produce meaning through allusion to other
texts; indeed, knowledge of other texts may be essential for any meaning to
be generated at all:

> In this sense, Godard is like Ezra Pound or James Joyce who ... no longer
> insist on speaking to us in their own words, but can be seen more as
> ventriloquist's dummies, through whom are speaking – or rather being
> written – palimpsests ... in which meaning can no longer to said to express
> the intention of the author or to be a representation of the world. (Wollen
> 1985: 506)

The BBC TV second series of *Gangsters* (1978) crammed allusion into its text.
For example the first episode, *The Dictates of Shen Tang*, included a *North By
North West* (US, 1958) pastiche, and the protagonist, Kline, being rescued by
a character from the BBC radio soap *The Archers*, accompanied by that
programme's theme music.

While not *all* the allusions that, arguably, actually constitute the text of
Gangsters need to be understood to follow the narrative, audiences are likely
– especially thirty years later – to struggle to make sense of the programme
unless they can recognize most of the references. Some of the allusions in
series two include:

- the Saturday Morning Serial
- Fu Manchu movies of the 1920s and 1930s
- Kung Fu films
- *The Avengers*
- *Monty Python*
- Laurel and Hardy
- *Who Do You Do?*
- *Batman*
- W. C. Fields
  (Kerr 1981: 75)

Certainly, if my students' response to episode one of series two is anything to go by, the text is virtually incoherent to younger audiences.

Pleasure versus un-pleasure

Conventional cinema aims to entertain (and thereby generate profit for its makers). Counter cinema aims to make the audience think. All the categories described so far serve, in counter cinema, to alienate the audience, to deny them entertainment, to make them think and, ultimately, to change them.

Counter cinema takes its definition of art from the formalists, who believed the function of art was to 'make strange' the world. The world of conventional cinema is a familiar place; even in alien settings there are good and bad guys, and maidens in distress who need that particular man to come to the rescue. The world of counter cinema is ambiguous and eschews conventional representations and entertainment.

However, this doesn't mean that pleasure is necessarily eradicated. Many get pleasure from thought-provoking texts, and, as Wollen notes, Brecht himself didn't 'turn his back on entertainment' (1985: 507).

Fiction versus reality

In conventional cinema, the fictional world is created as if it were real. BBC TV's period dramas are renowned for an attention to detail that signs itself as being 'as it really was'. This is, of course, an illusion; it is merely a representation. Counter cinema deals consciously with representations and informs its audience of the fact. The belief is that, by demonstrating to the audience that it is seeing a representation (showing actors ad-libbing while applying make-up, for example, in *A Cock and Bull Story*) then truth is, in some way, being shown. Sally Potter is a filmmaker who problematizes representation. For example:

> In *The Tango Lesson,* reflexivity is inscribed in the metafilmic narrative: A film director is preparing the film that has unfolded in front of our eyes. But reflexivity is at the same time presenting a more subtle way in the sense that real life director Sally Potter is doubled as a diegetic character, namely a film director called Sally Potter. (Jerslev, n.d.; accessed online)

Wollen demonstrated that counter cinema has its own rules, its own mode of representation in fact, defined by its opposition to conventional cinema. It arose out of a time of political turmoil epitomized as May 1968, where 'fiction [was deemed to] = mystification = bourgeois ideology' (1985: 508).

During the 1970s, counter cinema flourished, funded in Britain by the British Film Institute. Because of its non-commercial nature, many of these oppositional, alternative texts were only produced because they were funded by public money. This source tended to dry up during the 1980s as 'market forces' took over. Inevitably, any text that sets out to create, say, un-pleasure for an audience can only hope to address a small coterie of people. It is no accident that oppositional texts tend to disappear once commercial logic holds sway, since it is this very logic that these texts oppose (see Box 3.9).

Box 3.9   *Tout va bien* as counter cinema

Tout va bien was written and directed by Jean-Luc Godard and Jean-Pierre Gorin. It is a fascinating, if difficult, text dealing with the role of the film-maker and intellectual in post-May 1968 France.

The film's opening sequence clearly defines itself as counter cinema in a number of ways. During the titles a clapper-board, and the film's title, is heard continually: we are not going to be allowed to forget we are watching a film called *Tout va bien*. There follows a voice-over dialogue, between a man and a woman, concerning the requirements of film-making:

> *Man*: 'I want to make a movie.'
> *Woman*: 'That takes money.'
> (sequence of cheques being signed for *Tout va bien*)
> *W*: 'If we have stars, we'll get money.'
> *M*: 'Okay, we'll have stars.'
> *W*: 'What are you going to tell Montand and Fonda? An actor won't accept a part without a storyline.'
> *M*: 'A storyline?'
> *W*: 'Yeah, usually a love story.'

The institutional basis of film-making is immediately revealed, and the fact we are dealing with fiction rather than reality is emphasized. Without money, there is no film; without stars, there is no money; without a love story, there are no stars: it seems that the only stories that can be told are love stories.

Yves Montand and Jane Fonda were big box office attractions in the 1970s, and their appearance in a counter cinema text may well be unique; film stars are usually only found in mainstream cinema. Both Montand and Fonda appeared in the film because of their 'left of centre' political convictions, and their presence allowed money – as the dialogue said – to be raised to make the film. Another star to support radical film-makers was Julie Christie, in *The Gold Diggers* (UK, 1983).

Following the dialogue, we see Montand and Fonda, as Jacques and Susan, walking along a riverbank and talking lovingly to one another. Except that we see them walking along the riverbank twice, though their voices do not suggest this discontinuity. The editing process is fore-grounded and we see the same event twice, though the dialogue suggests it only happened once.

Godard and Gorin do provide us with the love story, against the back-drop of industrial strife in France. Parallels are drawn between Jacques' and Susan's personal and professional crises; he makes advertisements, she is a reporter.

The voice-over explains, 'we shall see farmers, farming, the workers, working; and the middle-class, middle-classing ('bourgeoisie, bourgeoisie-ing')'. Narrative is not hidden as an invisible structuring device, but high-lighted, emphasizing the text's narrative intransitivity.

Having a relatively large budget allowed Godard and Gorin to work in a studio. The set for the factory sit-in is a *tour de force*: a tracking-shot takes us from one room to the next, and the building is ultimately revealed to be without a 'fourth' wall, which has allowed us to see inside; once again the mechanics of cinema are foregrounded.

The use of film stars immediately sets up the possibility of identification, something that is antithetical to counter cinema. However we are, at least momentarily, estranged from this by seeing both stars working in the sausage factory when workers explain the poor conditions they have to suffer: stars do not work in factories.

Both management and union leaders engage with the camera in long monologues that, while they wittily satirize both groups, at the very least risk boring the audience, so un-pleasure is felt!

If you attempted to watch *Tout va bien* without thinking about the film, then you would probably only experience boredom, despite some fascinat-ing sequences like the interminable tracking shot in the supermarket toward the end of the film. Counter cinema insists that its audience thinks; not to do so leads to a failure to read the text.

As noted earlier, hegemony works to recuperate anything opposing the dominant ideological line:

'Recuperation' involves conceptualising continual and flexible cultural processes whereby radical and oppositional ideas, images and movements are taken on, or sucked in by dominant culture(s), to become part of the culture of domination. Not only do the oppositional ideas and practices lose their bite, but they can function to make it appear as if change has been effected. (Brunsdon 1986: 119–20)

Indicative of this might be that the top result of a Google search of the internet (in March 2008) for 'radical media' offered a commercial media company that stated: 'We believe that the future belongs to those who can connect with an audience in lots of different ways. Which is why @radical.media has evolved into a multi-disciplinary integrated media company' (http://www.radicalmedia.com; accessed March 2008)

The company produces films, music videos and advertising and integrates marketing messages into entertainment. The heritage of May 1968 seems to have been lost, and politicians, such as Blair and Sarkozy, have been determined to bury it. However, if radical formal experimentation has diminished, alternative representations have continued to be created.

We shall pick up on this in the next chapter in relation to the representation of gender. The final section of this chapter looks at the history of Western images and highlights how what might start as 'the shock of the new' can readily be recuperated into becoming a convention.

3.10 A history of Western images

What follows is a very brief 'history of images' – or, more accurately, of Western images. This has two uses: first, all images have histories that contribute to their meaning; and second, when we are analysing images from the past we need to be aware of the codes current at the time of the text's creation; as noted earlier, they may well have had very different meanings to their contemporary audiences. This history demonstrates how different world-views, or ideologies, led to different modes of representation.

Beginnings

In 1994, a rich hoard of 18,000-year-old cave paintings was discovered in the Ardèche, France. These examples of early naturalistic art suggest that images are as much a fundamental part of the human psyche as story-telling. We can only speculate as to the images' spiritual significance. Despite this, it is likely that the subject matter, which often consists of beasts that were hunted for food, helped prehistoric humanity to contemplate this crucial task while at rest. (The fact that we do not put images of the local supermarket on the walls of our homes suggests that obtaining food is a lot easier now, at least for the more privileged people of this planet.)

It is unlikely that the prehistoric artists imagined that we, thousands of years in their future, would one day be the receivers of these images. Millennia have elapsed since primitive times, and our plethora of cultural artefacts means that we would appear alien to our ancestors. However, with the benefit of history, they would not appear alien to us, as we know that, in some way, they are related to us.

Egyptian painting

The Sphinx and pyramids of Egypt are staple tourist attractions. Both, of course, are probably familiar to most of us as images of ancient artefacts. The Western world is probably more familiar with ancient Egyptian culture than it is with modern Egypt, possibly because of the Tutankhamun curse and exhibitions, the regular appearance of the Egyptian mummy in horror movies, and the legend of *Cleopatra* (fostered by Shakespeare's play and one of the most expensive films ever made, the eponymous financial disaster of 1963, starring Elizabeth Taylor).

EXERCISE 3.5

Examine Figure 3.1 and try to determine what, today, is unconventional about ancient Egyptian images.

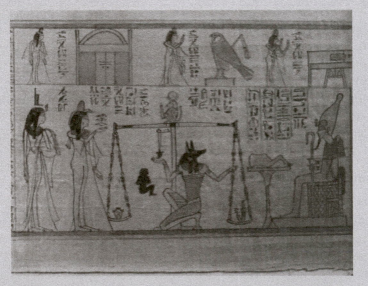

Figure 3.1 Funerary papyrus of the Princess Entiu-ny (1025 BC)

(*Source: Book of the Dead: Princess Entiu-ny & Osiris*, from SuperStock)

You have probably concluded that Egyptian art is non-naturalistic, because human beings look strange. Wrong. The ancient Egyptian mode of representation is simply different from our own. Heads were shown in profile; eyes from the front, as was the torso; and arms and legs were shown from the side. The ancient Egyptians were not a deformed race; their mode of representation in the visual arts was to portray different parts of objects from the most characteristic or recognizable angle. This makes sense when we realize that, potentially, we can get much more information from this representation than we can from what appears to us to be a naturalistic perspective.

Greek painting

The ancient Greeks had an idealistic view the world; they represented the world as if it consisted of ideal types, rather than how it was in reality. This Platonic view, named after the philosopher Plato, is similar to the idea, mentioned in Chapter 2, that the signified is a mental concept. Greek landscape painting was not, as a consequence, interested in the actual environment:

> In the Hellenistic period ... artists ... tried to conjure up the pleasures of the countryside ... These paintings are not actual views of particular country houses or beauty-spots. They are rather a collection of everything which makes up an idyllic scene. (Gombrich 1989: 77–8)

A realistic portrayal of the place was not important for the Greeks; they were concerned with the representation of it as an ideal – in this case, the idyllic countryside. It was not even necessary for Grecian artists to visit the place they were representing, and any attempt to draw a map of the area represented is doomed to failure. The idea of a place is portrayed, and this is the pictorial equivalent of the signified.

This convention was not wholly a result of the Greeks' world-view. A visual representation of the world as individual human beings might see it could not be created until the mathematical laws that govern perspective were understood. It is probable that the reason the Greeks had an idealistic view of the world was precisely that they did not understand these laws.

Feudal painting

The feudal period of history is characterized by a strict class system in which the king (occasionally the queen) is subordinate only to God and is followed in the hierarchy by royalty, representatives of the Church, the land-owners and, at the bottom, the peasantry. The system was strict, with no social mobility (except, possibly, through the Church).

In the feudal world, the dominant view was religious, and placed the Earth at the centre of the universe, God in heaven and Satan in hell. This is a particularly conservative view, which effectively makes society unchangeable; in contrast to this, the bourgeois sense of history is one of progress through time. In feudal times, however, progress was not thought possible, for the world had already attained the best possible state. As in Greek painting, we find that this world view is expressed in feudal painting.

For example, the size of a person in a painting represented not their size relative to other people in the painting, but their importance in the hierarchy. In his fascinating *The Story of Art*, E. H. Gombrich described 'The Entombment of Christ' from a thirteenth-century Psalter:

> The expression of intense feeling, and this regular distribution of figures on the page, were obviously more important to the artist than any attempt to make his figures lifelike, or to represent a real scene. He does not mind that the servants are smaller than the holy personages, and he does not give any indication of the place or the setting. (Ibid.: 147)

Servants were smaller because they were less important than Christ, and not because they were midgets. As in Greek art, the sense of place was irrelevant, because time and place are not important in a world-view that denies change. In fact, despite appearing completely natural to us, the detailed organization of time did not become important until inter-continental trading began. In order to navigate, ships used the sun by day and the stars at night. Because the sun's and stars' positions vary throughout the year, and are dependent on where you are on the globe, it became necessary to know the exact time in order to work out your exact position.

It wasn't until the development of capitalism (money-lending and business) in Venice in the fifteenth century that a new world-view – that of what is called the bourgeoisie – began to supplant feudalism.

This is not the place in which to try to draw together the historical strands that led to the development of the bourgeois world-view that has dominated the Western world for so long. It is sufficient, for our purposes, to say that the Renaissance, when the 'lost' learning of ancient civilizations was discovered by the Western world in Constantinople, was partly a cause and partly an effect of the development of bourgeois dominance.

Renaissance painting

The bourgeois world-view is centred on the progress of the individual. As noted earlier, in feudal times it was virtually impossible for individuals to live a life other than the one they were born into. However, in a bourgeois society, while accidents of birth are still very influential, social mobility is possible, and this is usually determined by wealth.

Once again, the expression of this world-view can be found in the work of artists from that era, and because of the emphasis on the individual, it was necessary that paintings should create an individual perspective from which to view the world. The 'multi-angled' views of Egyptian art, the ideal types of Greece, and the symbolism of the feudal era are all inappropriate to a world where the individual's position at a particular time, and in a particular place, are the defining factors.

In the wealthy, merchant city of Florence, in Italy, in the early years of the fifteenth century, Filippo Brunelleschi discovered the mathematical means of creating perspective. For the first time, a two-dimensional plane could look like three-dimensional space, the illusion of depth was created, and paintings began to look like a 'window on the world'.

Ironically, while Renaissance painting's verisimilitude gives the impression that we can look at people and scenes from the past exactly as they appeared at the time, this is an illusion created by the artifice of the artists. The conventions of ancient Egypt and Greece are obviously representations to modern eyes. However, at the time of their creation the conventions were as 'invisible' to audiences as contemporary conventions are to us, though images using the Renaissance perspective, also called the Quattrocento perspective, simply appear to be three-dimensional:

> The conception of the Quattrocento system is that of a scenographic space, space set out as spectacle for the eye of a spectator. Eye and knowledge come together; subject, object and the distance for the steady observation that allows the one to master the other. (Heath 1981: 30)

This coming together of 'eye and knowledge' is crucial to the understanding of the modern, bourgeois conception of representation. Knowledge is, literally, in the eye of the beholder, and the beholder is an individual – 'I'. Quattrocento perspective is determined neither by the inflexible sense of order that characterized feudal painting nor the idealism of the Greeks. It addresses the individual spectator and was part of the change in representational conventions that were, in turn, part of the emergent bourgeois ideology that was starting to 'see off' the residual feudal ideology.

Although the subject matter of Renaissance painting was often religious in nature, the patrons of the artist would also be represented as important characters within the frame, presumably in the hope that this might secure their place in heaven.

It is grossly over-simplifying the history of images to leap across a few periods of history and conveniently forget what lies in between. However, we are discussing Media Studies and not Art History, so we bridge 400 years to the creation of photography.

Photography

As Walter Benjamin, in his seminal essay 'The Work of Art in the Age of Mechanical Reproduction', says, 'the presence of the original is the prerequisite to the concept of authenticity' (Benjamin 1979: 15). In the age of mechanical reproduction, however, there is no guarantee of authenticity; everything might be a copy, at least to the untutored eye. Mechanical reproduction changed the way people looked at artefacts.

Benjamin saw this lack of authenticity as being wholly liberating, because it meant the 'aura' of the original was eliminated. People are free to examine artefacts in their own particular context, and artefacts of great cultural value are now accessible not only to the elite, but to a much wider audience.

Paradoxically, while mechanical reproduction, in Benjamin's terms, destroyed the authenticity of art, in other ways it seemed to guarantee authenticity. With the invention of the camera it appeared, for the first time, that reality could be reproduced without the intervention of human subjectivity, hence the notion that 'the camera never lies'. (Writing had been reproduced mechanically since Gutenberg's printing press, but the meaning generated by words, which are wholly symbolic, is not influenced to any significant degree by the typeface.)

The first commercial photography process, daguerreotypes, could not, in fact, be reproduced, as they were 'developed' directly on a metal plate. Other systems, using light-sensitive film, came to dominate and could be copied; this system has only recently been superseded by digital technology.

In the early days, capturing images took minutes, rather than fractions of a second, and often created pictures that were surreal in character. If moving figures were present during the exposure, these would probably not appear at all, and even as technology progressed they would appear only as ghost-like figures, as if superimposed upon the background.

In fact, these early photographs inspired the development of Impressionist painting, a form we hardly regard as 'realistic' today. Aaron Scharf shows how the painters Corot and Monet 'represented their subjects, not as the eye would see them but as they might be recorded by the camera' (1983: 172). It is ironic that Impressionism, which is the subjective impression of reality based on a *melange* of colours, should be inspired by a mechanical apparatus that was deemed to be objective at the time.

Artists also used photographs as an aid in more traditional forms of painting. Courbet, for example, used photographs as the basis for some of his paintings, as it is obviously far easier to take a photograph of a scene into a studio than to take the easel and palette outdoors, where the artist is at the mercy of the weather.

Photography also inspired the use of 'realist' subjects in painting, though. It was conventional in nineteenth-century paintings to concentrate on 'worthy' subjects – which meant, in essence, middle-class people and settings. The advent of photography legitimized the use of virtually anything as a suitable subject, including what was seen as the seedier (working-class) side of life. The art Establishment often derided such paintings as daguerreotypes, thus honouring the tradition of Establishment ridicule, and fear, of new technology.

As we shall see in Chapter 4, which considers the history of realism in the art of the Western world, mainstream art has a mimetic function; that is, it mirrors life. With the invention of photography, it appeared, for the first time, that reality could be represented using technology rather than being 'processed' through the consciousness of the individual, and therefore subjective, artist. This objectivity is illusory, as will be demonstrated in Chapter 5.

Photography appeared to have a privileged access to reality because of its iconic nature (see section 2.3). Cinema had even greater claims for verisimilitude for, as early film theorist Siegfried Kracauer put it, '(cinema) satisf(ied) at last the age-old desire to picture things moving' (Kracauer 1979: 7).

While Kracauer believed the mechanical aspect of cinema allowed it to fulfil the project of realism, Andre Bazin, an influential theorist who founded the important film journal *Cahiers du cinéma*, believed the photograph created a metaphysical realism:

The aesthetic qualities of photography are to be sought in its power to lay bare the realities. It is not for me to separate off, in the complex fabric of the objective world, here a reflection on a damp sidewalk, there the gesture of a child. Only an impassive lens, stripping its object of all those ways of seeing it, those piled-up preconceptions, that spiritual dust and grime with which my eyes have covered it, is able to present it in all its virginal purity to my attention and consequently to my love. (1967: 15)

Both Kracauer and Bazin offer a 'naïve' view of the form, as neither takes into account the ideological construction of the images in the first place, or the ideological basis of any readings made of those images. All images are representations and, as we have seen, one can only fully analyse representations by deconstructing the ideological basis of the artefact as well as the ideological basis of the audience's reading of the artefact.

It may seem that the history of images up to this point has been the gradual development towards the 'window on the world' that cinema and photography appeared to be uniquely placed to provide. However, in the mid-nineteenth century the glass started to become blurred by Impressionism, and was later shattered by Cubism.

In some ways, Cubism is a return to the Egyptian aesthetic, as it acknowledges that paintings are created on a two-dimensional surface and therefore three-dimensional objects have to be 'opened out' in order for us to 'genuinely' see more than one aspect of the image's contents. This shattering of perspective was particularly suited to the *zeitgeist* of the years following the First World War, and it is considered, along with modernism, in Chapter 4: 'Braque offers the restless view of a spectator in constant motion [however] it is important to note that the Cubists were interested in depicting reality, in creating a new way of looking at the real' (Sturken and Cartwright 2001: 120).

Despite the fragmentation of perspective by Cubism as part of the modernist aesthetic, mainstream conventions are little changed from those of the Renaissance, a tribute to the durability of the bourgeois world-view that portrays itself as 'natural'. It seems obvious to modern eyes that representations of objects should look like the objects that are portrayed, but this belief ignores, of course, that what was obvious in ancient Egypt, Greece, and in the feudal era, now looks peculiar to us. Similarly, our ancestors would probably have been confused by images that appear natural to us.

What should be clearer now is that an historical, or diachronic, investigation of images shows (to a degree, as the further back into the past we go, the hazier our knowledge usually becomes) the way an image's codes are a product of a particular era and society. While it is not necessary for us to know the original meaning of these codes in order to make a reading of the image, knowledge certainly adds to our understanding. We can still analyse historical images synchronically, without historical knowledge, and create a meaning, but our analysis of historical images is more powerful if we have some idea about their cultural background.

Realism, then, is a set of conventions that sets out to portray 'reality as it is'. However, behind the rhetoric there is always an ideology that is structuring the world-view. As we have seen, the roots of modern, Western realism are found in the Renaissance, when the emerging ideology of the bourgeoisie was first making an impact. The emphasis on the individual in literary artefacts was a result of the shift from feudalism, as was the individual address facilitated by the Renaissance perspective.

The concept of ideology also enables us to see links between different art forms – here, literature and painting – and show how these are expressions of a particular ideological system. Clearly, this is a very powerful and holistic way to understand texts and society. However, we must avoid the reductionism that makes a simple leap from the apparently all-encompassing dominant ideology, whatever that might be, to all media texts, for there are always exceptions to the rule. It is common, though, for mainstream texts to reflect dominant power structures.

4 Representation

4.1 Introduction

In the first three chapters of this book we considered how media language is used to communicate with audiences. This communication is inevitably a representation: the media can only 're-present' the world. It mediates between the audience and what is being represented. This chapter uses Richard Dyer's typography of representation, with an emphasis on examples and case studies, followed by sections on the representation of gender, and how genre can strongly influence representation, with reference to the Western. The final section considers propaganda and public relations.

4.2 Dyer's typography

Richard Dyer describes the typography of representation as consisting of:

1. re-presentation, which consists essentially of media language, the conventions that are used to represent the world to the audience; 'representation insists that there is a real world, but that our perception of it always mediated by [the media's] selection' (1985: 44).
2. being representative of, for example, 'to what extent are representations [of groups] typical of how those groups are in society?' (ibid.: 45). In this, the use of stereotypes is very important.
3. who is responsible for the representation, 'that is, in the sense of *speaking for and on behalf of*' (ibid.). In this, we must consider how the institution creating a media text influences representation.
4. what does the audience think is being represented to them; 'what does this [text] represent to me; what does it mean to other people?' (ibid.). As we saw in our investigation of preferred readings, audiences can make different readings of media texts from the one offered.

4.3 Re-presentation

As we learnt from the earlier chapters, meaning is communicated by codes and conventions. Different media may have different conventions; however, many texts, particularly generic texts, have their own conventions, which are used regardless of the medium. For example, soap operas have specific conventions of narrative and character representation that hold true whether broadcast on radio or on television. Formal conventions are also transferable across media; for example, most mainstream audio-visual texts use the rules of continuity editing outlined in Chapter 1.

In our consideration of textual analysis, we have concentrated on the tools of analysis, and it is through the application of these tools that we can understand how the text represents its subject matter. Most texts have messages, and these messages are structured by the values of the producers.

Stuart Hall (1997b) outlined three approaches to understanding how meaning is created through representation:

1. *reflective approach* – where representations simply reflect reality
2. *intentional approach* – where our understanding of reality is created by representations (the opposite of 'reflective')
3. *constructionist approach* – where representations create, or construct, meaning, but this is based on a material reality (a mix of the 'reflective' and 'intentional' approaches).

Media Studies is usually concerned with the third approach, because it avoids the naïve assumption that texts offer a simple 'window on the world', but also avoids the trap of assuming that the world has no effect on meaning. We noted in section 3.8 that discourses are powerful influences in the creation of meaning. However, these discourses can only be effective if they represent a recognizable reality. For example, feudal discourses, which suggested that all knowledge was contained in books such as the Bible, could not explain why the Earth was not the centre of the universe – see section 3.10.

4.4 Types and stereotypes

The use of character types has a long history, particularly in literature. Types are characters who are defined by what they represent rather than being genuine individuals. The type is signified by a character's appearance and behaviour and, unlike the stereotype, is primarily used in media texts rather than by people in everyday life.

Erwin Panfosky described the types derived from the theatre, which were used in early cinema: 'the Vamp and the Straight Girl ... the Family Man, and the Villain, the latter marked by a black moustache and walking stick ... A checkered table cloth meant ... a "poor but honest" milieu' (Panofsky 1979: 254).

Types were particularly useful in early cinema, which could not use dialogue to establish character. The types described above are still recognizable today, though we would perceive the early representations as being crude. In *film noir*, for example, the Vamp has become the *femme fatale* (often in the pay of the gangster/boss Villain), who takes the Family Man away from his wife/girlfriend, Straight Girl. So in *Out of the Past* (US, 1947), Kathie, in fact on the run from bad guy Whit, seduces Jeff away from Anne.

Types do not conform to the bourgeois notion of character (which will be described later) as they are too simplistic. Stereotypes, on the other hand, offer more sophisticated shorthand about characters and people in the real world.

Stereotypes

EXERCISE 4.1

Write down a list of images and ideas you associate with contemporary New York; then write down everything you can think of about students, and compare your lists with someone else's.

It is likely that your list for New York will include some or all of the following: skyscrapers; yellow cabs; crime; exciting; dirty; poor; rich; September 11; violent. ... It is also probable that your construction of this stereotype is not affected by whether you have been to New York, or not; of course, if you have personal experience of the place, then your understanding of it is likely to be different from that of those who have never visited.

The list you have drawn up about students, however, may differ greatly from the dominant student stereotype, which states that students are: lazy (they stay in bed as late as possible); sexually promiscuous; into soft and hard drugs; dress scruffily; have long hair. As you are almost certainly a student, you will know that this stereotype is only sporadically true. (There is also a stereotype for the 'swotty student' or boffin-type.)

Figure 4.1 is a spread from a media education magazine, *in the picture*, where the editor gave A-level Media Studies students an opportunity to represent themselves. Compare their portrayal with your own: does theirs' 'ring true'?

Stereotypes are very common, so common that even the concept of 'stereotype' itself has a stereotype. Tessa Perkins, in 'Rethinking Stereotypes' (1997), described the assumptions many people hold about stereotypes:

- stereotypes are always erroneous in content
- they are pejorative concepts
- they are about groups with whom we have little/no social contact; by implication, therefore, they are not held about one's own group
- they are about minority groups (or about oppressed groups)
- they are simple
- they are rigid and do not change
- they are not structurally reinforced
- the existence of contradictory stereotypes is evidence that they are erroneous, but of nothing else
- people either 'hold' stereotypes of a group (believe them to be true) or do not
- because someone holds a stereotype of a group, his/her behaviour towards a member of that group can be predicted.

Perkins challenges these assumptions and defines the concept in a far better way. She also distinguishes between recognizing a stereotype and believing in it; many know of the 'dumb blonde' stereotype – but does anyone believe it to be true?

Perkins suggests the following are characteristic; a stereotype is:

(a) *A group concept*: It describes a group. Personality traits (broadly defined) predominate.
(b) *It is held by a group*: There is very considerable uniformity about its content. Cannot have a 'private stereotype'.
(c) *Reflects an 'inferior judgemental process'*: ... Stereotypes short-circuit or block capacity for objective and analytical judgements in favour of catch-all reactions ...
(d) (b) and (c) give rise to *simple structure* ... which frequently conceals complexity (see (e)).
(e) High probability that social stereotypes will be *predominantly evaluative*.
(f) *A concept* – and like other concepts it is a selective, cognitive organizing system, and a feature of human thought. (1997: 80)

All we need is a good listening to

What are the pressures of being a student? Hanson School sixth formers think that parents, teachers and friends need to know more about the students they pressurise and that the media representation of students is inaccurate.

PARENTS

– They want their children to succeed because when they were at school they never had the opportunity to continue their education. This is especially true for women who have equal opportunities now and aren't expected to stay at home.

– They moan on at their children about doing homework and spending time on work. They don't allow their children a social life.

TEACHERS

– I find it very difficult to talk to teachers. I never know where to put myself and I'm always worried I'll say the wrong thing. I can never relax and I just don't feel comfortable with them. If teachers had a bit more personality, I wouldn't feel as nervous.

– They constantly tell us we must work towards our futures and this pressurises us into making hasty decisions about careers.

– You get a big speech on how you will be treated like an adult (just so long as you act like one) and at a time when you're trying to discover just what being an 'adult' might mean this sounds like a gift from the gods ... but you still get your Homework

journal checked and it seems that some teachers can't make the adjustment from GCSE to A Level themselves.

– They seem to think that their's is the only subject we take. They don't seem to realise that it all adds up to a heavy workload.

FRIENDS

– "Can I see you tonight?" "But I've got an essay to finish".

– Girls are under more pressure than boys. Boys put on the pressure in a relationship, to have sex when the girl isn't ready, to deny that she is "seeing someone else". But most of all students have to decide on how often they can afford the time to see a boyfriend or girlfriend.

MEDIA

– They portray students as typical, naïve teenagers. We want to be treated as individuals rather than classed as a group. We want to develop our own independence rather than be limited in the freedom we possess.

– Newspapers don't promote the image of the student constructively. The reports show students as joyriders, drug abusers and suicide cases. In reality students need to be self-motivated.

independent, reliable and able to cope under pressure. Crucially they need part-time jobs to help finance themselves, proving skills in time management as well.

Figure 4.1   Students represent themselves

An easy life or a hard road?

In the media, especially the popular press, students have a rough time. The only way to achieve a good image for a student seems to be to commit suicide or arrive at some other horrible fate, whereupon they are commended and become the hardest working, greatest achieving student in the world. For those less fortunate there is the media image of the drug taking, drink crazed idiot who fits his work in between having a good time. We show you both sides of student life, judge for yourself which is nearer the truth...

THE MEDIA PORTRAYED STUDENT?

THE REAL STUDENT?

STUDENT 1

STUDENT 2

Media Portrayed Student?

The Real Life Student?

6.00 a.m. Arrive home from party totally smashed out of my skull. Smoke a joint and then go to bed.

11.50 a.m. Get up to go to crappy 11.00 Lecture.

12.00 p.m. Arrive at lecture, get out pen and pad and go back to sleep due to terrible hangover.

3.00 p.m. Lecture ends. The bell wakes me up. Photocopy Swotty's notes and go home.

3.20 p.m. Arrive home and write essay on the meaning of life.

3.30 p.m. Make tea.

4.00 p.m. Go to chippy.

5.10 p.m. Watch Home and Away and Neighbours – purely for educational reasons.

6.00 p.m. Ring friends and arrange to meet outside Duck and Bucket. Hang clothes out of window ready to wear later.

9.00 p.m. Get to pub. Buy friend a half, lace it with laxatives for a joke. Friend is violently sick.

10.00 p.m. Gatecrash party and get off with cute girl. Leave her alone when I see her boyfriend.

12.00 a.m. Go to all night rave. Buy a couple of Es to get the party going.

6.00 a.m. Arrive home smashed out of skull. Smoke a joint and go to bed.

6.00 a.m. Get up and start getting ready for uni. Maybe do a little work on my essay if there is time.

7.00 a.m. Set off for lecture as the only accommodation I could get is miles away.

8.30 a.m. Arrive and prepare myself for lecture. Skip breakfast and put money towards a pushbike to get me here quicker.

9.00 a.m. Lecture starts. Write copious notes but still not sure I've got everything.

12.00 p.m. Can't afford a proper dinner, salad will have to do.

1.00 p.m. Go to another couple of lectures.

5.00 p.m. Set off to go to my job in a bar as it is easier to get there than to get home.

6.00 p.m. Arrive at work-place and start writing essay. Skip tea which I can't afford and don't have time for.

8.00 p.m. Start pulling pints.

12.00 a.m. Arrive home and get back to writing essay. Go to bed when I have finished.

6.00 a.m. Get up and prepare for uni.

13

As an example, research published in 2008 suggested that the differences between the North and South in Britain are as much based on stereotype as geography:

> Half of northerners associate the south with 'wide boys' and pinstriped businessmen. Two thirds brand southerners snobs, with more than half citing arrogance as a southern characteristic ... And southerners appear just as scathing. One in five says they see mining villages and chip shops as defining images of the 'bleak' life 'up north'. (Hill 2008)

Perkins' conception of stereotypes is clearly evident here, with large proportions of both groups of northerners and southerners understanding the other in pejorative terms. The research suggested that the popular and long-running soap operas *Coronation Street* (Granada Television, 1960–) and *EastEnders* (BBC, 1985–) are influential in the maintenance of these stereotypes. However, neither of these soaps particularly reflects the regions in which they are set: Salford (Manchester), and the East End of London, respectively. For example, of the 4,437 households listed in the 2001 census for the Shadwell ward (where *EastEnders'* Albert Square is set) only 2,131 consist of members of the same ethnic groups (which, of course, wouldn't necessarily be white). So the other 2,306 households were of mixed ethnicity (source: http://neighbourhood.statistics.gov.uk/dissemination/LeadTableView.do?a= 3&b=5941759&c=shadwell&d=14&e=16&g=346888&i=1001x1003x1004&m= 0&r=1&s=1204740467046&enc=1&dsFamilyId=173; accessed March 2008). This diversity is not evident in *EastEnders*.

These stereotypes, of course, are not new. Esther Adams examined some common myths of the North and found they often had long genealogy. For example, *the North as ugly/beautiful* (to southerners and northerners, respectively) can be found in the grimness of the (early-twentieth-century) novels of D. H. Lawrence and paintings of L. S. Lowry; while the awesome landscape of the Lake District was celebrated 100 years before that by William Wordsworth (Adams 1997). While the 'grim up North' stereotype is simple as a concept, it can lead to a complex view of the place. The North is seen as:

- polluted
- uncultured
- poor
- populated by simple folk
- suspicious of outsiders
- characterized by large families and drunken husbands

- violent
- rural
- plagued by bad weather
- cold.

From the first three words of the stereotype we can extrapolate a great deal. The fact that the stereotype is, largely, rubbish doesn't mean that it isn't effective, either as a tool to denigrate a region and its people, or as a way of characterizing a milieu in a fiction text.

Having defined stereotypes, Perkins then goes on to categorize six groups that are prone to stereotyping:

1. *Major Structural Groups*: colour (black/white); gender (male/female); class (upper/middle/working); age (child/young/adult/old) ...
2. *Structurally Significant and Salient Groups*: ethnic groups (Jews/Scots); artists and scientists; mothers-in-law; adolescents in the 1950s ...
3. *Isolated Groups*: social and/or geographic isolation. Gays; American Indians ... gypsies ...
4. *Pariah Groups*: gays; blacks; Communists in USA?; junkies? ... Groups here will also belong to another group (1–3).
5. *Opponent Groups*: upper-class twit; male chauvinist pig; reds; fascists ... These contrast to others in so far they are often developed by protesting, deviant or oppressed groups, about their opponents ...
6. *Socially/Ideologically Insignificant Groups*: milkmen; redheads. (1997: 81–2)

To the Major Structural Groups we should now add teenagers, a group who also regularly inhabit the Pariah Group. To the *Pariah Groups*, in Britain at least, we can add asylum seekers, and Muslims (see below), who are being placed increasingly in this group.

While the media has a very strong influence on the dissemination of stereotypes, it must be remembered that they were not created by the media; they are concepts that are part of everyday life. Walter Lippmann defined the idea of stereotypes in 1922; Richard Dyer (1993) described four functions of Lippmann's definition, namely:

- an ordering process
- a 'short cut'
- a way of referring to 'the world'
- an expression of 'our' values and beliefs.

An ordering process

Just as human beings' senses filter out much of what they perceive, stereotypes serve to order our reality in an easy-to-understand form and are an essential part of making sense of the world and society. The fact that stereotypes offer an incomplete view of the world does not necessarily make them false; there is, in any case, no such thing as a complete view of the world. Having stereotypical knowledge about New York is more useful for audiences watching a news story about the city or a feature film set there, than having no knowledge at all.

Short cuts

Because they are simplifications, stereotypes act as 'short cuts' to meaning. We can characterize New York in a dozen words, which will be sufficient for most purposes. We do not, for example, need to research the city thoroughly to understand, say, *NYPD Blue* (20th Century Fox, 1993–2005), or any movie set there.

Despite being used as a short cut, stereotypes can still give us more than just a basic knowledge of the subject being typified. For example, while a 'macho man' is defined primarily by his physical strength, we also learn from the stereotype that such men are of below-average intelligence, have a 'Neanderthal' attitude towards women, possess conservative views, and are sexually attractive. To adapt Perkins, the stereotype also refers immediately to macho man's sex (which refers to his status in society), his relationship with women, his inability to think; and to men who are not macho, to whom the opposite applies. The simple two words 'macho man' are a short cut to a more complex set of assumptions that reflect society's values. As Perkins says, stereotypes are both simple and complex.

One of the most powerful 'short cuts' to meaning is stereotypes' use of iconography. For example, yellow cabs are in New York; red buses in London; an intellectual wears spectacles and so on. (Iconography should not be confused with Peirce's definition of an icon; iconography is, in fact, an example of Peirce's indexes – see Chapter 2.)

A way of referring to the world

Stereotypes have their origin in the real world. They are social constructs and, as such, are a type of re-presentation. However, stereotypes are also used in fictive texts; stereotypes in fiction are not just social constructs, they are also aesthetic in nature.

When discussing fiction, stereotypes are often contrasted with the novelistic character, or, in E. M. Forster's (1976) terms, 'flat' versus 'round' characters. Novelistic characters have a greater aesthetic value in Western society because they are seen as being more 'true to life', more rounded, than stereotypes. 'Novelistic' characters, which can obviously appear in any fictional text, are considered in section 6.2.

Stereotypes are views that most people recognize, otherwise they could not work as stereotypes. However, we must ask where these views originate; they could hardly spring up simultaneously among members of the population. Stereotypes are most frequently used by individuals about people or peoples they do not know. It follows, then, that they must have received this stereotype from others. The media, in its various forms, is one of the main sources of information and it is very likely that it is a crucial influence in stereotyping.

The media's role in the representation of Isolated and Pariah Groups is particularly important. By definition, these groups have been marginalized in society and so are likely to be under-represented within the media. Leslee Udwin, producer of *East is East* (UK, 1999), described the difficulty she had in getting finance for the film:

> You have no idea what kind of bigotry we came up against ... It bordered on racism. We had number-crunching people saying, 'We don't believe a film that encompasses Asians can have a broad appeal.' Why the hell not? Why don't people say that about a film with Londoners? (Quoted in Minns 1999: 7)

The film did turn out to have a broad appeal; however, the representation of the Muslim father was problematic. Based on Ayub Din-Khan's autobiographical play, he was presented as an intolerant tyrant who wasn't averse to physically abusing his white, English wife. Dramatically this worked, in the sense his children were caught between his 'Eastern' aspirations and the Western society in which they lived. However, representations of Muslim fathers are not exactly numerous in British film, and so the character, George, by default, took on the 'burden of representation' for Muslim fathers. In addition to this:

> any negative behavior by any member of the oppressed community is instantly generalized as typical ... Representations thus become allegorical ... Representations of dominant groups, on the other hand, are seen not as allegorical but as 'naturally' diverse ... A corrupt White politician is not seen as an 'embarrassment to the race' ... Yet each negative image of an underrepresented group becomes ... sorely overcharged with allegorical meaning. (Shohat and Stam 1994: 183)

In the post-9/11 climate, Muslims, arguably, have shifted in mainstream Western media from being in an Isolated to a Pariah Group. Politicians have sought to define Western democracy – the Americans characterize it as 'freedom' – against the more feudal characteristics of Islam, and this has been replicated in the media, particularly the press (newspapers).

Since *East is East*, the British film industry, no doubt on the back of the earlier film's success, has produced a number of films centring on the experience of British Asians, including *Bend It Like Beckham, Anita and Me* (both 2002) and *Love + Hate* (2005). *Yasmin* (2004) and Channel 4's *Britz* (2007) focused on the post-9/11 climate for Muslims in Britain.

It's not only ethnic minority groups who find themselves under-represented in the media. The British working class, often vaunted during the Second World War, central to the Ealing films of the 1940s and 1950s and the British New Wave of the 1960s, now find themselves a Pariah group, often dismissed as 'chavs'. Outside soap operas, the working classes are often absent from mainstream texts. This may be because, since the decline of large-scale production industries, their economic importance has diminished.

One exception was *This is England* (UK, 2006), which focused on skinheads in the 1980s. Writer-director Shane Meadows goes against the skinhead stereotype (violent, male and stupid) in a scene where 13-year-old Shaun's mum berates a 'gang' of skinheads for cutting his hair. They are apologetic and promise not to do it again.

An expression of 'our' values and beliefs

We have acknowledged that stereotypes have their basis in the material conditions and social practices of society, so it should come as no surprise that stereotypes are an expression of the dominant ideology. Stereotypes serve to naturalize the power relationships in society; they have a hegemonic function, so the fact that women are often stereotyped as being subservient to men – whether as 'dumb blondes' (see below) or housewives – legitimizes their inferior position. In this way, the importance of the difficult and time-consuming work of running a household is diminished, because it is women's work; and women are diminished because they do housework.

In 2008, evidence of the stereotype's durability was seen in *Beat the Blondes* – a game show where the contestant can win by asking one of the fifty blonde women a question in the hope that she can't answer it. The 'blondes' can also win by getting the question right; of course, they also provide multitudinous 'eye candy' for the audience, thus offering evidence of the reactionary state of the television industry.

The fact that stereotypes are an expression of values explains that, while they refer to the world, they aren't necessarily an accurate representation of it. For example, racist stereotypes are expressions of racist ideology, not because black people are inferior. Stereotypes are not true or false, but reflect a particular set of ideological values. They are, in fact, mythic (in Barthes' sense) figures, representing social values in a concise fashion. The degree to which a stereotype is accepted as being 'true' or not is dependent on an individual's knowledge of the group in question and the degree to which they are prejudiced. However, they do present themselves to be 'common sense': 'The consensus invoked by stereotypes is more apparent than real; rather, stereotypes express particular definitions of reality, with concomitant evaluations, which in turn relate to the disposition of power in society' (Dyer 1993: 14).

The fact that travellers, for example, are maligned as a lazy, sponging, thieving group of people is an expression of the bourgeois belief in the importance of the home as a stable place where the nuclear family can flourish. Similarly, the 'dumb blonde' stereotype is common, in Western society at least, because it serves the purpose of patriarchal ideology.

The 'dumb blonde' stereotype

The 'dumb blonde' stereotype is an interesting construct which has gained wide currency in the media. Clearly, hair colour is not related to intelligence; so where does this stereotype come from? Blondeness may be deemed attractive in British and North American society because of its comparative rarity (a rarity compromised by the sale of blonde hair dyes); in Scandinavia, dark hair is accorded the same exoticism, probably because it's unusual in that location. A blonde is often thought of as being sexually attractive, but why is it 'necessary' that she should also be dumb?

It is here that this stereotype's reference to the world becomes a clear expression of ideological values. If a woman was sexually attractive *and* intelligent, then it is likely that she would not wish to take on a subservient role in any relationship; bourgeois ideology's patriarchal bent defines the dominant role as male.

Similarly, the racist stereotype of black people being like animals has its origins as an ideological construct. It boggles the civilized mind that Christian people could justify to themselves that slavery was morally right; however, their rationale was relatively simple: black people are like animals and thus can be treated as such. Therefore, it was justifiable to own them as slaves. Black people were characterized as 'Sambos', who were docile, lazy, untrustworthy, ignorant and simple. It is likely that much of the discrimination that black people suffer today has its origins in slavery which, after all, was only abolished in USA after the 1861–5 Civil War.

Gillian Swanson described the constituent elements of the dumb blonde type; they possess: 'strange logic; innocence and naivety; manipulativeness; humour; a body which is emphasised; a childlike nature; adult 'knowingness' and seductiveness' (1991: 131). Clearly, many of these attributes are contradictory: adult and childlike; innocent and seductive and so on. We can examine how this stereotype operated in a men's lifestyle magazine, *Loaded*, at the height of its popularity in the 1990s.

Loaded is a 'lad's' lifestyle magazine: laddishness is characterized primarily by an enjoyment of sexist representations of women, representations that reduce females to sex objects. Other interests that feature highly in 'laddishness' are sport, booze and music. *Loaded* was launched in 1994 and, despite the entry into the market of competitors such as *Maxim* and *FHM*, established a circulation of around 250,000 copies a month. This would have been unthinkable in the early 1980s, as there were no general interest magazines for men on the market. *Arena*, launched in 1986, was the first to establish a foothold in the niche market. This early pacesetter, however, did not concentrate on sexist representations of women. *Loaded*, and its ilk, however, defined women almost wholly by their sexuality.

Baywatch babe, Donna D'Errico, features on the cover of the November 1996 issue (see Figure 4.2); her breasts are clearly the focal point, particularly because they overhang her name. Her backside is also visible and sticking out invitingly; this is a trope of representing women as sex objects – they are often required to pose in a twisted way so that both the breasts and buttocks are visible. She is also blonde. Visually, and typical of the stereotype, she is defined by the shape and pose of her body and her 'inviting' expression of parted lips. However, the anchorage also indicates sophistication: '*Baywatch* babe on philosophy, science & religion'. Despite the suggestion of childishness in the use of 'babe' there is a suggestion of an intellect behind the breasts, an attribute obviously absent from the stereotype. In order to make sense of this contradiction, we must understand *Loaded*'s use of irony as a metalanguage.

The advertising contained in *Loaded* suggests a primarily middle-class (ABC1 as sociologists and advertisers define them) readership. The first five advertisements in the January 1997 edition featured: Guess jeans; Marlboro cigarettes; Nike; Vodazap pagers; and Base shoes. Analysing the advertising is the best way of creating an audience profile short of getting the actual readership figures. The magazine's strapline is 'for men who should know better': the implication being that middle-class men should know better than being sexist. Irony acts as a distancing device: by stating the ridiculous, that the

for men who should know better   NOVEMBER 1996 £2.50

shooting stars
George Dawes fingers Ulrika. Blimey!

go on, give us a game
life in the Premiership reserves

space
the band, not the empty area around us

**wouldn't touch yours
with a bargepole**
loaded goes up a canal

hong kong hard'un
Jackie Chan chops them out

steve coogan
Portuguese man of phwoar

DONNA

BAYWATCH BABE ON PHILOSOPHY, SCIENCE & RELIGION

frankie dettori .... **man u** .... **ghosts**

Figure 4.2   Cover of *Loaded* magazine

'bimbo', Donna D'Errico will be profiled from an intellectual standpoint, the magazine is knowingly acknowledging its own sexism, which, the rhetoric goes, makes defining women as sex objects acceptable. In the August 1996 issue, a photoshoot was listed in the contents as, 'Bikini clad girls on Hawaiian beaches? Oh, go on then', and sexual innuendo is manifest in many of the headings on the front cover. For a consideration of gender in contemporary magazines, see section 5.5.

4.5 Who does the re-presenting?

Media representations are usually a product of institutions, whether large broadcasting organizations or small independent companies. Even novelists, who are probably the most independent of media practitioners and theoretically restricted only by any generic conventions they are using, are published by large organizations that inevitably have an influence on what they produce.

Analysis of institutions is quite difficult, because our only access to them is usually through the texts themselves. Virtually everyone watches television, but very few people are able to see the programmes being made, and even less to have an opportunity to discuss the modes of representation used by the media practitioners. We are often, armed with our theories and tools of analysis, left only with the text.

In Media Studies, it is a commonplace assumption, but a true one, that media institutions are dominated by stereotypical white, middle-aged men, and media production reflects this bias. White, middle-aged men dominate Western society itself, both politically and economically, so it is logical that the producers of cultural meanings should reflect this dominant group. However, in recent years, many Western countries have become markedly more multi-cultural, but this has yet to be reflected in the make-up of media institutions – for example, in the national British press ('Fleet Street'):

> The number of members of racial minorities in editing positions across all of Fleet Street is tiny. One thinks of Peter Victor, who news edits the Independent on Sunday, or Malik Meer on the Guardian's Saturday Guide, as possibly the only two who run a significant-sized department ... most of the main desks ... are run by entirely white teams. (Harker 2008: 8a)

We have seen how representation serves to reinforce the dominant ideological views, but we must avoid the teleological position that all mainstream media products are, *per se*, sexist, racist, middle-class material, because they aren't. For example, as mentioned in section 3.8, the Equal Opportunities discourse of the 1980s led to a number of police series, such as *Juliet Bravo* (1980–5), focusing on female protagonists.

One way of looking at how the media reproduces the dominant ideological discourses is to analyse how media professionals' practices and agendas serve to naturalize this value system.

4.6 Audience and representation

We have already considered how audiences read texts, and noted that while the preferred reading, or representation, may be accepted by those in the audience who make a 'dominant' reading, others have the option of 'negotiated' or 'oppositional' readings.

As in considering institutions, our access to information about audience response is severely limited, often only to the responses of friends and ourselves. The media's audience research is rarely of much help in the academic sphere, because media institutions are usually concerned with quantity of audience and their democratic profile rather than understanding how a text is read; Hollywood previews are an exception to this – if the test audience doesn't like a film, then reshoots are likely to follow.

Clearly, our individual response is important and needs to be articulated in any analysis, but wild generalizations should be avoided. It is safer to restrict analysis of audience response to decoding the preferred reading and suggesting both negotiated and oppositional readings.

The influential magazine of film theory, *Screen*, seemed to believe, in the 1970s and 1980s, that the text would wholly determine an audience's reading. Ironically, given the leftist political position the publication adopted, this seems little different from F. R. Leavis's belief in the tyranny of the text.

In the 1980s, an ethnographic form of audience research was favoured. This was derived from anthropology, and researchers were meant to immerse themselves in the audience, or culture, being studied. While this is certainly an advance on the, basically, psychoanalytical theories of *Screen*, it is not without its problems (see Morley 1992).

However, one way of illustrating how audience readings change through time is to consider texts that were controversial when first seen and compare with that initial reading today's reactions. In 2007, the British Board of Film Classification (BBFC) refused the video game *Manhunt 2* a certificate, which effectively prevented in from being sold in Britain. If past examples are anything to go by, it's quite possible that in a few years' time people will wonder what the fuss what about; indeed, the ruling was overturned a year later, on appeal. The regulation of media texts becomes more liberal because audiences become used to more explicit representations of sex and violence. How texts are read when they are first released is likely to be very different years later. Two films from the post-Second World War years illustrate this.

The Wicked Lady (1945) was the first British film to be censored in the USA. The narrative focused on a bored aristocratic lady, played by Margaret Lockwood, who sought excitement with a highwayman, James Mason.

Presumably, it was her penchant for black leather, as much as the implied adultery, that led the American censor to demonstrate his disapproval. Now the film appears to be incredibly tame, if mildly entertaining. On its release, however, it seemed to be pushing back the boundaries of censorship and clearly thrilled its audience:

> At the age of 12 year I thought it was a great film and voted it the Odeon film-goers 'film of the year' 1947, or was it 1946 (memory's going). Anyway I though the very beautiful Lady, being bored with her life and wimpy husband, met her match in the handsome highwayman. She was looking for excitement and adventure, and found it in him. While she was very wicked he was, I thought, cruel and mean and didn't really care for her as she did for him.
>
> I like the Pat Roc character, very gracious and refined, just the opposite to the Lady. I think her character loved the husband, was it Griffith John? I may be wrong, but it was a memorable film, remembering it over 47 years shows that. (Patricia Lacey [aka the author's mum], 1995)

Censorship gives us information about society's mores, albeit one defined by (institutional) regulation rather than the audience. Another film that was censored because of its apparent immorality, this time in Britain, was *The Wild One* (US, 1953).

This film, as Richard Falcon (1994) makes clear, is a fascinating case study. It wasn't just censored; it was banned completely! It eventually received a certificate from the BBFC (at that time called the British Board of Film Censors)) – only in 1967, when it was given an 'X' (18) rating. When the video was certified in 1986 it received a PG (Parental Guidance – defined as being appropriate for 'General viewing, but some scenes may be unsuitable for young children'). Clearly the text, *The Wild One*, has not changed since the early 1950s, but the BBFC's attitude has. This 'liberalization', however, does not happen in isolation from audiences: how audiences read *The Wild One* now is very different from in the past.

Based on a real incident, *The Wild One* stars Marlon Brando as Johnny, leader of a gang of bikers who invade a small town and cause trouble. What upset the censors most was the narrative's refusal to condemn the gang's actions and mete out suitable punishment. This led the Board to fear 'copy-cat' actions from Teddy Boys in Britain:

> 'Having regard,' they told the producers at Columbia, 'to the present wide-spread concern about the increase in juvenile crime, the Board is not prepared to pass any film dealing with this subject unless the compensating

moral values are so firmly presented to justify its exhibition to audiences likely to contain ... a large number of young and immature persons.' (Mathews 1994: 128)

Whether the film inspired violence in the USA or not, it appeared to have a great influence on young people. The iconography of the film became symbols of rebellion for teenage youth, who were being stifled by conformism in Cold War America. As Brando said in his ghosted autobiography:

[I] never expected [the film] to have the impact it did. I was as surprised as anyone when T-shirts, jeans and leather jackets suddenly became symbols of rebellion. In the film there was a scene in which somebody asked my character ... what I was rebelling against, and I answered, 'Whaddya got?' But none of us involved in the picture ever imagined it would instigate or encourage youthful rebellion. (1994: 175)

As can be seen from Figure 4.3, the iconography now looks more 'gay' than 'youthful rebellion'; an example of how codes can change through time.

While *The Wild One* clearly had an impact on audiences in the USA at the time of its release, the cultural changes since the early 1950s mean that audiences now read the film very differently; and this is acknowledged institutionally by its PG certificate.

Below are some readings from A-level students in England made after watching *The Wild One* in 1995:

'Timid and weak.' (*Paul Watmough*)

'Johnny ... by today's standards shows extreme sexism in the way he acts toward Mary.' (*Alistair McDonald*)

'The film *Wild Ones* [sic] is quite tame in comparison with some of today's films. There is not a lot of violence, and no swearing or sex.' (*Samantha Ryan*)

'I found the film to be ... entertaining in a humorous rather than violent way.' (*Vicky Bastow*)

'I felt the things that the gang did were amusing, and felt attracted to their way of life. Perhaps it is because of this attraction to their behaviour that it was banned, as it tends to glamorize rebellion.' (*Nicola Wormald*)

'The character of Johnny would have undoubtedly provided a role model for '50s youth and, although he leads a motorcycle gang, he appears to be

Figure 4.3   Marlon Brando as 'the wild one'

a very sensitive character. His relationship with Mary proves this. I had no unsocial urge to turn over a parked car or run down an old man.' (*Jonathan Cockcroft*)

The dominant reading of this text is now very different from the one in the 1950s. However, the meanings of all texts do not change as radically as this one. A text such as *The Seventh Seal* (1956), for example – a meditation on death in a medieval setting – is likely to change far less than those that deal with contemporary issues.

When dealing with texts that appeal to a particular audience – a youth audience in the case of *The Wild One* – it is essential to take into account the influence of a sub-culture. Members of different sub-cultural groups share particular cultural codes and will read texts differently from the way that a mass audience will.

Other factors influencing readings are the expectations generated by media coverage. For example, when *Reservoir Dogs* (US, 1991) was released, it was very difficult to see the film without prior knowledge of the notorious torture scene. It is probable that, in years to come, audiences will read the film differently, possibly with less emphasis on the torture and more on the film's generic antecedents, just as *The Wild One* now has different readings from those originally made. Away from the 'mediation' provided by the media, future audiences will see the film in a different context.

Genre is also a very strong factor that influences readings of texts, and the next section considers how the codes and conventions of the Western represent the 'Wild West' of nineteenth-century America.

4.7 Genre and representation: the Western

Genres, by their nature, have a particular way of re-presenting the world. They are a paradigm that producers use to create texts and audiences use to read them. This is most clearly defined as a repertoire of elements consisting of typical narratives, iconography (visual and aural signs), characters and settings. In some genres, such as comedies and thrillers, the use of elements is non-existent or very loose; comedies are most obviously described as texts that attempt to make audiences laugh, and:

> The concept of 'thriller' falls somewhere between a genre proper and a descriptive quality that is attached to other, more clearly defined genres – such as spy thriller, detective thriller, horror thriller. There is possibly no such thing as a pure, freestanding 'thriller thriller'. (Rubin 1999: 4)

Genres such as gangster texts and Westerns are far easier to classify and were among the first to be considered by genre theorists in the late 1960s. The Western was a staple genre during Hollywood's Golden Age (approximately the 1920s–1940s) and into the 1950s. During the 1960s, the upheavals in American society, and the Vietnam War, were apparent in the changes in modes of representation used by the Western, for example, in *The Wild Bunch* (1969) and *Little Big Man* (1970).

Westerns experienced a barren period in the 1980s: '1984 was ... the year in which Westerns were recorded as having a market share of zero in the cinema' (Neale 2002: 290). In the 1990s, though, the Western had something of a box-office renaissance with films such as *Dances With Wolves* (1990) and *Unforgiven* (1992). Despite its box office success being decidedly patchy by the end of the decade, the new century saw the genre being successful on television, with *Deadwood* (2004–6), and – critically at least – in the cinema with *Open Range*

(2003). The final months of 2007 alone saw the release of *Seraphim Falls*, *3:10 to Yuma* and *The Assassination of Jesse James by the Coward Robert Ford*.

The Western genre originated with the novels of James Fenimore Cooper; whose book, *The Last of the Mohicans*, was twice given the Hollywood treatment, in 1936 and 1992, and is characterized primarily by the myth of the frontier. The frontier was a specific place and time, which receded westwards from the moment the Founding Fathers landed until the end of the nineteenth century. At the frontier, various thematic clashes were enacted. Jim Kitses described the binary oppositions that structure the Western:

THE WILDERNESS	*CIVILISATION*
The individual	**The community**
freedom	restriction
honour	institutions
self-knowledge	illusion
integrity	compromise
self-interest	social responsibility
solipsism	democracy
Nature	**Culture**
purity	corruption
experience	knowledge
empiricism	legalism
pragmatism	idealism
brutalisation	refinement
savagery	humanity
The West	**The East**
America	Europe
the frontier	America
equality	class
agrarianism	industrialism
tradition	change
the past	the future

(Kitses 2004: 12)

The frontier is the, often imaginary, geographical space that lies between the wilderness and civilization. It is an ambiguous place that is neither wholly wild, as it is inhabited by Europeans (in this conception, Native American Indians were originally defined as savages), nor wholly civilized, as the law often had little or no power. This non-prescriptive taxonomy, Kitses

suggested, should be used to view the individual film against [this] matrix ...
to illuminate where it falls in relation to genre traditions (ibid.: 14).

While there are problems with this framework, as it lacks 'the [gender],
ethnic or racial terms which underpin most aspects of frontier (or western)
mythology' (Neale 2000: 135), it is nevertheless useful as a starting point.
Frontier mythology has been central to America's conception of itself and is
most clearly expressed, generically, in the Western. More than 100 years later,
long after the frontier had 'closed', the myth still shapes American consciousness; in, for example, *Star Trek*'s 'Space, the final frontier ...'. However, as Jack
Kerouac discovered in his novel *On the Road* (1957), there is in reality
nowhere else to 'boldly go', whatever the myths suggest.

It has been argued that, far from sustaining America, the frontier myth in
fact weakens it, because meaning is created primarily through violence:

> It is by now a commonplace that our (American) adherence to the 'myth of
> the frontier' – the concept of American as a wide-open land of unlimited
> opportunity for the strong, ambitious, self-reliant individual to thrust his way
> to the top – has blinded us to the consequences of the industrial and urban
> revolutions and to the need for social reform and a new concept of individ-
> ual and communal welfare. Nor is it a far-fetched association that the murder-
> ous violence that has characterized recent political life has been linked by
> poets and news commentators alike to the 'frontier psychology' of our recent
> past and our long heritage. The first colonists saw in America an opportunity
> to regenerate their fortunes, their spirits, and the power of their church and
> nation; but the means to that regeneration through violence became the
> structuring metaphor of the American experience. (Slotkin 1973: 5)

This 'self-reliant individual', the model bourgeois personality, is in the
Western invariably male. What follows is a consideration of how what values
the heroes of Westerns represent.

The Western hero

To read society from films, as this section will do, is a highly dodgy process.
Hindsight structures what we're looking for but, on the other hand, it would
be highly surprising if the *zeitgeist* didn't inform how genres evolve. Genres
are 'the same but different'; in order to engage audiences, genres must stay
fresh and 'speak' to their addressees. So while we should be careful in our
suggestions about how a particular genre variation – in this context the
changing Western hero – relates to society, it doesn't mean we shouldn't speculate about what it *might* be saying.

In the aftermath of 9/11, Susan Faludi argues, America was in a desperate need of heroes. She describes *Spirit of America* (2001), a three-minute short film consisting of a montage of screen heroes described by the director as '"reluctant but defiant revenge takers"' (2007: 7). One character, Ethan Edwards of *The Searchers* (1956) (see Box 4.1), played by John Wayne, features twice: '"Wayne is the quintessential American hero ... He's a rescuer"' (ibid.).

Wayne was associated with the Western throughout his career and was a major box office star for thirty years. He first came to fame in *Stagecoach* (1939), featuring Wayne as the Ringo Kid, who avenges his family. Although Ringo is on the wrong side of the law, he is clearly a 'good guy' who's doing the right thing ('what a man's gotta do'). In this he is a typical Western hero: while he epitomizes the individual, in Kitses' oppositions he is also a defender of the community (against the Indians, who attack the cross-section of society in the stagecoach). Ringo kills the bad guys and leaves the community, with the prostitute Dallas, who'd been expelled by 'good citizens', to go and form a family in a place free from prejudice. The Western hero represented an ideal American: his integrity and honour was important in civilizing the wilderness (he was also male and white).

By the 1950s, the Western hero was not necessarily as straightforward to portray. In *High Noon* (1952) – a film reviled by Wayne – the hero cannot rely on the community to support him in his duel with the bad guys. The McCarthy witch-hunts – the infamous senate hearings where people were asked to 'name names' about who had been a member of the Communist party – had a direct influence on the film, as three of those involved in its production were called to the hearings. Drummond suggests that the hero's integrity, a 'given' in previous Westerns, was:

> no longer simply associated with personal power and charisma [but] rather with suffering and with the loss of personal and social potency, in a substantial revision of masculine identity increasingly typical of the new cinema of the post-war years. (1997: 82)

Jim Kitses notes how the heroes in director Anthony Mann's Westerns typically have:

> a highly-developed moral sense, while being at the mercy of an irrational drive to deny that very side of his nature. The hero also has a strong sense of chivalry, society's cloak for instinct and strong feeling, which vanishes when he is under stress. (2004: 142–3)

Mann's films were made in the years following the Second World War, and it is likely that the experiences of veterans of the war shaped a more complex view of morality. While the war against fascism was clearly a just war, the effect of the violence experienced by those involved left its mark for many years afterwards. The *film noir* genre, in particular, which thrived just after the war, undercut the 'conventional affirmation of heroic masculinity' (Krutnik 1991: 88) of the hero of thrillers.

In *3:10 to Yuma* (1957) the hero is 'split' between the family man (Dan Evans) and the gang leader (Ben Kane). While Evans struggles to prove his masculinity to his wife, the charismatic Kane is decidedly on 'the wrong side of the law'. In the 2007 remake, in an interesting change, Evans has to prove his 'manhood' to his son. This supports Faludi's suggestion that, post 9/11, the US media seemed obsessed with the return of patriarchal values at the expense of gains made by the women's movement in the 1960s–70s. In twenty-first-century America, proving one's manhood is apparently a wholly male activity.

If representing the 'pure' Western hero was no longer tenable in the post-war period, the 1960s saw further revisionism in the light of social turmoil – particularly the civil rights movement – and the Vietnam War. Hollywood star Henry Fonda, whose persona was forged in the 'good guy' roles of *Young Mr Lincoln* (1939) and in *The Grapes of Wrath* (1940), played Frank in Sergio Leone's 'spaghetti Western' *Once Upon a Time in the West* (Italy–US, *C'era una volta il West*, 1968). The first time he is seen, he shoots and kills children.

In *The Wild Bunch*, the 'hero', once again, is split, this time between Pike and Deke, ex-partners who find themselves on opposite sides of the law; Deke's been blackmailed to track Pike. The film starts with a 'slaughter of innocents' – echoing what was happening in Vietnam – caught in the cross-fire:

> Notions of honour seem outdated in a world where technology (motor cars, machine-guns) increasingly dominates and realpolitik and business (represented by the rapacious railroad) are more powerful than love and honour. (Buscombe 2006: 225)

For Pike, death is preferable to a world without honour. Clint Eastwood offered a different take on this by revisiting his 'man with no name persona', forged in 1960s' 'spaghetti Westerns' with *Unforgiven* (1992). He plays William Munney, one-time gunslinger turned pig farmer, who is determined to bring his family up properly. However, the call of violence proves too much, and the climactic massacre suggests that psychotic slaughter is at the heart of the West.

While the 'revisionist' Western, where the Indians were recast as victims, had been in evidence since the 1960s (for example, *Cheyenne Autumn*, 1964, directed by John Ford), in the 1990s two films attempted to offer civil rights and equal opportunities discourse: *Posse* (1993) and *Bad Girls* (1994), which featured African-Americans and women as heroes. A preface to the former notes that one-third of cowboys were black; but in Hollywood black cowboys were almost wholly absent – a whitewashing of history. While the film does show how racism still blighted the lives of ex-slaves after the Civil War, as their town, Freedomville, is at the mercy of a local (white) sheriff, its couching of the 'hero' as a man driven by Oedipal conflict – his need to revenge his father – places it comfortably within the mainstream of Western discourse (and hence it is 'white').

Bad Girls starts similarly to *Stagecoach*, with the 'good folk' driving out the prostitutes. As a film with a badly troubled production history, the original director Tamra Davis being replaced by Jonathan Kaplan, it still manages to make some surprisingly telling points. Women's masquerade (see section 5.4) is emphasized when they play various roles to manipulate men, such as Eileen's 'New Orleans' lady. The women ('girls'?) are seeking to exploit one of their number's claim to land, but Anita finds that, because she is female, she cannot claim her land: 'I was worthless until I was married. I am worthless as a widow. I had some value as a whore.' Although the women do save themselves, the insistence that they should all look glamorous does undercut the seriousness of the film.

The television series *Deadwood* (2004–6) offered an interesting variant on the genre in focusing on the community rather than on a particular hero. As a television serial it has a wider 'canvas' on which to represent the West. However, in eschewing the usual (bourgeois) focus on the (individual) hero, it does represent a distinctive change. The setting is Montana in 1876, a place where there is no law:

> If Calamity Jane (with [Wild Bill] Hickok) offers us melancholic symbols of frontier virtues about to disappear, then Bullock represents the Westward expansion through capitalism, arriving with Sol Star not to prospect for gold but to set up a hardware store. (McCabe 2006: 64)

The first three episodes of series one include a narrative thread detailing the demise of Hickok, whose status as a celebrity was cemented in Wild West shows of the time. Keith Carradine's world-weary Hickok is merely waiting for death as he no longer, if he ever did, wishes to 'live up to' his celebrity. This theme is taken up in *The Assassination of Jesse James by the Coward Robert Ford* (2007). The Western hero as celebrity obviously echoes the contemporary obsession with celebs, and the emptiness of the celeb's existence, and of those who venerate him, is beautifully portrayed in the film.

Seraphim Falls (2006), unusually for a Western, strays from the realist mode at its climax. Once again, the hero is split between the protagonists; however, we do not know why Carver is pursuing Gideon and so don't know who is 'good' and who is 'bad'. This ambiguity is heightened, at the end, when the pair meet (or hallucinate a meeting with) Madame Louise (C Farr – Lucifer) in the desert. The pointlessness of revenge is emphasized, casting into doubt one of the central tenets of the Western – the revenge narrative. This meeting with the devil suggests a metaphysical element and so allows us readily to generalize the characters' behaviour to the mythic: America's pursuit of revenge after 9/11 is futile.

As Faludi points out (and see Box 4.1) the choice of Ethan Edwards as a quintessential American hero was deeply suggestive of a rather sick national psyche as the 'Duke [John Wayne] we were so desperate to 'welcome back' in the aftermath of 9/11, [was] a stone-cold killer and Indian hater who would stand guard over our virginal girls' (2007: 7).

The Western represents particular ideas of nationhood and is a potently American genre. The way the genre is used to represent its heroes can be seen as a marker of society's particular concerns at the time the films were made.

Box 4.1   *The Searchers* (1956)

This film is driven by a revenge narrative, in which Ethan Edwards (played by John Wayne) and Martin Pawley, his 'half-breed' 'nephew', search for his niece, Debbie, who was kidnapped as a child by Indians. Edwards' brother's family had been massacred when Debbie was captured. The narrative covers the massacre and the years of searching.

Like many Hollywood films, *The Searchers* uses film stars. John Wayne was one of the biggest box office stars in the 1940s and 1950s and is associated particularly with the Western. His well-established persona of a rugged individualist who lives by his own code is subverted, somewhat, by the psychologically disturbed nature of Edwards' character. Edwards' obsessive hatred of Indians is such that he intends to kill Debbie because she has been 'defiled' (had sex with) an Indian.

By the 1950s, the Western genre had reached a 'mature' stage and was starting to question the myths it was propagating. Ford's later film, *The Man Who Shot Liberty Valance* (1962) is an overt consideration of these myths. The presentation of the Wayne character as psychologically sick casts doubt not just on the heroism he represents in *The Searchers*, but in all of his films.

The film's representation of women is conventional for Hollywood at the time, with Vera Miles' role (Laurie Jorganson) being little more than the 'love interest'. The women are the homemakers who wait anxiously for their men to return from the wilderness. It is Laurie's mother who makes a statement about civilizing the frontier; women create a community to which men like Edwards, an individual and therefore an outsider (as revealed in the *mise en scène* of the opening, and in the closing shots), can never belong. Community spirit in Ford's Westerns is often symbolized by the singing of 'Let us gather at the river'; in *The Searchers* this takes place at the funeral of Edwards' family, but he brusquely cuts it short.

As with women, *The Searcher*'s representation of Indians as savages is true to generic type. It wasn't until revisionist Westerns that the genocidal nature of the frontier began to be acknowledged. Anyone wishing to see a true representation of what the West was really like can only conclude that the Western genre is a travesty of the truth. However, this misses the point; the crux of the Western is that it articulates the myths of nationhood, which are important for sustaining national identity, particularly in a very young nation such as the USA.

Ethan Edwards is a portrayal of a person who can only seek redemption through revenge. This individualism is at odds with the organic, agrarian society of the Western settlers. However, the original settlers' ideals of living by the natural law, like Thoreau at Walden, were soon to be

> overcome by the Jacksonian Democracy of the western man-on-the-make, the speculator, and the wildcat banker; (by) racist irrationalism and a falsely conceived economics (which) prolonged and intensified slavery in the teeth of American democratic idealism; and ... men like Davy Crockett became national heroes by defining national aspiration in terms of so many bears destroyed, so much land preempted, so many trees hacked down, so many Indians and Mexicans dead in the dust. (Slotkin 1973: 5).

Westerns do not represent the reality of nineteenth-century frontier America, but create and articulate myths of North American nationhood.

4.8 Propaganda and public relations

Propaganda attempts to persuade its audience of a particular political, or religious, point of view. It does this through attempting to convince the audience that its explanation of the world is the correct one, and adherence to the views it is propagating will benefit individual members of the audience. Public relations (PR) is the means by which governments, businesses, pressure groups and public services attempt to portray themselves, in the media, in the best possible light. The extent to which this is the same as propaganda is debatable; at one extreme there is little difference between PR and propaganda; however, PR is usually more subtle in both its content and how it is presented to audiences.

Because of the requirement for 'balance' in news and current affairs, party political broadcasts are the only legal form of propaganda allowed in British broadcasting. Newspapers are not so bound, and the owners are free to vent their prejudices, restrained only by the law and occasional censure by the Press Complaints Commission. PR companies, however, do not usually produce media texts, but attempt to influence the content of productions (one exception is the issue of video news releases – VNRs; these look like news reports and are designed to be broadcast, uncredited, by news organizations). This can range from the 'spin' of news management to the placement of advertorial material in magazines (advertorials look like editorial matter but are in fact simply marketing their content – examples are fashion pages towards the back of lifestyle magazines).

PR is also involved in attempts to influence government policy by lobbying politicians, producing reports, infiltrating pressure groups who oppose their clients, and even fabricating documents and/or websites:

> There are websites like Empower Peace (www.empowerpeace.org) which appears to representing a grass-roots campaign for world peace but which is, in fact, the creation of the US State Department promoting US foreign policy. (Davies 2008: 222)

In 1990, Kuwait was invaded by 'Saddam Hussein's' Iraq. The Kuwaiti royal family hired Hill and Knowlton, a PR company, to mobilize public opinion in the USA to support a war to liberate their country. One of the most vivid testimonies given to Congress was about the brutality of Iraqi soldiers, who flung babies out of their incubators. It was subsequently found that the 'nurse' testifying to this, Nayirah, was the daughter of the Kuwaiti ambassador to America, and that these 'facts' were false.

Distinguishing between information and propaganda is not necessarily straightforward, as propaganda is not necessarily lies; it can represent actual events, such as the Nuremberg rally in 1934 discussed below. To distinguish between 'information' and 'propaganda' it is necessary to analyse the way in which the audience is addressed and, if possible, ascertain the intentions of the text's producers. In propaganda, as Steve Neale (1977) has shown, the individual is often identified as a national citizen, so by addressing a mass, who are all of one nation or race, the text is addressing the individual. In addressing *one* nation it is obviously not going to be offering a (Bakhtinian) dialogue (see section 3.4). In Althusser's terms (see section 3.6), propaganda seeks to 'interpellate' the individual in the audience, the 'you' addressed by the text, into the text's view of the world. The intentions of party political broadcasts are obviously to get the audience to vote for the party; the clear signification – a voice-over states who the broadcast is for both at the beginning and end of the broadcast – of the text's provenance makes it obvious to the audience who is speaking. In America, political advertising, outlawed in Britain, also make it clear whom the text is supporting.

Propaganda's prime function, however, is to persuade audiences towards the producer's viewpoint, or to reinforce the views of those who already agree with them, rather than to inform. In this sense, advertising is propaganda; however, adverts are generally formally signified as being advertising, to enable audiences to 'put up their guard'. Advertising, in the UK at least, is also heavily regulated, so claims of a product's efficacy usually need to be proven.

Propaganda does not necessarily signify itself as such and is far more likely to manipulate or withhold information to suit its purposes. It is quite possible, in this sense, to consider many British newspapers as being propaganda promoting the ideological views of their proprietors. While propaganda may use 'facts and figures' to give the argument an apparently objective basis, it is distinguished by its appeal to emotions and prejudice rather than rational argument. It will play upon fears and anxieties while offering a solution – usually the political party, or pressure group, that is the producer of the text support. Sharon Beder investigated the role of large corporations in ridiculing the existence of 'global warming' for many years, and showed that:

> Corporations seek not only to influence legislation and regulation but also to define the agenda – what it is legitimate for government to consider and what can be discussed in the political area – thereby rendering those groups who have other agendas ineffective. (1997: 239)

It is not only corporations that are mendacious in their dealings with both the media and the public, however. Nick Davies describes how a Greenpeace press release exaggerated the number of deaths that resulted from the nuclear accident at Chernobyl in 1986 (2008: 41). However, this may simply be a case of Greenpeace using the same 'dirty tactics' as the anti-environmental lobby. Of course, it is always the audiences who lose out in such circumstances.

In many ways, the influence of propaganda is a product of the mass media, whose technological base makes it possible to disseminate information to large numbers of people. It is not, however, solely a product of the modern age; in the late sixteenth century it was recommended to Pope Gregory XIII that there should be a Cardinal for Propaganda in order to convert dissenting nations to the faith.

In section 3.7 we investigated how the ruling classes gain the consent of others to rule on their behalf – hegemony. The role of PR in this process was made explicit by the head of PR at General Motors in the aftermath of the Great Depression of the 1930s:

'The challenge that faces us is to shake off our lethargy and through public relations make the American plan of industry stick. For, unless the contributions of the system are explained to consumers in terms of their own interest, the system itself will not stand against the storm of fallacies that rides the air.' (quoted in Davies 2008: 180)

The capitalist system had failed during the Depression, and American business felt threatened by the alternative political system of communism. Hence many mainstream representations of communism were negative, and remain so at the time of writing.

Propaganda is only obvious as propaganda to an audience that is aware of its nature. This awareness may be the product of an 'oppositional' reading (as people loyal to a political party are likely to make of their opponent's publicity) or of contextual information (such as being told by a respected expert that a text's message is false). Clearly, a propaganda text cannot work as effectively if the majority of the audience of the text is aware of its true purpose.

In war, where truth is often said to be the first casualty, propaganda is a major weapon. During the war in the Balkans in the 1990s, state television was in the vanguard of the propaganda battle:

The Croatian government in Zagreb was still denying that (Vukovar) had fallen. Since there had been no surrender, there could not be any refugees, nor buses full of desperately thirsty people on the road to Zagreb. As proof, that evening, the Zagreb Television news described the heroic, irreducible resistance of the Croat fighters of Vukovar, the commentary given against a montage of artillery salvoes filmed at least three weeks ago, before the journalists of Zagreb TV had packed up and left the town. I then flipped to Belgrade TV, which was broadcasting a sequence of images of children's mutilated bodies – mutilated, it was claimed, by Croatian forces. (Hatzfeld 1994: 215)

Propaganda was also used to great effect by the Nazis in the 1930s and 1940s. One of the most effective proponents of propaganda in Nazi Germany was Joseph Goebbels, Head of the Ministry for Popular Enlightenment and Propaganda (interestingly, Goebbels did not feel the need to conceal his Ministry's function). He is often credited with enabling the Nazis to mobilize the German nation into the atrocities of the Holocaust.

The Frankfurt School of media theorists concluded that the co-operation of the bulk of the German people, who were not Nazis, was a result of the corrupting influence of popular culture, and they feared the same would happen elsewhere in the Western world. Their theories were influential for a time and still have a residue in 'common sense' discourses; this was dealt with in *Media Institutions and Audiences* (2002).

Nazi propaganda

Hitler appealed to a nationalism based on folklore, tapping into a yearning for the 'good old days' during the economic maelstrom and cultural decadence of the Weimar Republic. He used mass meetings to reinforce his ideological standpoint, impressing his audience with the scale of the meeting and making the audience feel part of a mass movement.

One of the most famous pieces of Nazi propaganda is Leni Riefenstahl's *Triumph des Willens* (Triumph of the Will); see Box 4.2 below. This film record of the Nuremberg Rally in 1934 probably earns its reputation today more from its undoubted visual power than from any particular influence it had on its audience at the time. While the rally was certainly important in consolidating Hitler's power – it came only days after the Rohm Putsch, when he wiped out opposition within his party – but it probably had little impact on the German population.

In the Rohm Putsch, Hitler had killed the leaders of the SA, the Brownshirts, who had continued advocating a populist socialist agenda, something that was anathema to the German Establishment. Brian Winston (1995) has shown that the propagandistic aim of *Triumph des Willens* was to reposition the Nazi party after it had gained power in the 1933 elections and to gain the support of the Brownshirts:

The film has, despite its mind-numbing repetitiveness and interminable length, a careful and coherent structure which articulates a quite clear social/public-education purpose ... Virtually every synch word is directed towards the SA problem and the renegotiation of the Nazi Party's populist stance in the aftermath of the putsch. (Winston 1995: 75)

It is a fascinating, and repelling, document to analyse, for it reveals much about how the conventions of filmic representation can be used for emotional, and propagandistic, impact.

Box 4.2   *Triumph des Willens* opening sequence analysis

The martial style of the music connotes militarism and nationalism. The Nazi emblem draws upon Roman iconography, as the Roman nation was also a militarist one. The low-angle shot emphasizes the power that Nazis possess. By bringing the shot to eye-level we are brought into a privileged position, a position we are given access to throughout this sequence.

The old-style lettering of the title emphasizes its longevity: it (Nazism) has always been with us, but only now is it fulfilling its destiny.

The title shown in the second shot suggests it is a documentary ('a record'), and this reality is shown, in the shot following, to have been sanctioned by the Führer. 'Hitler as god' is another of the structuring themes of the sequence.

The music becomes Wagnerian, with connotations of archetypal myths of creation. The music comments explicitly upon the titles at this point, a minor key emphasizing the sinister circumstances of Germany's defeat in the First World War, leading to the heroic theme associated with Hitler and Germany's rebirth.

A partisan view of history is clearly being created and reinforced by the music's emotional impact. Then the documentary's narrative begins, with Hitler's arrival at Nuremberg.

Shot 10 is clearly a point-of-view shot, but we are not sutured (shown the position of the point-of-view) until shot 23, when we see Hitler's aeroplane. This lack of anchoring within the sequence serves to create mystery and a god-like feeling of power as we see the descent from the clouds from Hitler's perspective. Of course, everything looks comparatively small from the air, though the buildings are impressive in their grandeur (clearly selected for this reason). In 1934, few people would have flown, giving the sequence the excitement of a space flight now.

The photography is stunning, the sun-gilded clouds emphasizing nature's beauty and power, myths on which Nazism drew, particularly in its representations of the purity of the mountains. As we descend from the clouds, among the first buildings we can see clearly, appropriately for a god, are a church and a building that has both the German and Nazi flags flying on it, emphasizing the interchangeability of the Nazis and the German nation.

Once Hitler's point-of-view is anchored, in shot 23, his shadow – in fact, the aeroplane's, but we identify it with Hitler, since we assume him to be in the aeroplane – is seen both on the buildings and on the minute people marching to greet him. (There is a similar scene in *The Third Man* (1948), in which Harry Lime points out that it is easy to kill people you perceive as insects.)

At last, after three minutes of descent, the aeroplane lands. Just before this, crowds are seen waiting in anticipation, shielding their eyes – obviously from the sun, but it could easily be from the bright aura of the Führer. Cheering starts, and the medium close-up of shot 34 brings us close to the masses of smiling, saluting Nazis. Shot 35 is a very striking composition creating the effect of people saluting into the sky, from where their 'saviour' has just landed.

The arrival concludes with our perspective safely within the crowd. Our privileged position is now denied us, leaving Hitler on his pedestal.

It is a powerfully constructed sequence, but only fascists could find it convincing now, as to us, Hitler has come to represent evil. In 1934, it appears that most people found the film boring. However, the rhetoric of the film's style works by giving us access to a privileged position squarely within the adoring masses that attended the Nuremberg rally. This is the 'you' that Neale defines as a function of propaganda, although rather than identifying 'you' as a national citizen, 'you' are placed as a Nazi.

Goebbels believed that feature films were, by far, a more potent force of propaganda than documentaries, as films were about entertainment and not 'preaching to the masses'. He believed that feature films would imperceptibly influence the audience, because they would be unaware that they were watching propaganda.

Goebbels controlled film production by nationalizing the German film industry. Only members of *Reichsfilmkammer* (Chamber of Film) were allowed to make films. However, the notorious propaganda feature films such as *Hitlerjung Quex* (1933) and *Jud Suss* (1940) did not appear out of a cultural vacuum. Ufa, Germany's premier film studio, had been producing 'mountain movies' since the late 1920s (Leni Riefenstahl, as an actress, starred in many of them). These films emphasized the racial purity of Aryan heroes by associating them with glaciers and mountains. The seeds of Nazi myths, and anti-semitism, were already part of German, and in fact, European, culture.

Although *Hitlerjung Quex* and *Jud Suss* are both clearly propaganda to our non-fascist eyes, they represent different styles of feature film. *Hitlerjung Quex*, with its heroic, sacrificial tale of the Hitler Youth (a vicious variant of the Boy Scouts) did not find favour with Goebbels. It was too overtly propagandistic. *Jud Suss*, however, was Goebbels' response to the trite and nauseating documentary *Der ewige Jude* (The Eternal Jew), commissioned by Hitler. *Der ewige Jude* left little to its (small) audience's imagination in its equation of Jews with rats; *Jud Suss*, however, used the technique of cloaking contemporary issues in costume drama, and employed conventional feature-film narrative to instil the message that Jews were evil and should be exterminated. Audience research at the time – albeit Nazi research – showed that the audience did make the equation.

So the most effective propaganda were the texts that appeared to be entertainment and yet carried a specific ideological message that was intended to influence audiences' attitudes. All films, in fact, carry an ideological message; however, Goebbels' films differed in that they were designed specifically to change attitudes; most films seek, usually 'unconsciously', to reinforce the dominant ideological view. It is interesting to compare an overtly fascist propagandistic film (albeit a documentary) with a Hollywood film made in the same decade that attempted to articulate explicitly the liberal values of New Deal America (see Box 4.3).

Box 4.3   *Triumph des Willens I, 42nd Street* and the New Deal

In *Triumph des Willens* there are numerous long shots of thousands of people moving as one, this creates abstract patterns that only the multitude of cameras – and the fact that much of what we see is from Hitler's god-like point-of-view – can capture. These sequences have great visual power.

The fact that, while National Socialism is undeniably disgusting, the film has moments of incredible aesthetic power, has caused problems for a number of film critics and led some to eulogize Riefenstahl as 'a great film-maker' while acknowledging that the subject matter is dubious. This view was encouraged by Riefenstahl, who claimed she was 'politically naïve' and was only concerned with making films, the content of them being incidental. This position is indefensible, as Susan Sontag, *in Fascinating Fascism* (Sontag 1976) demonstrated.

However, it is interesting to see how similar sequences in a Hollywood film can create a similar aesthetic effect and yet are, on the face of it, articulating values that are the opposite of fascism.

US President Franklin D. Roosevelt started his term in office, in 1933, during the 'Great Depression'. This originated in the Stock Market Crash of

1929, and was threatening the economic and social fabric of Western society. Roosevelt brokered a New Deal, a liberal attempt to intervene in the economic management of the country. The New Deal involved everybody 'pulling together' and the opportunity for a 'fresh start'.

Hollywood was affected drastically by the recession; takings and production were down, and investment and cash flow had been reduced to a trickle. This is not the place to embark on a thesis linking all Hollywood production to the New Deal, but at the time there was a thriving genre that seemed to reflect Roosevelt's values quite explicitly: the backstage musical.

The American Dream is that everyone, no matter how humble in origin, can be a success through hard work. Anybody can become president, even if, like Abraham Lincoln, it means going from the backwoods to the White House. As we saw in our consideration of the Western, the American Dream is a myth, an ideological construct designed to give society cohesion and make everyone feel they have a stake in the country. Mark Roth demonstrates that the Warner's 'backstage musicals' subtly varied this myth:

> But while the myth is supported by the plot, it is contradicted, or at least significantly modified, by the dance numbers in which we see the individual subordinated to the will of a single person – the director ... The message is that cooperation, planning and the guidance of a single leader are now necessary for success. (1981: 19)

In the backstage musical, an individual, through hard work and some talent, gets to become a star. However, to do this in the Great Depression requires a leader, and this leader – the director – represented Roosevelt. The interdependence of individuals in society is represented through the Busby Berkeley dance routines.

Roth also points out that the leads of *42nd Street* – Ruby Keeler and Dick Powell – are particularly untalented, suggesting to the audience that anyone can 'make it' (Powell did, however, make an excellent Philip Marlowe in *Farewell, My Lovely* (1944)). Keeler plays a chorus girl who gets her lucky break and becomes a star. Their very ordinariness possibly provokes an even stronger form of identification than mainstream cinema normally facilitates, positioning the audience as a 'you' in an almost propagandistic fashion.

The parallels between the New Deal and the 'backstage musical' are made clear in *42nd Street,* with the director, played by Warner Baxter, having lost his money on the financial markets. Warner Bros. also made the link between the film and Roosevelt's attempt at economic renewal explicit in their publicity material:

The next week, the *'42nd Street* Special' left Hollywood 'on the greatest ride since Paul Revere', carrying 'news of a Revolution in Picture Art!' and 'leaving a trail of millions of ticket buyers for WARNER BROS. NEW DEAL IN ENTERTAINMENT'. (Hoberman 1993: 32)

On the one hand, *42nd Street* is a Horatio Alger story as refracted through the Ziegfeld Follies: the virtuous Peggy Sawyer works hard, resists temptation, gets her break, and makes the most of it. On the other hand, the film offers the vision of some new, collective social order, founded on the industrial production of erotic fantasy, the joyous orchestration of the masses, the confusion between making love and making work. Even more than most musicals, *42nd Street* presents 'head-on', as Richard Dyer suggests in his essay on the use-value of entertainment, just 'what utopia would feel like'. (Ibid.: 68)

It takes little imagination to see the similarity between the abstract patterns that Berkeley creates out of people in his dance numbers and the dehumanized masses in *Triumph des Willens* (indeed Berkeley-style routines were featured in mainstream German cinema); however, one is a Liberal expression of community and the other a vicious ideology intent on slaughter. It is interesting to consider that, while both texts are produced with apparently opposing ideological aims, they are in fact the product of the same, bourgeois, aesthetic.

But are the aims of *Triumph des Willens* and *42nd Street* so different? As Roth concludes:

The image of a political leader as a large-scale Busby Berkeley is certainly ambiguous. The thrust of such an image is undoubtedly toward collective effort and subjugation of the will of the individual to the overall pattern dictated by the leader. But does this imply the ideal represented for Ruskin by the Middle Ages, or a socialist-communist ideal, or a Hitler–Franco type fascist dictatorship? (1981: 55)

It could be that the same aesthetic device, which makes startling abstract and concrete patterns out of people, can only reflect one ideological position. The needs of Hitler and Roosevelt were the same, obedience, even though one was a fascist and the other a liberal. In this sense, both are propagandistic texts but, in Hollywood texts, the values of the dominant ideology are articulated and packaged as entertainment.

Modern propaganda

As we shall see in section 6.5, news values construct and select events that will be defined as news. Herman and Chomsky take this a step further by suggesting that the selection of news is so heavily influenced by dominant ideological interests that it could be described more accurately as propaganda. They proposed five 'news filters' that compromise the way news is presented:

1. the size, concentrated ownership, owner wealth, and profit orientation of the dominant mass-media firms;
2. advertising as the primary income source of the mass media;
3. the reliance of the media on information provided by government, business and 'experts' funded and approved by these primary sources and agents of power;
4. 'flak' as a means of disciplining the media; and
5. 'anticommunism' as a national religion and control mechanism. (Herman and Chomsky 1994: 2)

Concentrated ownership

They explain that media organizations, as large businesses, have interests in common with governments, banks and other large corporations. Governments often seek the support of newspapers in order to gain favourable coverage of their policies. In return, the newspaper proprietors look for legislation that favours their businesses. For example, for many years, in both Britain and the USA, it was illegal to have controlling interests in both television and newspaper companies, as this was likely to restrict the plurality of views deemed necessary for a democracy to work effectively. However, in recent decades, in deference to free market economics, such restrictions have been lifted.

When Rupert Murdoch's News Corporation bought *Times Newspapers* in 1981, the purchase of *The Sunday Times*, because it was profitable, should have been referred to the Monopolies and Mergers Commission. Murdoch threatened to pull out of the deal if this was done and so threatened the newspapers with closure. The extent to which Murdoch's support of the Thatcher Government at the time led to his being able to buy both papers without referral to the MMC has since been the subject of debate:

> Woodrow Wyatt, a confidant of both Thatcher and Murdoch ... [boasted] he was responsible for there being no MMC referral ... while it is unlikely that Thatcher stayed her [trade] minister's hand on Wyatt's word alone, it

is entirely plausible that Wyatt lobbied hard on Murdoch's behalf. (Greenslade 2004: 378)

Greenslade goes on to describe the Murdoch-owned *Sun*'s vilification of Labour leader Neil Kinnock. It warned, before local elections, 'that voting Labour would cause sterling to collapse, drive companies to the wall and necessitate heavy borrowing because of high public service spending' (ibid.: 609). The campaign against Labour culminated in the front page on General Election day, 9 April 1992, featuring Kinnock's head in a light bulb, with the headline:

If Kinnock wins today will the last person to leave Britain please turn out the lights.

Labour duly lost the election, and there's been much debate about the influence of the newspaper, as it had, and still has, the largest circulation among the dailies, plus a predominantly working-class readership, the natural constituency of the Labour party. When Tony Blair became leader of the party, in 1994, he was quick to cultivate a relationship with News Corporation and Rupert Murdoch and received *The Sun*'s support in the three elections that he won. The Labour party of Blair, rebranded New Labour, was very different from the socialist party that Kinnock led.

Advertising income

Curran and Seaton (2003) demonstrated how, in the nineteenth century, advertisers disadvantaged left-wing newspapers in Britain: 'Left publications were also forced to close down with circulations far higher than some of their more right-wing rivals' (Curran and Seaton 2003: 50). Advertisers are unlikely to support a news organization whose agenda is not sympathetic to their businesses. American television is regularly threatened by the withdrawal of advertising if it screens 'unsuitable' material.

Public relations

PR has become an increasingly important source of news because of the increasing pressure on news organizations to make a profit. This squeeze on resources, meaning fewer journalists have to produce more copy, has also led to a greater reliance on public relations material.

Instead of investigating the claims of press releases, journalists, because of pressure of time and/or a lack of training, are increasingly likely to print them verbatim, without even checking the information the contain; Davies (2008) calls this 'churnalism'.

It must not be forgotten that 'public relations' also refers to the management of news by governments. For example, in the long-running Israel–Palestine conflict, compared to the Palestinians:

> The Israelis had twice as much time to speak ... [and] were more likely to be interviewed in calm, relaxed surroundings ... We asked a very experienced Middle East correspondent for the BBC to explain why these differences ... occurred ... [he said] the Israelis have a very well organised media and public relations operation [and] ... the Israelis limit what the Palestinians are able to do because of the impositions of their military occupation. (Philo and Berry 2004: 136–7)

Israel has a sophisticated news management system that is beyond the means of Palestinians. In addition, the fact that news very rarely explains the background to such long-running conflicts means that many viewers don't understand what is happening. As Philo and Berry show, 90 per cent of British students believed that the term 'occupied territories' referred to Palestinians occupying Israel and not, as is the case, the other way around.

Israel also benefits from generating 'flak'.

Flak

'"Flak" refers to negative responses to a media statement or program' (Herman and Chomsky 1994: 26). Flak is a tool that can be used by both governments and pressure groups. For example:

> when a 12-year-old boy, Abdullah Quran, was stopped while unwittingly carrying explosives at an army checkpoint, Israeli embassies called news editors to insist they cover the story and warn that failure to do so would be viewed as bias against Israel.
>
> When several news organisations failed to report it, an Israeli newspaper called for their correspondents to be expelled. (McGreal 2004)

While many resisted this pressure, at a risk of not being able to report from the country in the future, some took the easier option.

Since the advent of the internet as a mass medium, flak has become an even more widespread tool. For example, when the BBC transmitted the controversial *Jerry Springer: The Opera* it received over 50,000 complaints and:

The recently appointed controller of BBC2 and [the director of television] ... received a number of abusive calls after their numbers were printed on the website of a prayer group, Christian Voice, one of a number that have organised campaigns against the show. (Gibson 2005)

The Christian Voice website encourages people to contact decision-makers on a variety of issues, and puts their postal and email addresses on its website: http://www.christianvoice.org.uk/index (accessed April 2008).

In the case of *Jerry Springer*, the BBC refused to bow to pressure and broadcast the opera. However, the use of such tactics puts organizations under pressure to defend themselves, and some might take the easy option and avoid anything controversial.

Anti-ism

Herman and Chomsky's fifth point is now outdated only in the specificity of the 'national religion' as, since the fall of the Berlin Wall and demise of the Soviet Union, anti-communist rhetoric has greatly reduced. However, it is arguable that it has been replaced, post-September 11 (2001) with the 'war on terror' as a national religion. This is particularly the case in the USA, where for a number of years the press gave uncritical support to the Bush Administration's war on terror. In 2004, the *New York Times* published what was, in effect, an apology for less than robust reporting:

> But we have found a number of instances of coverage that was not as rigorous as it should have been. In some cases, information that was controversial then, and seems questionable now, was insufficiently qualified or allowed to stand unchallenged. Looking back, we wish we had been more aggressive in re-examining the claims as new evidence emerged – or failed to emerge. (Editors, 26 May 2004, http://www.nytimes.com/2004/05/26/international/middleeast/26FTE_NOTE.html?pagewanted=1&ei=5007&en=9 4c17fcffad92ca9&ex=1400990400&partner=USERLAND; accessed April 2008)

The premise of Adam Curtis's three-part BBC documentary, *The Power of Nightmares: The Rise of the Politics of Fear* (UK, 2004) suggested that the anti-communism that shaped the post-Second World War era, and lost its influence at the end of the Cold War, has been replaced by a vague catch-all idea that the electorate should be afraid:

> In the past, politicians promised to create a better world. They had different ways of achieving this. But their power and authority came from the

optimistic visions they offered to their people. Those dreams failed. And today, people have lost faith in ideologies. Increasingly, politicians are seen simply as managers of public life. But now, they have discovered a new role that restores their power and authority. Instead of delivering dreams, politicians now promise to protect us from nightmares. They say that they will rescue us from dreadful dangers that we cannot see and do not understand. And the greatest danger of all is international terrorism ... But much of this threat is a fantasy, which has been exaggerated and distorted by politicians. (Documentary introduction)

It is evident that the already vague line between propaganda and PR has become even more blurred, as both governments and pressure groups take up the tactics of 'spin doctors'. The news media struggle to come to terms with this – see section 6.5.

Two recent examples of propaganda centre on representations of George Bush on 11 September 2001. In *Fahrenheit 911* (2004) Michael Moore, using actuality footage, makes great play that the president read *My Pet Goat* for seven minutes after he learned of the second collision with the World Trade Centre. However, *DC 9/11 Time of Crisis* (2003), a dramadoc reconstruction, shows Bush pausing to finish his discussion with the class and then calmly leaving; there's no indication of the seven-minute 'delay'. Michael Moore's film was designed explicitly to unseat Bush in the election of 2004; *DC 9/11: Time of Crisis* is a hagiography. Moore's film, however, does have the advantage that he was using actuality footage.

Reading between the lines?

We can attempt to avoid being duped by propaganda and PR by looking for alternative sources of information; this has been facilitated greatly by the internet. For example, it is easy to find a variety of perspectives on the violence in Tibet of March 2008. In Britain, the *Daily Telegraph* reported:

The normally picture-postcard setting of the Tibetan capital had been transformed into something akin to a war zone. And like all war zones, there were reports that some, perhaps many, were dead. Two separate witnesses said more than 100 Tibetans had been killed. (Eimer 2008)

It is no surprise that the view of the *China Daily News* should be very different, as China runs Tibet. It quoted Qiangba Puncog, chairman of the Tibet Autonomous Regional Government:

Thirteen innocent civilians were burned or stabbed to death, he said, adding that calm had returned to Lhasa.

On Friday, violence involving physical assault, destruction of property, looting and arson broke out in urban Lhasa. Rioters set fires at more than 300 locations, including 214 homes and shops, and smashed and burned 56 vehicles.

In one case, a civilian was doused with gasoline and burned to death by rioters.

Sixty-one members of the armed police were injured, including six critically. (Wu Jiao 2008)

Of course, it is difficult to decide who is telling the truth. On the one hand, the right-wing *Telegraph* is likely to be critical of a 'communist' country such as China. However, as the media in China is state-run, it's highly unlikely that, if the *Telegraph*'s report was accurate, it would ever be reported.

In addition, there are not necessarily only two opposing viewpoints about events. Another view of the conflict was provided by the left-of-centre IndyMedia UK website:

Washington has obviously decided on an ultra-high risk geopolitical game with Beijing's by fanning the flames of violence in Tibet just at this sensitive time in their relations and on the run-up to the Beijing Olympics. It's part of an escalating strategy of destabilization of China which has been initiated by the Bush Administration over the past months. It also includes the attempt to ignite an anti-China Saffron Revolution in the neighboring Myanmar region, bringing US-led NATO troops into Darfur where China's oil companies are developing potentially huge oil reserves. (Engdahl, accessed April 2008)

Engdahl's view has the advantage of looking at the bigger ('geopolitical') picture and links events in Tibet to those in Darfur and the struggle to gain control over the world's diminishing reserves of oil. It is likely, however, that most would reject such a left-wing view since Western mainstream news organizations, such as the BBC, which tend to be the most trusted, rarely – if ever – offer this type of analysis.

In addition, the internet has facilitated the rise of citizen journalism, so it is possible to access eyewitness accounts of events and not rely only on news organizations; indeed, the latter are increasingly using such postings to inform their reports. For example:

On Friday there were large scale Tibetan protests in Lhasa, in the afternoon Public Security began to restrict the area, residents told not to go out, in the streets already see military troop transports, tanks and armored cars approach the demonstrators in Bajiao Square, government troops surround Lhasa's three largest temples, seal off the area. Xinhua English reports confirm police used tear gas, in addition to warning shots being fired. (posted at http://www.mutantpalm.org/2008/03/15/chinese-tweet-updates-on-lhasa.html on 15 March; accessed April 2008)

Current TV, available at http://current.com/, and on UK cable and satellite networks, is a site where citizen journalists are encouraged to post their own news stories or current affairs features. As these stories are working outside the mainstream news providers they regularly offer alternative views of what's happening in the world. A report on 'Chaos in Tibet' (http://current.com/items/88878416_chaos_in_tibet; accessed April 2008) included actuality footage of the rioting with news reports, presumably recorded 'off air', of the exiled Tibetan leader and a Chinese politician. It was posted on 27 March and had been watched, by 17 April, 358 times, clearly, a small number. The 'blogosphere' readily allows audiences to comment on postings and other contributions (wording in postings that follow is exactly as it appeared online):

I do believe we need to let the Chinese Government know how much we want Tibet to be returned to the Tibetan people by Boycotting all Chinese made goods. From now on, when I go to a store, if it say's made in China, I will no longer purchase these goods. Until there is a change. Anyone want to join me? (SNJ)

And:

good luck boycotting Chinese made goods, guess you'll have to stop buying EVERYTHING!! and White people need to shut up about Tibet, look at what they have done (colonialization of ALL OF THE WORLD SINCE 1492), so who are they to judge other peoples.ANd why just Tibet, why not free Hong Kong, Taiwan, East Turkistan, and Mongolia. Oh , thats right, white people dont know about Hong Kong, Taiwan, East Turkistan, and Mongolia.. THey just know what those electronic boxes tell them, just shut up .... and FREE TIBET!!! (CharlieMaiGreenRep)
    (Both http://current.com/items/88878416_chaos_in_tibet/responses; accessed April 2008)

The second comment is mildly abusive, a form of address that is prevalent in the blogosphere. Possibly, anonymity, and the fact the recipient isn't present, encourages the belligerent to air their views in direct fashion. Will access to a variety of views about news lead to a wider understanding of events, or confuse audiences to such a degree that they cleave even more to their prejudices?

All media texts re-present the world. Many seek to inform audiences, and many try to do so in as honest a fashion as possible, albeit in a way that will inevitably be influenced by the dominant ideology. Many, however, are designed to benefit the producer and so will represent the world in a way that suits them and not the audience.

5 Representing Gender

5.1 Introduction

The main purpose of this chapter is to consider in detail the representation of gender, as this is a concern for everyone, with an emphasis on the representation of women as they remain, in terms of the distribution of power, a minority. In doing so, we shall investigate a variety of theories about the representation of gender and apply them to a variety of texts in different media.

5.2 Representations of gender

Gender should not be confused with sex; gender is a social construction, whereas sex is biological. So in our analysis of gender we are examining how society's ideological values are apparent in representations; or how some producers attempt to challenge the dominant representations.

Content analysis is a quantitative technique that helps to avoid subjective impressions. For example, of the 170 women represented in the 2 February–6 March 2008 issue of the lads' mag *Nuts*, how many would you expect to be topless in the editorial pages? Given the magazine's penchant for naked female flesh, the actual figure of 40 (23 per cent) might seem surprisingly small. What percentage of topless men might we expect from a magazine aimed at women? The 1 January 2008 edition of *More!* included 86 men in the editorial, and 9 (10 per cent) were topless.

This technique is also useful for tracking patterns such as coverage of developing nations. For example: 'A report by Jennie Stone for 3WE concluded that the total output of factual programmes on developing countries by the four terrestrial channels dropped by 50% in the 10 years after 1989' (Glasgow Media Group 2005). This is clear evidence of a significant reduction in this type of programming; however, it doesn't tell us about the quality of the programmes. It could be that, before 1989, while there were more programmes, they focused on soft topics such as wildlife documentaries; and, while there are far fewer post-1989, these might be more serious in content. So while there are fewer factual programmes, we might in fact learn more about the developing world. (The true situation is that serious issues are far less likely to covered now than they were in 1989.)

So the technique's prime limitation is that it doesn't address meaning. For example, while stating that there are twice as many topless women than topless men in the magazines compared above does indicate a clear difference in the way genders are represented, it fails to consider how else both the topless men and women are being shown. For example, the first topless image in *More!* is of David Beckham (a celebrity and footballer), as shown in an advertisement for Armani (although it was originally an ad, here it is part of the editorial); he is frowning and gazing directly at the audience. Whereas the first topless woman in *Nuts* has her head tilted to one side, and 'It is the expression of a woman responding with calculated charm to the man whom she imagines looking at her – although she does-n't know him. She is offering up her femininity as the surveyed' (Berger 1972: 55).

As Berger noted in his classic, *Ways of Seeing*, '*men act* and *women appear*' (ibid.: 47). Beckham's frown interrogates the woman, whom he imagines looking at him, while the woman is 'offering herself'. Berger characterizes the way genders are represented as opposite to one another. Indeed, it might appear natural to consider the genders as opposites.

Such simplifications certainly over-generalize, but do serve as a broad template for how mainstream texts represent gender, even to the extent that the typefaces used by magazines are invariably hard edged if the audi-ence is male, and curvy for a female readership. Advertising, unsurprisingly, as it is central to the political economy of the media (that is, it is a form that

Table 5.1 Gender oppositions

Male	Female
active (do)	passive (talk)
dominant	submissive
hard	soft
intelligent	intuitive
(hard) muscles	(soft) curves
rational	emotional
strong	weak
thoughtful	impulsive

articulates most explicitly bourgeois-capitalist ideas), reinforces these traditional (patriarchal) oppositions:

> Analysis of ads suggests that gender is routinely portrayed according to traditional cultural stereotypes: women are shown as very feminine, as 'sex objects', as housewives, mothers, homemakers; and men in situations of authority and dominance over women. (Dyer 1982: 97–8)

Dyer drew upon Erving Goffman's book *Gender Advertisements* (1979) that:

> concluded … adverts frequently depict ritualized versions of parent–child relationship, in which women are largely accorded childlike states. Women were typically shown lower or smaller than men and using gestures which 'ritualized their subordination', for example, lying down … [and with] deferential smiles. (Gill 2007: 79)

In the thirty years since Goffman's study, we would expect that the representation of gender would have evolved to take into account women's increasing equality in Western society. Studies have found that women's freedom is now often expressed in consumerist terms: 'the traditional image of the 'wife–mother–housewife' is now being replaced by images of sexually assertive, confident and ambitious women who express their "freedom" through consumption' (ibid.: 81).

In other words, to become this 'ideal' woman, the target audience need only buy the product or service on offer; there's no need for any 'collective struggle for social and political change' (ibid.: 95).

However, it may appear that at least there is an acknowledgement that women do have active desires and can be confident enough to assert them. The 1998 Wonderbra advert, featuring Eva Herzigová and copy saying 'Hello, boys', arguably encapsulated this new idea of femininity. Angela McRobbie suggested that this image was indicative of post-feminism, the wearer of the bra was confident in her sexuality and actively soliciting 'boys'; however, her confidence was reliant on the display of her breasts: 'It was, in a sense, taking feminism into account by showing it to be a thing of past, by provocatively "enacting sexism" while at the same time playing with those debates in film theory about women being the object of the gaze and even female desire' (McRobbie 1996: 32).

More recently, the Opium perfume advert featuring the model Sophie Dahl lying naked, apart from a pair of high-heeled shoes, with one hand on her breast and her thighs parted, stimulated a debate about the extent to which this represented a self-contained female, in no need of a man, or sexual exploitation:

The Opium picture of the nude woman was really terrible ... Advertisers feel they have to shock to be memorable, to be effective – a problem that's become worse in the last five years. People are so used to these images they no longer see or react to the sexism. But when such intimate scenes are exhibited in public it threatens everyone, not just women. (Florence Montreynaud, the founder of the Chiennes de Garde ('guard bitches'), quoted in *The Independent*, 26 November 2000)

On the other hand:

Sophie Dahl's body is ... available for reading as an emblem of liberation, fun, self pleasure and pride, not only within an older libertarian tradition which celebrates porn, but also for a much wider readership for which sexy images have become the currency of the day. (Feona Atwood, quoted in Gill 2007: 38)

The context in which the ad was seen is also likely to have an effect on the reading. If the ad was in a women's magazine, then the latter view is more likely to predominate; however, if the same ad were in a men's magazine, it's likely that women would take the former view (the men, however, are likely to view the image with lust). While we would expect men to be more likely to see women as sex objects, theorists have suggested that the way we should see a text is inscribed in the text itself.

5.3 Ways of seeing gender

One of the most influential books in media studies, based on a BBC TV series, is John Berger's *Ways of Seeing* (1972). It examined how women were represented, primarily, as sex objects in advertising, but also in Renaissance painting. Berger established a clear link between representation and ideology; for example, in his analysis of Gainsborough's painting *Mr and Mrs Andrews*, he showed the intimate relationship between landscape painting and capitalism:

The point being made is that, among the pleasures their portrait gave to Mr and Mrs Andrews, was the pleasure of seeing themselves depicted as landowners and this pleasure was enhanced by the ability of oil paint to render their land in all its substantiality. (1972: 108)

Berger also describes how the representation of women in European oil paintings serves to subordinate them to the male, patriarchal, gaze:

One might simplify this by saying: men act and women appear. Men look at women. Women watch themselves being looked at. This determines not only most relations between men and women but also the relation of women to themselves. The surveyor of woman is herself male: the surveyed female. Thus she turns herself into an object – and most particularly an object of vision: a sight. (Ibid.: 47)

In his analysis of the nude, Berger shows how the conventions of female representations in oil paintings were still prevalent in pornographic magazines. Women are wholly defined as sexual objects, objects available for male pleasure.

By showing how power relationships are inscribed in the actual representations, Berger opened up a whole new area of academic enquiry; among the most influential contributions was Laura Mulvey's article 'Visual Pleasure and Narrative Cinema', first published in 1975. Despite Mulvey's thesis being modified since then – not least by Mulvey herself – it is still a touchstone of ideological criticism. As with Berger's analysis of European oil paintings, Mulvey showed how the male gaze structures narrative cinema.

The form of narrative cinema has been defined, through its economic dominance, by Hollywood. Any film-maker attempting to produce a mainstream narrative film is, in the Western world at least, in effect making a Hollywood movie. Mulvey contrasts this with independent cinema, which can use and create different modes of representation (similar to Wollen's definition of counter-cinema discussed in Chapter 3):

The magic of Hollywood style at its best ... arose, not exclusively, but in one important aspect, from its skilled and satisfying manipulation of visual pleasure. Unchallenged, mainstream film coded the erotic into the language of the dominant patriarchal order. (Mulvey 1985: 306)

As in European oil painting and pornography:

In a world ordered by sexual imbalance, pleasure in looking has been split between active/male and passive/female. The determining male gaze projects its phantasy onto the female figure, which is styled accordingly. In their traditional exhibitionist role women are simultaneously looked at and displayed, with their appearance coded for strong visual and erotic impact so that they can be said to connote to-be-looked-at-ness. (Mulvey 1985: 309)

As Roland Barthes described it, in one of his essays in *Mythologies* (1973), the stripper's dance is an integral part of creating the spectacle, legitimizing the male gaze by defining the strip as a performance which the display of a woman simply taking off her clothes could never be.

Mulvey goes on to explain how representing women as sex objects can freeze narrative flow while the spectators, and characters within the film, contemplate her eroticism:

> Traditionally, the woman displayed has functioned on two levels: as erotic object for the characters within the screen story, and as erotic object for the spectator within the auditorium, with a shifting tension between the looks on either side of the screen. (Ibid.)

As one of the defining tenets of Hollywood cinema is narrative flow, or transitivity (see section 3.9), these pauses of erotic display are potentially disruptive. Mulvey shows how the often-used character of the showgirl, whose narrative function is to be displayed, alleviates this tension by justifying looking at women in the narrative. This device also allows the spectator's look to be unified with that of the characters within the screen story. As we saw in section 3.10, the Quattrocento system works to allow the spectator to master the knowledge presented in painting; in Hollywood cinema, the film's form is structured to allow the spectator to master women.

Despite this:

> the moment of sexual impact of the performing woman takes the film into a no-man's-land outside its own time and space. Thus Marilyn Monroe's first appearance in *The River of No Return* and Lauren Bacall's songs in *To Have and Have Not*. Similarly, conventional close-ups of legs (Dietrich, for instance) or a face (Garbo) integrate into the narrative a different mode of eroticism. One part of a fragmented body destroys the Renaissance space, the illusion of depth demanded by narrative, it gives flatness, the quality of a cut-out or icon rather than verisimilitude to the screen. (Ibid.)

Although there is the potential that these close-ups may break the narrative flow, the ideological function served is to portray femininity as something abstract and mystical. While men are filmed as part of their environment, the eroticized close-ups of women serve to define them not as individuals, but as fragmented beings who exist only for the male gaze.

The function of the male hero, who drives the narrative through his actions, is to be the bearer of the spectator's look:

so that the power of the male protagonist as he controls events coincides with the active power of the erotic look, both giving a satisfying sense of omnipotence. A male movie star's glamorous characteristics are thus not those of the erotic object of his gaze, but those of the more perfect, more complete, more powerful ideal ego. (Ibid.: 310)

Hollywood narrative invariably concludes with the male protagonist 'getting the girl'. By means of identification with him, the spectator possesses her too.

The positioning of the spectator in the male protagonist's point of view is especially evident the first time we see the female lead of a film. We invariably begin by seeing the male hero looking, and then, with an eyeline match cut, see the woman he is looking at.

EXERCISE 5.1

Make a note of whether this happens in the next ten mainstream movies you watch.

Annette Kuhn (1985), drawing on Mulvey's ideas, demonstrates how males and females are shot differently by looking at cross-dressing films. Her analysis of the first appearance of Marilyn Monroe (Sugar) in *Some Like It Hot* (1959) is particularly illuminating. The awkward walking of Jack Lemmon (Daphne) and Tony Curtis (Josephine), in drag, is contrasted with the fluid movement of Sugar: as Daphne says: 'Look at that! Look how she moves! It's just like Jello on springs. Must have some sort of built-in motor or something. I tell ya, it's a whole different sex!'

The gag is reinforced by filming the characters' walks in the same way, but before we see Sugar, we see Daphne and Josephine looking, and then see what they are looking at – Sugar:

on the one hand, Josephine and Daphne, pretending to be women, seem to receive the same sort of visual treatment as the 'real' woman, Sugar. At the same time, however, the shifts of point-of-view between the camera on one side and Josephine/Daphne on the other mark these characters as masculine. (Kuhn 1985: 72)

Mulvey's analysis is influenced by psychoanalysis, and while this discipline is undoubtedly an important tool in ideological criticism, its roots in the theories of Sigmund Freud are problematic. Freud's theories are asocial (that is, they do not take society into account), and although they aspire to scientific status, they are also highly idiosyncratic.

What happens if the male body is at the centre of the narrative, which is often the case in Westerns, musicals or action movies? Steve Neale attempted to relate Mulvey's ideas to the representation of heterosexual males. Neale points out that: '"male" genres and films constantly involve sado-masochistic themes, scenes and phantasies or that male heroes can at times be marked as the object of an erotic gaze' (1993: 8).

Neale refers to Paul Willemen's contention that 'spectacle and drama in [director Anthony] Mann's films tend both to be structured around the look at the male figure' (ibid.) and:

> The (unstated) thesis behind these comments seems to be that in a heterosexual and patriarchal society, the male body cannot be marked explicitly as the erotic object of another male look: that look must be motivated in some other way, its erotic component repressed. The mutilation and sadism so often involved in Mann's films are marks both of the repression involved and of a means by which the male body may be disqualified, so to speak, as an object of erotic contemplation and desire. (Ibid.)

In musicals, the dancing of actors such as Gene Kelly and Fred Astaire insists that their body be looked at and, like the appearance of the female lead, the performance stops the flow of the narrative: literally, show-stoppers. As Steve Cohan points out, Astaire is 'feminized' in his performance of 'Let's Kiss and Make Up' in *Funny Face* (1957):

> In this case ... it is the female star who looks on and a male star who performs for her benefit, and the two close-ups of (Audrey) Hepburn watching ... feature her smiling to signify the pleasure she takes in looking at Astaire. (1993: 60)

However, Astaire offers a spectacle of performance rather than eroticism; Hepburn's look is an appreciation of Astaire's actions rather than of passion for him. At the end of the number, 'the dance closes without a reverse shot of her looking, as Astaire takes his bow in acknowledgment of the audience's spectatorship more than hers' (Neale 1993: 22).

Rosalind Gill suggests that men are also feminized when represented as sex objects in advertising: 'they have particular facial features which connote a combination of softness and strength – strong jaw, large lips and eyes, and soft-looking, clear skin' (2007: 98).

'Women's' pictures, melodramas, have also, in part by having women as the protagonists, challenged the dominant way of seeing. Like musicals, melodramas can be defined, generically, as narratives 'inaugurated by the eruption of (hetero)sexual desire into an already firmly established social order' (Neale 1980: 22). For example, in the opening of *All That Heaven Allows* (1955), directed by Douglas Sirk, Jane Wyman, playing a middle-aged, slightly dowdy widow, Cary Scott, is seen gazing at the gardener – Rock Hudson's glamorous young 'hunk'. The action movies of the 1980s and 1990s did introduce an interesting variant on the traditional representation of gender: see section 5.6.

Ultimately, Mulvey's ideas proved to be too reductive, because they necessitated that audiences make the dominant reading in taking on the male gaze 'constructed' by the film. As noted in Chapter 3, audiences were released from their shackles by Stuart Hall *et al.* (1980) by emphasizing that we could make our own readings of texts. This fluidity in reading was matched by an increasingly fluid conception of gender.

5.4 Gender, masquerade and the queering of the gaze

Mary Ann Doane pointed out that, when men dress as women, it is humorous; while vice versa is sexy. In a patriarchal society, it makes sense that a woman would want to be a man, but why would a man want to be a woman? So, 'while the male is locked into sexual identity; the female can at least pretend that she is other' (2000: 502).

Doane, and others such as Judith Butler (1999), argued that the patriarchal construction of what it means to be feminine can be resisted with masquerade:

> The masquerade, in flaunting femininity, holds it at a distance. Womanliness is a mask which can be worn or removed. The masquerade's resistance to patriarchal positioning would therefore lie in its denial of the production of femininity as closeness, as presence-to-itself, as, precisely, imagistic. (Doane 1982: 81–2)

If femininity is conceived of as a performance, then any sense that it is 'natural' is negated. However, much depends upon how a text is read by the audience. *Sex and the City* (TV, 1998–2004; film, 2008) apparently featured a strong, independent woman, Carrie Bradshaw; however, Angela McRobbie reads Bradshaw's 'performance' of femininity as:

> This endless masquerade (glancing in the pocket-mirror, touching up her make-up, catching sight of herself in shop windows, doing girlish twirls in front of the full size mirror) shows how *Sex in the City* works as a

provocation to second-wave feminism and how it enacts a kind of gender re-stabilisation by summoning the ghost of the old disapproving feminist, (did she ever really exist?) only to dismiss her in a flash by overdoing, quite hysterically and fearfully, the comforting rituals of femininity. (2008)

Bradshaw's 'masquerade' of femininity, her performance of 'girly' behaviour, served to undermine her 'independent woman' status. If, however, Bradshaw's performance as a woman, or actor Sarah Jessica Parker's performance as Bradshaw, had been ironic – that is, highlighted its artificiality – then it would have been drawing attention to the unnatural nature of being feminine. Doane calls this ironic performance of femininity 'double mimesis': ' "double mimesis" occurs in the woman's film at moments in the text where the woman appears to produce a reenactment of femininity, where her gestures are disengaged from their immediate context, made strange' (1987: 181).

Doane uses as an example *Stella Dallas* (1937) where the mother (played by Barbara Stanwyck) exaggerates, cringingly, her 'embarrassing mother' role so that her daughter won't feel guilty when leaving for a better life. While the daughter is fooled by her mother's performance, the audience is not, and so Stella Dallas epitomizes the self-sacrificing mother and in doing so draws attention to the fact that such self-sacrifice is meant to be a female role: 'The masquerade mimics a constructed identity in order to conceal that there is nothing behind the mask; it simulated femininity to dissimulate the absence of a real essential feminine identity' (Robertson 1996: 12).

Contemporary definitions of femininity are increasingly circulated in celebrity culture. McRobbie argues that 'there is now an inflated and accelerated interest' (2006) in celebrity culture, and 'In recent years the commercial domain (rather than the welfare state) has established itself as the primary public space in which the parameters are set for what constitutes acceptable codes of femininity' (ibid.).

On the one hand, there has been the rise of the 'ladette', a woman who behaves in typically 'laddish' ways, which seems to offer a form of equality in representation of gender: if men can behave badly, why can't women do the same? However, there is often a double standard at work, suggesting that while it is 'natural' for men to behave in an immature fashion, women, really, should know better:

The ironic norms of contemporary popular culture do little to protect figures such as Jordan, Chantelle and Jade from once again incurring the 'cheap tart' or 'stupid girl' status they had been assured had long been excised from the statute book of equal opportunities. (Ibid.)

Pop star Pink's music video *Stupid Girl* addresses this issue. The video dramatizes 'bad' and 'good' angels whispering into a little girl's ears appropriate ways to behave. The 'bad' angel – which is the devil – suggests that having big breasts, a fake tan, fashionable clothes, and behaving in a ditzy fashion is the way to go; while the 'good' angel asks 'What happened to the idea of a woman president?' The bad angel's models are celebrities, such as Paris Hilton and Christina Aguilera (all played by Pink). The video suggests that the little girl should ignore such role models, and at the end she does pick up a football rather than play with her Barbie dolls.

In playing most of the types of women represented in the video, Pink is highlighting the masquerade involved. At one point she pulls an emergency chord that inflates her breasts so that she can 'compete' with a particularly large-breasted woman. However, if Pink's song is progressive as it rejects the type of femininity designed to appeal to men, it is also regressive because it criticizes the women as being 'stupid' rather than the men who demand such representations.

Masquerade has also featured in the work of Madonna over nearly three decades. The title of her second album, *Like a Virgin* (1984), emphasized her preoccupation with sex. Although this is not unusual in pop music, Madonna is not usually represented in the traditional (patriarchal) passive role of being. The video for *Material Girl* (1985) is a pastiche of the *Diamonds Are a Girl's Best Friend* musical number, featuring Marilyn Monroe, from *Gentlemen Prefer Blondes* (1953). Madonna has invoked glamorous stars on a number of occasions, particularly in *Vogue* (1990), and in alluding to previous sex symbols she is necessarily commenting on her own role as a sex icon.

While *Material Girl* appears to celebrate consumer society, and the lyrics suggest that all she wants is money, the narrative of the video finds her going off with a menial truck driver. However, the audience knows that, in fact, the suitor (played by Keith Carradine) is in fact rich; he is the Prince Charming character.

Madonna's use of pastiche, *Express Yourself* and *Oh Father* (both 1989) are based on *Metropolis* (Germany, 1927) and *Citizen Kane* (1941), respectively, and the fact that her appearance changed radically with each new album emphasizes the performative nature of 'Madonna the pop star':

> Madonna knows she is putting on a performance, and the fact that this knowingness is part of the performance enables the viewer to answer a different interpellation from that proposed by the dominant ideology, and thus occupy a resisting subject position. (Fiske 1989: 105)

It could be argued that Madonna is, like Stella Dallas, drawing attention to the masquerade of femininity. However, Madonna primarily represents herself – and she is a rare example of a female 'player' in the music industry – as a sex symbol. So while she is drawing attention to the constructedness of female sexuality, she is simultaneously reinforcing the validity of simply defining women in terms of their sexuality. This is why Madonna has been the focus of so much feminist debate; the question is whether 'Madonna fuels or dismantles those stereotypes, whether she represents a retrograde and antifeminist image of oppression, or embodies a new vision of powerful and independent femininity' (Robertson 1996: 125).

While sexuality has been Madonna's main concern, she has also taken on patriarchal institutions such as the Catholic Church, with her black Jesus in the *Like a Prayer* (1989) video, and Pepsi Cola who got 'burned' by the controversy that surrounded the video as they'd built a campaign around the song. (The fact that a black Jesus was deemed controversial does suggest that the problem was with those outraged by the representation rather than Madonna herself).

The extent to which Madonna creates subversive representations of femininity depends on the audiences. However, working in the mainstream, as pop music inevitably does, means that it is very difficult to overcome conventional representations:

> When Madonna argues ... that the video for *Express Yourself* ... does not exploit women because she chained *herself* to the bed, she asserts her ability to control current stereotypical, pornographic, and hierarchical discourse, thus obscuring the fact that she is spoken by those discourses and incapable of speaking them. (Ibid.: 134)

In other words, because the discourse of pornography is used in *Express Yourself*, it must inevitably degrade women. As Foucault (see section 3.8) suggests, (in this context) pornographic discourse is inscribed by patriarchy to such an extent that it is impossible to use it and not speak with a patriarchal voice.

One way in which we *might* be able to circumvent such a monolithic position (as both theorist and spectator) is by 'queering' our way of seeing. There are a variety of ways of defining 'queer'; for our purposes the following definition is most useful:

> 'queer' refers to a variety of discourses that have grown up in opposition to or at variance with the dominant, straight, symbolic order. (Ibid.: 9)

While mainstream texts are invariably heterosexual, and patriarchal, this does not mean that audiences cannot read 'against their grain'; or, in Hall's terms, make oppositional readings (see section 3.3). It can also refer to:

representations of 'queer' characters (lesbian, gay, bisexual or transgendered) ... [and] homosociality, camp, hypermasculinity, and gender and/or sexual ambiguities are all aspects of queerness. (Jones 2002: 109a)

Hence *Brokeback Mountain* (2005) 'resists' categorizing its protagonists as homosexual: they are simply human beings who sexually desire one another. Some 'straight' texts can also be read in a 'queer' fashion. For example, the 1980s cop show *Cagney and Lacey* (1982–8) focused on two women cops, one of whom was married. The homosociality of their relationship allowed ('queer') audiences to speculate about whether they might not be displaying sexual desire for each other. Indeed, when Lacey was giving birth, with her husband absent 'Cagney was represented as a stand-in anxious partner/expectant father. Here the possible lesbian subtext was so near the surface as to be almost on the grain with not too much to read against' (Jennings 2004: 38).

The 'lesbian subtext' suggests that the programme was conscious of its 'queer' possibilities. Other texts are more obviously queer, such as *Xena Warrior Princess* (1995–2001):

XWP is not so much capital-L 'Lesbian' as it is queer, an interpretive landscape where gender roles are uprooted and hetero-, homo-, and bisexuality coexist in the space of possibility. It both flirts with and sidesteps questions of sexual identity, but it never buys into them, [but rather] questions conventional assumptions of compulsory heterosexuality and binary gender roles. (Stein 1998)

The role of fandom is important in queer readings as they can 'normalize', for a queer sub-cultural group at least, readings that are, to a greater or lesser extent, against the grain. Xena and her travelling partner, Gabrielle, could never actually 'come out' as lesbians because of the commercial prerogatives of such a mainstream text; when Ellen DeGeneres' character 'came out' in the sitcom *Ellen* (1994–8), the show was cancelled a year later.

Box 5.1 Representing minorities: lesbians on television

As *The Celluloid Closet* (US, 1995) shows, for many years, homosexuals were represented via negative stereotypes, such as the sissy, or wholly absent from film and television. However, in recent years, the positive representation of gays and lesbians has, in Britain at least, been a feature of mainstream media.

Jeanette Winterson's novel, *Oranges Are Not the Only Fruit* (1985), was adapted for BBC television in 1990 by the author, produced by Phillipa

Giles and directed by Beeban Kidron. It concerns the 'rites of passage' of Jess, who was born into a 'fundamentally religious' Christian family and discovers herself to be lesbian. Julia Hallam and Margaret Marshment argued that:

> The makers had very consciously adopted a strategy that would ensure a supportive response to the issue of lesbian identity. Playing off the representation of one unpopular minority position (religious fundamentalism) against another (lesbianism), they aimed to secure a reading in sympathy with the protagonist Jess and her predicament rather than with the fundamentalist sect who persecute her. If we were right, then viewers who accepted this preferred reading would be accepting a definition of lesbianism directly counter to dominant ideological positions concerning 'normal' sexuality. (1995: 2)

Hallam and Marshment's investigation into the responses of 'ordinary women' found this to be the case and concluded that, despite the overall diversity of the readings, they 'remained within a recognizable "we" of common experiences and common pleasures which seemed to owe much to our common positions of women' (ibid.).

Here we are touching on specifically female discourses that get little airing in the mainstream media. When women are given control to make texts then, potentially, they will offer distinctive ways of seeing that are normally stifled by the male dominated management of most media companies – all the main creative 'voices' of *Oranges* were female. Despite the programme's success, Phillipa Giles continued to have problems getting 'female' projects 'off the ground' unless they contained a male-orientated 'narrative thrust'.

Oranges Are Not the Only Fruit shows how a text broadcast by a mainstream institution can offer discourses alternative to those of the dominant ideology. The Open University programme, *Women in TV: Taking the Credit*, pointed out other texts as being particularly feminine, including *Making Out*, *Culloden* and *Street Girls*.

By the twenty-first century, such narrative strategies appear no longer to be necessary, if the success of dramas such as the Sarah Walter adaptation of *Tipping the Velvet* (BBC, 2002) and *Queer As Folk* (2000–5) are anything to go by. Shanaz Shakir's (2006) investigation into same-sex kissing in mainstream television included the soaps *Coronation Street* and *EastEnders*, crime series *The Bill*, and *Buffy the Vampire Slayer* (1997–2003). The majority (albeit from a small sample size) responded with 'indifference' to the kisses in the soaps.

> However, homosexual characters, unlike heterosexual ones, tend to be defined primarily by their sexuality. This is also true of ethnic minorities; if they are represented, then race is likely to be an issue. Being defined by one's sexuality is, however, a step-up from being defined as 'deviant, tragic, predatory and/or comic figures' (Jones 2002: 109b) as was the case for many years.

Implicit in Doane's use of the idea of masquerade is that, while women in the main consent, hegemonically, to perform 'femininity', men are free from this demand and can simply be themselves. Chris Holmlund contests this with an interesting reading of *Tango and Cash* (1989), starring Sylvester Stallone and Kurt Russell. He describes the 'butch clone' as a male, gay masquerade:

> The butch clone's muscles and macho attire, in particular, ensure he looks 'like a man', and a working-class man at that. He is living proof that, as Lacan hints, masculinity, not just femininity, is a masquerade. (Holmlund 1993: 219)

He goes on to list various scenes in the film which (almost) overtly offer a queer reading. Despite being a hypermasculine action movie:

> Stallone's and Russell's biceps, calves, pecs, abs, and butts are displayed for their – and our – gaze as they stand naked in the prison shower. They look each other up – and down. Cash drops the soap. (Ibid.: 221)

This playfulness on the (potential) homosexuality of heterosexual males is also evident in the video shop scene in *Bad Boys II* (2003) and the interplay between Pierce Brosnan and Woody Harrelson in *After the Sunset* (2004). Maybe the normative idea of hetero- or homosexuality needs to be more fluid; a point taken up by Judith Butler.

Fluid identities: gender and new technology

This chapter has considered gender as a dichotomous concept; however, drawing on Judith Butler's (1999) ideas:

> 'the sexes' are not 'not unproblematically binary in their morphology and constitution'; and, further, that if 'the immutable character of sex is contested, perhaps this construct called 'sex' is as culturally constructed as

gender ... ranges of secondary sex characteristics such as facial and body hair and muscle mass; more instances of sexual dimorphism (babies born with both penises and vaginas) than we realise. (D'Acchi 2002: 91)

The fact that this conception of gender seems peculiar, and perhaps disturbing, to many is evidence of how entrenched the 'binary opposition' of gender is in our psyche. One of the ways in which the bourgeois dualistic, mind/body, construction of identity can be undermined can be seen in a postmodern construction of humanity in which the body is entwined with machines: 'the apparent mind/body dichotomy is superseded by the *tri*chotomy of mind/body/machine (Bukatman 1990: 203).

This theme is taken up in many science fiction texts (see Lacey 2005), manga such as *Neon Genesis Evangelion* (1995–6) and the films of David Cronenberg. With the arrival of new media technologies, audiences have had opportunities to experiment with their sense of self, from first-person shooter games to role-playing simulations:

[A] theme that emerged among our participants was the belief that Second Life enabled them to express themselves in ways that were unavailable to them in real life. Whether it was being more outspoken, better looking, or wealthier, SL provides an opportunity for users to live the life or be the person they want to be offline. (McKeon and Wyche n.d.; accessed April 2008)

Despite this freedom to express themselves, it appears that the tropes of gender representation are rife within cyberworlds, as masculinity and large breasts were popular with the avatars:

Although an argument might be made for the ways chests and biceps on male characters act as symbolic sexual characteristics, they are simultaneously able to represent power. This can be contrasted with the way large breasts *only* act as sexual markers and their meaning remains fairly one dimensional. (Taylor 2003)

Of course, it is no surprise that the cyberworld should mimic, at least in some ways, the world we live in. The desire to 'live out' a fantasy self also suggests that mainstream representations have a very strong hold on audiences. On the other hand, we might consider that game players, or Second Life visitors, feel that they need to conform to the norms of bourgeois society in order to be treated with any respect; this could also be a self-fulfilling prophecy. In addition, it is obviously very easy for avatars to be different to the person's actual sex. This playfulness with gender is, arguably, central to gaming:

> Representational characters in games cannot be ignored, yet such considerations need to be reconciled with the fact that computer games are actualized through play: the user is a *player*, as well as a viewer, a reader, a consumer and a spectator. (Carr *et al.* 2006: 162)

The ludic dimension is central to gaming and, perhaps, to virtual worlds such as Second Life; though capitalism quickly established itself in the latter, with individuals making money out of 'products'. The extent to which this immersive play alters the way we understand, and make, media texts is, as yet, unclear.

5.5 Gender in magazines: *More!* and *Nuts*

More!, published by Bauer (a German-based company), describes itself as:

> The only lifestyle weekly for women in their early 20s. Famous for its outgoing personality and irreverent tone, *More!* also offers a unique mix of celebrity gossip, beautiful fashion and beauty shoots, relationship advice, amazing real-life stories and lifestyle content, in a glossy, aspirational weekly package. (http://www.baueradvertising.co.uk/magazines/portfolio. asp?ID=19; accessed March 2008)

In order to appeal to both its target audience and advertisers, *More!* must have a distinct idea of what it means to be a female in her early twenties. This means that 'magazines inevitably draw up the boundaries of a fixed gender identity, which in turn is assumed to be the natural sign of an original sexual demarcation as female' (McRobbie 1996: 181).

More! define its reader's lifestyle as follows:

> *More!* readers are 18–30 (average age 24), and have a real passion for life. They're upbeat, positive and love to have a laugh. The average reader is in her first job and first home, and loves to spend her money on a 'celebrity' life.
>
> In many ways she's quite similar to one of their favourite celebrities, Coleen. She wants to look good at all times and invests in her image. She loves make-up and beauty products and will splash out on designer items, but when it comes to shopping for her wardrobe she's a shrewd bargain-hunter and is most likely to be found elbowing her way to the front of the queue in Primark for the latest catwalk copy.
>
> Like Coleen, her friends and family come first, and she's happiest when she's surrounded by people she cares about. (http://www.baueradvertising. co.uk/magazines/portfolio.asp?ID=19; accessed March 2008)

Figure 5.1   *More!* front cover 2008

Coleen (McLoughlin) is a celebrity whose claim to fame is that she was the long-term girlfriend and is now the wife of English footballer, Wayne Rooney. This is a marker of contemporary popular culture: McRobbie describes how women's magazines of the 1990s had shifted away from fashion and beauty (and in the 1970s it was romance) to sexuality (see Box 5.2), while in the 'noughties', being like a celebrity is paramount.

The front cover of the 1 January 2008 issue of *More* featured 'real-life love' on *Coronation Street* and '*BB* [Big Brother] Celebs Dress Up As ... 2007's Biggest Stars' (see Box 5.3).

Box 5.2   *More!* in the 1990s

Generically, *More!* is a lifestyle magazine that, increasingly in Britain, means it is about sex and more sex. Even established lifestyle magazines, like *Cosmopolitan,* have been increasing their erotic content; the August 1995 issue of the magazine featured '40 ways to arouse a man' and '12 pages of erotic explosive intimacy'. The male equivalents, which have been mushrooming in recent years, are slightly more sedate: *Maxim*'s August issue featured 'six hot sex tricks every man should know'. The readership profile of these magazines is older than *More!*'s 15–24-year-olds, which may explain why the publication with the younger target audience contains more sex. More competes in the same market as *Sugar* and *Just Seventeen* (now defunct).

As you can see from the front cover, all the stories, with the exception of that concerning Naomi Campbell, are about sex. The design is brash, with a lurid purple background, and eye-catching; the contents are unashamedly about lust (8-page special: 'tackling his tackle, the hard facts about the male member'). The model is not outrageously 'beautiful', and, with her lack of smile could even appear a bit dopey, thus not setting too high a role model for the magazine's readers. Her attractiveness appears to be more the product of her make-up, emphasizing that everyone has a chance to become attractive. When *More!* featured Pamela Anderson on the front cover she was anchored by the critical 'Pamela, is marriage her biggest boob yet?' While *More!* is interested in glamour, it is a glamour that most can manufacture, and not the elitist perfection sported by many lifestyle magazines with an older readership profile.

The lifestyle of *More!* readers is not supposed to be glamorous, it is signified as being normal. The fact that a social class profile of the readership is not included in the magazine's media pack suggests that it may have a large 'working-class' component, which is less attractive to advertisers. (Of course, the glamour associated with magazines like *Cosmopolitan* is probably not in evidence in many of that magazine's readers' lives either.) On a monthly basis, *More!*, which is published every week, is more expensive than *Cosmopolitan*; however, the weekly price is easier for a younger audience to 'shell out' in one go. Annual subscriptions are probably something the advertising manager only dreams of, while *Cosmopolitan* sells them aggressively.

More!'s content is gossipy, the 'real-life drama' of 'I'm sleeping with my sister's husband', giving it a British tabloid newspaper feel. Film, television and pop stars are also given space, as is fashion. The articles tend to be short in length and the inside pages are as 'busy' as the front cover. It is full of conventional material about icons of glamour and sexuality, presented in easy-to-read 'bites'.

More! is probably an excellent 'sex education' publication, which serves a basic need, particularly when public information on the subject is scant and puritanical (a British Minister for Health prevented the publication of a health education pamphlet on the grounds that it was 'smutty' – I wonder what he thinks of *More!*?).

However, *More!*'s representation of young women suggests there is only one subject on their minds. This places it centrally within mainstream media that represent women predominantly as sex objects. The motto 'smart girls get more!' suggests that if you're not having regular sex, then you're thick.

McRobbie points out, drawing on Butler (1999), that in defining the norm there is an inevitable 'silent exclusion' of those who don't fit:

> women who veer from the path of normative ... exist, like [lesbian and] black women, as a category in the magazines [that] sign that we now live in a more open, multicultural, sexually diverse society. (1996: 181–2)

So the inclusion of people who are lesbian, gay or of ethnic origin is a marker of liberal society that is inclusive, despite the fact that their simultaneous marginalization because they are 'different' reinforces the dominant ideological values. This is an example of hegemony in action: a group is included and

Figure 5.2   *More!* front cover 1995

Box 5.3   Celebrities and the imagined community

Benedict Anderson suggested that nation states gained their sense of identity through an 'imagined community':

> It is *imagined* because the members of even the smallest nation will never know most of their fellow-members, meet them, or even hear of them, yet in the minds of each lives the image of their community. (Anderson 1991: 6)

Unsurprisingly, the mass media is crucial in the formation of the 'imagined community' (though not in a monolithic way, as there are always competing versions even if they vary only a little), and Anderson showed how the origins of national consciousness coincided with the first mass medium: the printing press:

> Before the age of print, Rome easily won every war against heresy in Western Europe because it always had better internal lines of communication than its challengers. But when in 1517 Martin Luther nailed his theses to the chapel-door in Wittenberg, they were printed up in German translation and 'within 15 days [had been] seen in every part of the country'. (Ibid.: 39)

Luther's works represented a third of all books sold in Germany between 1518 and 1525. It is unlikely that Protestantism could have succeeded without the printing press, which was also exploited by early capitalists. Luther's protest against Catholicism represented, and contributed to, the ideological shift from feudalism to capitalism, and the 'imagined community' offered by celebrities in the twenty-first century is strictly consumerist in nature.

Celebrities are, from this perspective, people we all can know and gossip about. For example, in July 2004, the *Daily Star* ran several pages on Charlotte Church's holiday, including several shots that emphasized her breasts and/or buttocks. We learnt who she was on holiday with, how she was having fun, and what she looked like when she had had a tad too much to drink. Readers are encouraged to keep buying the newspaper to follow the on-going narrative of Church's holiday. Church came to fame as an 11-year-old singing 'serious' music. Part of the fascination for *Daily Star* readers may be in seeing Church's transformation into a sexually attractive woman and the fact that, artistically, she came from the apparently repressed world of 'classical' music.

Whether the celebrities are used to attract an audience, by anchoring shows such as MTV's 'celebrity choice', or to sell particular products through advertising, they exemplify 'The historical transition in the meaning of "the popular" from "the property *of* the people, through packaging *for* the people, to consumption *by* the people"' (McGuigan 1992: 127).

Celebrity culture is enmeshed in the consumer culture of late (if its days are in fact numbered) capitalism. However, one democratic aspect of current celebrity culture is that it appears possible that everyone, as Andy Warhol suggested, 'can be famous for fifteen minutes' (the 15 minutes being spun out for as long as possible by celebs' agents). In this sense, we can all possibly become part of the 'imagined community' of our nation. However, who (and what they represent) is allowed to become a celeb is heavily dependent on the gatekeepers. And given the entertainment-driven consumerism of celebrity culture, political issues (such as the role of Muslims in UK's imagined community) are only apparent by their absence.

If *anyone* can become a celebrity, and enjoy the luxury lifestyle that entails, then this helps to legitimate the democratic idea suggesting that power resides with the people. However, it has been argued that we are, in fact, living in post-democracy:

> a set of political arrangements which may retain the procedural characteristics of representative democracy but which are unable to give any meaningful expression to popular wills which might conflict with the demands of capital. (Gilbert 2003: 102–3)

So celebrities have a hegemonic function that disguises the fundamental inequality of capitalist society. Indeed, it is argued that celebrity culture is itself fascistic in nature, as it sets up 'strong leaders' for the 'weak masses' to follow.

(An earlier version of this was originally published in *in the picture*, issue 51, April 2005.)

so 'consents' to the norm; of course, it is likely that many non-heterosexual and non-Caucasian peoples won't read the texts in this way.

Gill noted how:

lesbian women rarely appear in mainstream adverts *except* in [a] highly sexualised manner [and] it often seems as if gay masculinity is primarily a

> style identity, not a sexual one, signified by attractive bodies and faces and
> beautiful clothes. (2007: 101)

That said, Gill also suggests that 'normal' femininity is now characterized by 'fractured hegemonies'; that is, there are a variety of identities on offer. However, while equal opportunities, once only part of a feminist discourse, is now an accepted right, 'independence is constructed around the idea that [women] are "born to shop"' (ibid.: 187). Similarly, while it is acceptable for women to be sexually active, this 'is undercut by the emphasis on reading boys, and getting to know what they want' (ibid.: 185).

In section 4.4 we considered an early, mid-1990s, issue of *Loaded* in relation to the dumb blonde stereotype. By 2007, *Loaded*'s circulation had declined to 115,000, reflecting the decline of the 'men's monthly' lifestyle market. This decline was accelerated in 2004 by the arrival of the weeklies *Nuts* and *Zoo Weekly*, whose 'nipple count' – see content analysis in section 5.2 – far exceeded that of the original men's monthlies. When *Loaded* and *FHM* were launched, their focus wasn't primarily on women's bodies; now, this is the case, as the April 2007 front cover of *Loaded* suggests: 'Jana & Lucy. The planet's most eye-popping boobs now in 3D'. This playful (childish?) tone is also evident in *Nuts*: '100 Sexiest Footballers' Wives! Crikey! You'll get a groin strain looking at this lot!' (29 February–6 March 2008).

While the original lads' mags traded heavily in irony, the tone of *Nuts* is much more 'schoolboy smut'. For example, in the issue cited above, a picture of actor Gemma Merna has the caption: 'The *Hollyoaks* honey defended the show last week when she claimed they were all "serious actors". We don't know about that, but you're seriously gorgeous, Gemma!' (page 8). And footballer Craig Bellamy's wife is anchored by: 'The widdly West Ham striker may be a bit of a hothead on the pitch, but we're sure that when he gets home, he gets over-excited in a completely different way!' (page 61).

This puerile tone of *Nuts* is indicative of:

> a continuing downmarket drift in men's print media, an increased reliance
> on British bawdy porn conventions, and an intensification of lad charac-
> teristics, most clearly evidenced by a shift away from a concern with style
> and grooming and towards more stereotypically masculine interests such
> as sport, gadgets and machines. (Attwood 2005: 4–5)

This contrasts with the use of irony, in the magazines of the 1990s, that 'allowed' men, as the original *Loaded* strapline put it, 'who should know better', to enjoy sexist images in a guilt-free fashion. That is, they believed they weren't aping the 'Neanderthal' attitudes of earlier generations, as they weren't taking the representations seriously: 'To offer a political critique of the magazines is to miss the point of the joke and place yourself outside a mediated laddish community' (Jackson *et al.* 2001: 78).

The *Nuts* media pack doesn't describe its audience as Neanderthal, but as follows:

MALE	85%
AVERAGE AGE	27
WORKING FULL TIME	62%
BC1C2	74%
CIRCULATION:	270,053
READERSHIP:	1,048,000

http://www.ipcmedia.com/mediainfo/nuts.pdf; accessed September 2008

Media packs are designed to sell audiences to advertisers; the BC1C2 refers to the predominantly lower-middle-class and upper-working-class readership of the magazine. ABC1s, the middle class, are usually more attractive to advertisers, as they tend to have more 'disposable income'. It would be interesting to know what proportion of that figure consists of C2s, as they would be less appealing to advertisers. The 'schoolboy smut' tone of the magazine is similar to the *Daily Star*'s, and 30 per cent of that newspaper's readership consists of C2s.

Nuts does not appear to be particularly interested in representing men, other than footballers who are shown as typical lads. More upmarket lads' mags, such as *Esquire* and *GQ*, however, do include pages on grooming: '*Men's Health* in particular focuses on the body as an "unfinished project" which can be disciplined, thus warding off stress, uncertainty and decline' (Jackson *et al.* 2001: 91). This 'project' requires, of course, the purchase of various grooming products to hone the 'machine' that the male body is represented as. In comparison, if the male body is a project to be improved, the female body is, characteristically, a problem:

> McRobbie (1982) has shown how the 'teenage press' typically constructs the girl's body and therefore her sexuality as a series of problems – breasts the wrong size or shape, spotty skin, lifeless hair, fatty thighs, problem periods. The list is endless. The advertisers, of course, who are the ones who benefit economically from these magazines, always have a product that can, at a price, solve the problem. (Fiske 1989: 102)

Representations must evolve as society changes. It is widely suggested that Western society offers equal opportunities to both men and women, assuming they are white and not disabled. This equality has extended to Hollywood, where the female action hero is no longer conspicuous by her absence.

5.6 Female action heroes

Although the 'action' genre certainly wasn't new, it established itself as an important source of income for Hollywood in the 1980s. At that time, muscular bodies defined the biggest stars of the genre: Arnold Schwarzenegger and Sylvester Stallone. The muscular body was de-emphasized in the 1990s, when actors such as Keanu Reeves in *Speed* (1994) and the *Matrix* trilogy (1999–2003) and Leonardo DiCaprio in *Titanic* (1997) could play credible action leads. Female action heroes weren't wholly absent during that time. Carol Clover's study of the horror movie of the late 1970s and 1980s suggested: 'The fact that the horror film so stubbornly figures the killer as male and the principal as female would seem to suggest that representation itself is at issue' (Clover 1992: 47). However, Laurie Strode, one of the first of Clover's Final Girls, in *Halloween* (1978) required a man to 'finish off' the monster, Michael. It wasn't until *Alien* (1979) that one of the most iconic of the female action heroes, Ripley (Sigourney Weaver), was introduced. She was the only survivor of a crew attacked by the eponymous creature (the character was, however, originally intended to be male). She subsequently defeats aliens in three further films, demonstrating her leadership skills as being superior to those of the males in the narrative; in the fourth film, *Alien Resurrection* (1997) she returned part-alien herself.

Terminating the female action hero

Another science fiction film with a female action hero – *The Terminator* (1984) – featured Sarah Connor (Linda Hamilton) as a waitress (a traditional, low-grade, female job) who has to contend with a virtually indestructible cyborg. By the end of the film she has become a female action hero; it is she who finishes off the terminator-monster, but: 'It could be argued that ... She only becomes a match for the terminator when she has been impregnated by Reese and placed in touch with a more ancient femaleness [that is, being a mother]' (French 1996: 51).

Connor, as an action hero, is even more compromised in the sequel, *Terminator 2: Judgment Day* (1991). Arnold Schwarzenegger, the original Terminator, is transformed into a caring father figure, while Sarah becomes a gun-toting, muscular individual, bordering on the psychotic and virtually incapable of motherly affection. The conclusion of *T2* offers hope for the future ('No fate'): will the new nurturing man together with the new aggressive woman save the world? Susan Jeffords thinks not:

> It is ... John Connor and not Sarah Connor or the Terminator who holds the real power of these films, and marks himself as the hero of Hollywood sequels, for it is he who survives the destruction of the 'old' masculinity, witnessing teary-eyed the Terminator's destruction. As he stands above the melting Terminators, audiences are to recognize in John Connor not only the father of his own and the human future, but the new masculinity as well. (1993: 260–1)

John Connor is shown, early in the film, behaving in a criminal fashion. However, he does stress to his Terminator that 'you just can't go around killing people', as his mother is intent on doing when she goes to Dyson's house:

> audiences can conclude that the aggressive and destructive 1980s male body that became the target for both ridicule and hatred may not have been *inherently* 'bad,' but only, in some sociologically pitiful way, misunderstood. And who, finally, does Terminator 2 suggest *does* understand this obsolete but lovable creature? None other than John Connor, the 'new' man himself. (Ibid.: 261)

According to Jeffords, then, the representation of Sarah Connor is not a radical departure from the 'damsel in distress'. She fails to save the world by killing Dyson, and it is left to men (like the one her son will become) to make the world a less aggressive place, with the emphasis placed on fathering.

While the first film was a relatively low-budget independent production, the sequel was touted as the most expensive movie ever made (though it was still independently-produced), and so it is no surprise that the values it offers are more mainstream. It is easier to offer alternative representations if a film is independently made, and with a low budget.

Can women make a stand against patriarchy?

Blue Steel (1990) was both independently produced and directed by a woman, Kathryn Bigelow. In it, Megan Turner (Jamie Lee Curtis, who also played *Halloween*'s Laurie Strode) is a rookie New York cop who, at the start of the film, graduates from the police academy. Her family, though, is noticeably missing from the ceremony. Turner's wife-beating father hates his daughter for becoming a cop. Turner's close friend, Tracey, and her family act as 'stand-ins' for the celebratory photographs. Soon after, Turner shoots and kills a gun-toting thief, but the weapon is stolen by Eugene Hunt, a psychopath who is a trader on the New York Stock Exchange. As the thief then appears to have been unarmed, Turner is suspended for using 'unreasonable force'. Hunt becomes obsessed with Turner and starts shooting people with bullets on which he has inscribed her name. Turner then teams up with sensitive detective Nick Mann to catch the killer. Meanwhile, Turner has embarked on an affair with Hunt, not knowing she is also hunting him. Later, Hunt murders Tracey, with Turner in powerless attendance.

Blue Steel deals with the relationship between male power and violence and is unusual for a 'cop' film in having a female lead. However, the film is not just a 'cop' movie; like *Near Dark* (1987) it mixes genres and has elements of *film noir* and horror, and even ends in a Western-style shoot-out.

Film noir deals with the dark side of the human psyche, usually with a criminal context, and in an urban, nocturnal (and often rainy) setting. Classic *noir* movies include *The Maltese Falcon* (1941), *The Lady from Shanghai* (1948) and *The Big Heat* (1953). The main female character in *noir*, the *femme fatale*, is usually a sexually powerful creature that corrupts 'good' men and receives her punishment at the film's end. *Blue Steel* reverses this, to an extent, by making the psychotic male – Hunt – the *'homme fatal'* to whom Turner is sexually attracted.

After the credit sequence, Turner is seen graduating among hundreds of other similarly uniformed individuals: she is the only female cop we see. The *mise en scène* often uses a shallow depth of field, allowing only one individual to be in focus; this is usually Turner, but a black cop is given similar treatment, emphasizing his kindred status: they are both in subordinate positions in American society.

Narrative conflict is immediately introduced with Turner's absent family. Tracey, who tells Turner how proud she is of her, is a married mother and represents 'normal' femininity. In contrast, Turner's family is shown to be dysfunctional; her father represents patriarchal power that he uses to brutalize women. In a climactic scene, Turner arrests her father but takes him home when he breaks down in tears, confessing he does not know why he beats his wife. On their return, Hunt has entered the Turner home posing as a boyfriend, emphasizing the male power which Turner, in releasing her father, has just failed to subdue.

Turner's main problem is that she is simultaneously a victim of male power and a member of a repressive agency of patriarchy, the police. (Jamie Lee Curtis's own androgyny emphasizes the maleness of her profession.) When she arrests her father, she is using the forces of patriarchy against, in this discourse, 'one of its own'.

The instrument of male power is the gun, represented as a phallic symbol; when Hunt and Turner are apparently about to have sex early in the film, we find he is interested only in her gun. The title sequence also plays on this symbolism, with extreme close-ups of a Smith & Wesson, shot in a blue light, thus fetishizing the weapon. The insertion of bullets further suggests the equation of male (sexual) power and violence.

EXERCISE 5.2

Analyse Figure 5.3, taken from the scene in *Blue Steel* where Turner shoots the thief in a supermarket, and Figure 5.4 from *Thelma and Louise* (1991).

Figure 5.3 emphasizes the 'maleness' of Turner's character, with the 'classic' gun-holding pose of a cop, her grim expression, and her uniform. Turner's

Figure 5.3   Still from *Blue Steel*

Figure 5.4 Still from *Thelma and Louise*

journey through the supermarket shelves, when she shoots the thief, is shown in some detail, emphasizing both her nervousness and fear. Clearly, these emotions are motivated by her status as a 'rookie', though the emphasis they are given may indicate a female sensitivity that allows such 'non-macho' feelings to be displayed.

The setting for this scene is very important. Shopping, conventionally, is a female activity, but in this film roles are reversed somewhat: it is Hunt who holds the shopping basket. Turner's familiarity with such an environment is completely destroyed by her terror as she makes her way toward the thief.

Hunt is incapable of the normal, tender sex that Turner and Mann share, and when he rapes Turner he is portrayed as an animal, ferociously copulating. It may seem, then, that the portrayal of Turner as a female victim is rather conventional, despite her being the central character. However, she is shown to be assertive in her relationships with men and she kicks Hunt off her as she is being raped, escapes from hospital to pursue him, and eventually kills him in a shoot-out.

Despite the ability of Turner's character to motivate narrative, an ability usually reserved for male characters, the narrative conclusion subverts any assertiveness she may have shown. In order to escape from the hospital she must don a male uniform, and she is left literally speechless after the shoot-out and taken into comforting male arms.

Blue Steel articulates the possibility of females using patriarchal power systems and concludes, in my reading, that any attempt to do this will fail.

The woman simply becomes a tool of men; she cannot, ultimately, make a stand alone against patriarchal power.

Thelma and Louise (1991) is similar, thematically, to *Blue Steel*; here the men, with the exception of the Harvey Keitel character, are either wimps or deceptive. Thelma (in Figure 5.4), played by Geena Davis, is holding the gun is a similar fashion to Turner in *Blue Steel*, though clearly she is not a professional. What I find fascinating in this image is the comparison between Thelma's and Louise's expressions: there is a certain vulnerability about Thelma's expression that might be considered feminine; Louise's, however, is aggressive. Does this mean Louise has a masculine expression, or is it because of the way gender is defined in our society leads us to use such terms?

Thelma and Louise is a fascinating road movie, with both a Western and an 'action' element, as the women's journey takes them out of the grasp of patriarchal society:

> Drawing on a long history of representations of freedom and self-respect, the film traces the women's increasing ability to 'handle themselves', a tracing that follows their ability to handle a gun. Thelma can barely bring herself to handle her gun, a gift from her husband Darryl, at the start of the film – picking it up with an expression of distaste, in a rather 'girlish' fashion. As the narrative progresses, she acquires both physical coordination, which denotes self-possession, and the ability to shoot straight. When the two women shoot out the tanker, they happily compliment each other on their aim. (Tasker 1993: 139)

Despite their ability to 'handle themselves' and guns, which in Hollywood terms is a male characteristic, Thelma and Louise have nowhere to go in contemporary society, hence they drive over the edge of the Grand Canyon at the end.

While there are progressive representations of women in mainstream cinema and on television, they remain exceptional. Mulvey's (1985) description of the way Hollywood cinema tries to make us see, while not being the definitive formula it appeared on publication, is still a powerful tool for unravelling some of the ways women are represented in mainstream audiovisual media.

Mulvey's work can also be applied to television that, in many ways – because of the dominance of the major networks – is even more politically conservative than the film industry. However, with women being deemed so important to advertisers as they, traditionally, make most of the consumer purchases, it is hardly surprising that some representations of female action heroes should have 'slipped through' the gaps.

Female heroes on television

Christine Geraghty described how soap operas are a particularly 'feminine' text as they 'overturn the deeply entrenched value structure which is based on the traditional oppositions of masculinity and femininity' (1991: 41). She contrasts them with *Hill Street Blues* (1981–7) and *Miami Vice* (1984–9), both traditionally masculine cop shows. However, during the 1980s, *Cagney and Lacey* featured two women who just happened to be cops.

As mentioned in section 3.8, in Britain there were also a number of female police protagonists articulating an equal opportunities discourse. The first episode of *Juliet Bravo* (1980), written by Ian Kennedy Martin, who'd also scripted the very masculine police series *The Sweeney* (1975–8), focused on the first day at work for the newly-promoted Inspector Jean Darblay. The novelty of having a woman in charge is remarked upon, and one of her subordinates comments, 'Give her five minutes to put on her face.'

Things are even harder for DCI Jane Tennison in *Prime Suspect* (1991), as some of the men in her team try actively to undermine her authority. However, she uses skills that the men in her team don't have, such as recognizing the provenance of a murder victim's clothing and speaking to female prostitutes with respect, and so succeeds in capturing the 'prime suspect': '*Prime Suspect* emphasizes its vilification of "patriarchy" through its presentation of Tennison herself, whose qualities as a *woman* accentuate the flaws of the male-centred system around her' (Tomc 1995: 49).

Tennison's success is played out against her dysfunctional private life; it seems she can't have both a high-powered career and give domestic comfort to her partner. This highlights the domestic expectations that often accrue to women: they are meant to manage both a home and a career.

Prime Suspect is a cop series conceived in the 1990s. In the 2000s, one of the most successful programmes featuring a female action hero was *Heroes*. In the first season (2006–7) only two out of twelve characters featured on the BBC *Heroes* characters' page (www.bbc.co.uk/drama/heroes/characters; accessed December 2007) were female: Claire Bennett and Niki/Jessica Sanders. The sexual attractiveness of both women is emphasized: Claire as a cheerleader, and Niki runs an internet porn business. There are other females in *Heroes*, but they are all killed off, and only one has a non-traditional female role, as a mechanic. This suggests, as *Heroes* was the topped-rated 'scripted' series in its first season, that patriarchy's grip is still strong.

If female action heroes were in short supply in the twentieth century, then the plethora of them in the twenty-first might seem symptomatic of a more equal society. However, one of the important characteristics of the action heroine was that she should be a 'babe'.

Hollywood female action heroes in the twenty-first century: the action babe

Of course, using the millennium as a dividing point is over-simplistic. However, within the first decade of the twenty-first century, the numbers of female action heroes increased significantly: *Charlie's Angels* (2000 and 2003), *X-Men* (2000–6), *Lara Croft* (2001 and 2003), *Resident Evil* (2000, 2004 and 2007), the *Kill Bill* films (2003 and 2004), *Elektra* (2004), *Aeon Flux, Mr and Mrs Smith* and *Sin City* (2005). In addition, outside Hollywood, the crossover success of the Chinese films *Crouching Tiger, Hidden Dragon* (*Wo hu cang long*, 2000) *Hero* (*Ying xiong*, 2002) and *House of Flying Daggers* (*Shi mian mai fu*, 2004) all featured Zhang Ziyi in an action role.

Of the Hollywood films, all, with the exception of *Charlie's Angels* and *Mr and Mrs Smith*, are adaptations of comic books or video games. Hollywood's adaptation of comic hero *Tank Girl* (1995) turned the punk character, which had a wide lesbian appeal, into an anodyne, much more conventionally good-looking woman. Commercial interests dictated that the strong female character should form 'eye candy' for the (heterosexual) male audience.

We've already considered Xena (see section 5.4) but it's worth contrasting her with:

> some other female warrior vehicles, most notably the Alien series and the Terminator films ... where the female hero becomes both masculinized and monstrous in her pursuit of her goals, XWP embodies a much more satisfying feminist message. (Stein 1998)

The difficulty any non-mainstream text has, when adapted by Hollywood, is the changes deemed necessary to give the text a mass appeal. While it's possible to be commercially viable in a niche market, it's not possible to spend an estimated US$62m (plus prints and advertising) on *Aeon Flux* (2005) and simply reproduce a live-action version of the cult MTV cartoon. As the creator of the original, Peter Chung, said of his involvement with the film: 'For the most part, the suggestions and notes that I've made were pretty much not used. In some cases, they were paid attention to and used as a guide for a direction not to take. They ended up doing the opposite of what I suggested in my notes' (Thill 2006).

An example of a television series successfully adapting a movie is *Buffy the Vampire Slayer* (1997–2003). Sarah Michelle Gellar, like Xena, became a lesbian icon, though it should be noted that an attractive-looking heroine does not necessarily detract from a strong personality. *Buffy* creator:

Joss Whedon has stated that the essential idea behind *Buffy* was to reverse the horror movie convention of the powerless woman. Both Whedon and many of the commentators on the show referred to it as explicitly feminist. Starting as the air-brained shallow teen cheerleader stereotype in the film and the first episode of the TV show, Buffy progresses to being a strong independent woman. However, she maintains her 'female' characteristics and challenges the typical representation of the successful female in a man's world who adopts 'masculine' characteristics. (Murphy 2006: 65)

In this, Buffy has a similar trajectory to Claire Bennett in *Heroes* (2006–) who is a stereotypical cheerleader, except for her super-powers, for much of series one before developing into a more rounded character. Bennett is also blonde and emphasizes the necessity of good-looking leads; something obviously not restricted to women:

The term 'action babe heroine' is intended to capture the yoking together of the 'soft' and 'hard' elements which comprise this fantasy figure. She is at once ... a 'babe' and, equally importantly, she is 'fit' ... stressing the idea of the body beautiful as the healthy, exercising, worked-on, athletic body. (O'Day 2004: 205)

The 'action babe' was epitomized by Angelina Jolie's *Lara Croft* films. Jolie's curvaceous body fitted the original video game conception. Of more interest, from a gender perspective, is *Mr and Mrs Smith*, an action-screwball comedy hybrid, where the 'battle of the sexes' is made lethal by having the protagonists as contract killers. Despite being a mainstream Hollywood movie, and a major financial success, the film toys with gender roles. Jolie's female team is represented as being far more efficient than Pitt's sidekick, Vince Vaughn's misogynist slacker. The two are matched throughout in terms of their action ability; arguably, in fact, Jolie's character is a tad more efficient.

Similarly, *Elektra* changes the generic trope by focusing not only on the action babe but reversing the Oedipal narrative, where a male character finally 'lives up to his father', by having a young girl 'look up to' Elektra, who both saves her and helps her to realize her own superpowers. The film was not popular; could it be that action movie fans don't want to see women at the centre of the narrative? At the time of writing (April 2008) the film has an exceptionally bad 4.9 rating on the internet movie database. The film is, however, conventional, in having an older male 'master' figure who brings out the best in Elektra.

Elektra also holds back on eroticizing Jennifer Garner's body, apart from a close-up of her backside near the beginning. This acts as a 'promise' of erotic display, but it's not until the climax that we get to see Elektra clearly, in her distinctive red outfit. This reticence is at odds with most representations of the action babe. Marc O'Day argues that both Lara Croft and Alice, of *Resident Evil*, are knowingly eroticized, as the latter 'makes sure that Alice gets wet in the laboratory so that her nipples show through her dress and, in the film's denouement, returning us to her naked body as she wakes alone in the Racoon City hospital' (2004: 214).

The first *Resident Evil* film is interesting in its use of Michelle Rodriguez as Alice's partner. Unlike Milla Jovovich's Alice, Rodriguez plays a far more 'masculine' role, which illustrates:

> the typical construction of Latina action protagonists as inherently fierce and fearless [and] confirms that Hollywood creatives do not quite know what to do with the physically capable Latina action protagonist ... [and gives] primacy to the white characters. (Beltran 2004: 195)

It is possible that Rodriguez's character, Rain Ocampo, can be so 'masculine' because she is Hispanic. So the 'deviance' of the representation is 'contained' by being non-white and, in Hollywood terms, therefore not the norm.

While Hollywood has offered a far more active role to women in the 'action' picture, it still, on the whole, insists that they are 'babes'. This is evident in *Sin City* (2005), where all the women are prostitutes and spend their time in their underwear or stripping. The fact that they are also very effective at defending themselves does not negate their sexual objectification. However, the men in the film are hardly role models of masculinity either, so it is possible to read the film as misanthropist rather than misogynist.

Why should so many of these female action heroes derive from comic books? It's possible that the non-realist narrative world that most of these comic books create allows a greater freedom of representation, as anything that goes against the norm isn't necessarily challenging tropes in 'our' world. However, as is clear from this brief survey, even female action heroes are objectified sexually in most cases. As Lisa Coulthard notes, regarding the *Kill Bill* films (2003 and 2004):

> the film's depiction of female violence is entwined with discourses of ideal-ized feminine whiteness, heterosexuality, victimhood, sacrificial purity, maternal devotion, and eroticized, exhibitionistic, sexual availability. (2007: 158)

So white, masculine supremacy is, in all the films with the exception of *Mr and Mrs Smith*, questioned only to be ultimately reaffirmed. For an example of a female action hero who triumphs against patriarchy, we have to turn to the *Female Convict* (Japan, 1971–3) series, featuring Meiko Kaji in the eponymous role. Although these films are 'pink' (exploitation) movies, this extraordinary character – aided by an exceptionally stylish *mise en scène* – does not compromise in her battle against male hegemony.

Box 5.4   Female heroes in anime

Japanese anime has grown enormously in popularity in the last few years in the West. The films of Miyazaki Hayao in particular have found appreciative Western audiences. Much of the appeal is no doubt rooted in the spectacular visual style; however, it's also likely that the cultural differences between Japanese and Western texts offer novelty value.

Miyazaki's heroes are invariably feminine, though *Porco Rosso* (1992) is a pig; the heroes are usually young girls (*shojo*) on the verge of womanhood. This is explicitly the case in *Kiki's Delivery Service* (1989), when the tradition of the 'world' Kiki belongs to demands that she leave home when she's thirteen to find her way in the world. As Susan Napier points out, this idea of female independence is particularly abhorrent to traditional Japanese culture. Though not strictly an action hero, Kiki is required to demonstrate her skills to save 'the boy' at the climax:

> it is Kiki who rescues Tombo, solidifying her passage on the road to genuine independence. Liberated form her own worries by her concern for someone else and capable of fast and efficient action. (2005: 164)

However, in most anime, the male takes on the hero role, though they often lack the certainty that characterizes Western heroes. For example, in *Neon Genesis Evangelion* (*Shin seiki evangerion*, 1995–6) Shinji is often a morose and reluctant hero. Shinji is an adolescent boy who is thrust into a 'rite of passage' where he has to save humankind. His tentative masculinity is emphasized by a visual joke, in the second episode, where he is 'caught' naked by the older girl, Misato. His genitals are covered from the audience's eyeline by a pack of toothpicks. He's shown to be in awe of the 'older woman', and this is emphasized in the *mise en scène*, when she says 'isn't this nice', referring to having Shinji stay with her, while thrusting her breasts toward his face; this is followed by a cut which features her bottom in the foreground. Misato is simultaneously shown to be both dominant and a sex object.

This non-typical hero, seen from a Western perspective, is also evident in *hentai*, pornographic anime where males are either monstrous demons or pathetic voyeurs. The genre also features one of the most outrageous female heroes, La Blue Girl, a *ninja* trained in 'sex magic arts' that she uses in her battles with demons.

One of the most distinctive of *anime* action heroes is Major Kusanagi of *Ghost in the Shell*, released as three films (1995, 2004 and 2006) and as a TV series, the *Stand Alone Complex* (2002–5). While Kusanagi is undoubtedly feminine – she's seen naked in the first film – she is in fact a cyborg. Brian Ruh argues that, unlike the manga on which the film is based, the nudity is not an example of sexual objectification. He suggests that it is part of the film's critique of traditional Japanese society where, in Buddhism, 'a woman has to be reborn as a man before she can reach enlightenment' (Ruh 2004: 136).

5.7 Cindy Sherman: who are women?

EXERCISE 5.3

Analyse the image in Figure 5.5, 'Untitled Film Still No. 21, 1978'.

Figure 5.5   Cindy Sherman: 'Untitled Film Still No. 21, 1978'

The work of New York photographer Cindy Sherman deals explicitly with the representation of women. In her early work she used herself as the model for a series of photographs called 'Untitled Film Stills' and, later, simply 'Untitled'. Though a title such as 'film still' implies a frozen moment of a narrative, the lack of title liberates the image by not anchoring it to an explicit, preferred reading. The ambiguity this creates forces the audience to make its own interpretation of the images. What Sherman's images mean is mainly constructed in the audience's mind. Sherman's 'philosophy of representation' is as follows:

> The central theme is identity, the roles people play, real or forced on to them by society. 'I wanted to show that the characters were as confused and frustrated by the roles they had to play as I was,' [Sherman] says ... She speaks of 'wanting a man to look at it in expectation of something lascivious, then feel like a violator ... I guess I'm trying to make people feel bad for certain expectations. (Barnes 1994)

While she resists anchoring her work with specific captions, Sherman does use recognizable types, such as the sexy blonde (*Untitled No. 103*) and tomboy (*Untitled No. 104*), but the universality of the types are undercut by the fact that all the images are of Sherman herself. Sherman is both the producer of the text and the represented, and she uses a variety of photographic styles and disguises.

In a culture where we are used to seeing females represented primarily as sexual objects, or mothers, the ambiguity of Sherman's images resist simplistic categorization and forces the audience to consider other meanings. It is likely that such unanchored and unconventional imagery will create a varied response in audiences, thus probably revealing their own prejudices and expectations. It is very likely that women will read Sherman's images differently from men. Judith Williamson sees Sherman's images as:

> 'Essentially feminine' ... [but] they are all different. This not only rules out the idea that any one of them is the 'essentially feminine', but also shows, since each seems to be it, that there can be no such thing ... The identities she acts out may be passive and fearful. But look what she does with them, what she makes [shows] she is in control. (1983: 13)

Because of this intentional ambiguity, Sherman emphasizes Doane's (see section 5.4) idea of the masquerade. As Williamson says:

> When I rummage through my wardrobe ... I am not merely faced with a choice of what to wear. I am faced with a choice of images ... [dressing] is not just [a question] of fabric and style, but one of identity. (Ibid.: 102)

Sherman has the 'artistic' freedom to make very different representations of women from the predominantly male perspectives that are presented in mainstream media.

The extent to which you feel that the post-feminist era is one that is characterized by actual equality between the genders, or is an equality defined by patriarchy, is obviously dependent on your reading of the world. It is clear that many feminists, from the second wave of feminism (1960s–1970s), are not convinced that the battles for equality that they fought have been won:

Thus, the new female subject is, despite her freedom, called upon to be silent, to withhold critique in order to count as a modern, sophisticated girl. Indeed, the withholding of critique is a condition of her freedom. There is a quietude and complicity in the manners of generationally specific notions of cool and, more precisely, an uncritical relationship to dominant, commercially produced, sexual representations that actively evoke assumed feminist positions of the past in order to endorse a new regime of sexual meaning based on female consent, equality, participation, and pleasure, free of politics. (McRobbie 2007: 340)

In this view, the prevalence of lap-dancing clubs, in the UK at least, is certainly *not* an index of sexual equality. As Kate Symons (private conversation) put it, 'How likely is it that what women want is *exactly* the same as what men want?'

6 Representation and Reality

6.1 Introduction

In Chapter 3 we considered four ways of approaching the analysis of representation. In this chapter we investigate representations that are based explicitly on the world. We are not concerned, however, with the 'real world', but with the conventions used to re-present the real world. We shall consider the conventions of two different modes of representation: realism (including naturalism), and modernism.

Media texts cannot show reality as it is; by their nature they mediate. Even our perception of the physical world is mediated, if only by our senses. Realism is a form of representation that has a privileged status because it signs itself as being closer to reality than other forms of representation, such as 'genre' texts. Realist texts can, of course, be fiction. The 'reality' they purport to show may be signified to be typical of 'everyday life', such as in soap opera and the films of Ken Loach.

Our starting point will be a brief history of realism, which will serve as a reminder that all representations are the result of conventions produced at a particular time and place determined by the dominant ideology. What appeared to be realistic in the past is as likely to appear contrived now; we should not forget, however, that contemporary modes of realism are likely to be seen in this way by future generations.

There then follows an examination of realism in film and different modes of documentary. These sections are primarily theoretical and are also intended to serve as a historical background explaining how ideas of realism have evolved. History is crucial in giving context to the contemporary. There then follows a section on how the world is represented by news, the media form that is most bound up in representing the world in as immediate a fashion as technology will allow.

The chapter concludes with a short section on how Hollywood cinema, in particular, has represented the events in Iraq and, finally, how non-Western media producers can use different modes of representation and certainly represent the world differently from those in the West.

6.2 Defining realism

What has constituted realism over the past few hundred years has changed constantly:

> Historical realisms are: the realism that opposed romanticism and neo-classicism (c 1850); the realism that was distinguished from naturalism at a time when the concept seemed in danger of dilution (c 1890, but revived later, eg by Lukacs); the realism that was affirmed against modernist tendencies (formalism, abstractionism, futurism, etc.), particularly in the Soviet Union (c 1930); the various realisms within modernism (verism, surrealism, hyperrealism, etc.), 'neo-realism' in opposition to 'Hollywood'. (Nowell-Smith n.d.: 1)

Confused? You are probably meant to be. Clearly, realism is a concept embedded within the ideological discourses of a particular time and, as such, is useful in understanding the historical development of aesthetics. Roland Barthes, writing about literature, defined realism as a form that tries to efface its own production. In this sense, mainstream cinema, as defined in Peter Wollen's antinomies (see section 3.9), is realism. In this definition, a modernist text, one that draws attention to itself as a text, cannot be realist. Realism strives for transparency; strives to appear natural:

> In Barthes' view, there is a literary ideology which corresponds to this 'natural attitude', and its name is realism. Realist literature tends to conceal the socially relative or constructed nature of language: it helps to confirm the prejudice that there is a form of 'ordinary' language which is somehow natural. This natural language gives us reality 'as it is': it does not – like Romanticism or Symbolism – distort it into objective shapes. (Eagleton 1983: 135–6)

Barthes' definition means that realism is inevitably constrained by the conventional codes in operation at the time the text is created. For example, old (a floating definition, dependent on how old you are) films can seem 'corny' to contemporary audiences because the codes used are different from those employed today; at the time, however, the film may have seemed the epitome of realism.

So perhaps we can be a little more specific in our definition: a realist text uses codes that efface its own production, and these codes are specific to cultures at any given time. What, then, are Western culture's conventions of realism as they are understood now?

These were shaped in the seventeenth and eighteenth centuries. Ian Watt has described the philosophical basis of 'realism and the novel form' as a world-view that, as we shall see, still holds sway today. Its intellectual origins were in the ideas of René Descartes.

Descartes

Descartes' philosophical formulation, *cogito ergo sum* ('I think, therefore I am') describes truth as being a pursuit of the individual. This contrasted with the hitherto dominant belief, set out by the Greek philosopher, Plato, that truth was universal and existed independently of individuals. Plato's universe was unchanging, and therefore there was no need for individuals to pursue truth; everything was already known.

In the novels created in such profusion since the seventeenth century, however, we have characters that are the cause and starting point of human actions. It matters little whether characters are stereotypical or 'rounded' as long as they are the cause of a convincing effect. The novel is concerned with psychological motivation, with characters acting on the basis of their experience. Even in novels where fate takes a hand, such as Thomas Hardy's, late-nineteenth-century, *Tess of the D'Urbervilles, Jude the Obscure* or *The Mayor of Casterbridge*, the emphasis is on the individual.

Before the novel broke with tradition in creating new plots, writers largely recycled previously-used stories. Shakespeare, for example, used old stories, history and mythology as the basis of his plays, material that reflected feudal ideology and offered a world-view that emphasized the unchanging nature of the world. Because in feudal times there could be nothing new, the essentials of human experience had already been investigated: all that remained were variations in the ways of telling archetypal tales.

The novel's new emphasis on the individual at the expense of story allowed, in Watt's words, for 'the total subordination of plot to the pattern of the autobiographical (and this) is as defiant an assertion of the primacy of individual experience in the novel as "cogito ergo sum" was in philosophy' (1972: 15). This autobiographical emphasis is epitomized, as Watt shows, in Daniel Defoe's *Robinson Crusoe* (1719).

'Particular people in particular circumstances'

As truth could be seen to be the pursuit of specific goals by individuals, these individuals obviously had to be particular, rather than general, and they had to exist in a recognizable circumstance, or social background. Once again, this was in opposition to literary tradition, which, deriving from Greek literature, insisted upon general human types set against a conventional literary background. For example, the Pastoral had an idyllic countryside setting populated with shepherds and sheep.

Indeed, when considering complex 'novelistic' characters, which are intended to represent real people, we should consider the following qualities:

a)   particularity – the character is unique rather than typical;

b)   interest – the particularity of characters makes them interesting;

c)   autonomy – characters have a 'life of their own', they are not blatantly a function of the plot;

d)   roundness – characters possess a multiplicity of traits rather than one or two which 'types', or flat characters, possess;

e)   development – characters should develop in the narrative; they learn from experience;

f)   interiority – characters have an interior life; this might be shown by giving access to their intrapersonal communication and, again, emphasises their particularity;

g)   motivation – there are clear psychological reasons for characters' actions, often derived from their particularity;

h)   discrete identity – the character must be signed to exist beyond the text in which they appear, in other words, they usually have a past and a future beyond the text;

i)   consistency – while characters must develop, they must also possess a central core, an ego-identity, that does not change.

(see Dyer 1979: 104–8)

These qualities are inevitably ideological constructs:

the bourgeois conception of the individual/character ... that stress[es] ... particularity and uniqueness tends to bar, or render inferior, representation of either collectivity and the masses or the typical person/character [and] history and social process in which explanation is rooted in the individual conscience and capacity rather than I collective and/or structural aspects of social life. (Ibid.: 108)

The more a text is designed for the mass market, the more types are likely to be used; however, these are still 'particular people in particular circumstances'.

Proper, rather than characteristic, names

In John Bunyan's *The Pilgrim's Progress*, written in 1678 and 1684, the main character is called Christian and meets Faithful and Hopeful. Their names are really descriptions of the characters. The places visited are allegorical in nature: Vanity Fair, the Hill of Difficulty and the Delectable Mountains. By contrast, the novel uses 'normal' names; however, these could also indicate character, for example, eighteenth-century novelist Samuel Richardson's Mrs *Sin*clair and Sir Charles *Grand*ison. Contemporary Hollywood is not averse to using names that inform us of character; the Jason *Bourne* character's lack of identity in *The Bourne Identity* (2002) and so on might suggest he hasn't been born yet.

Time and space

Convincing characters must exist in a particular time and place. The philosopher John Locke described how personal identity was reliant on memory conceived as consciousness through time. Once again, this contrasts with Plato's universals, where time has no role in the creation of meaning, as the ideal types are fixed and universal.

In the modern novel, we demand that the setting, whether historical or contemporary, signifies itself to be accurate. If an author introduced motor cars in a novel set in the eighteenth century, we would instantly spot the anachronism. However, period dramas are not always historically accurate; BBC TV's 'classic' serials, despite their reputation for verisimilitude, include props that were not contemporary with the setting because modern audiences associate them with the time of the text. Similarly, we can accept futuristic, science fiction settings as being accurate (which, of course, we cannot know) so long as they are conventional to the genre.

As mentioned earlier, the actions of a novel's characters must be motivated by their experience (their past); this emphasis on the temporal is, once again, at odds with the feudal belief in an unchanging, and unchangeable, world.

Time-scale within novels is often carefully constructed, whether it is a saga that crosses generations, such as *Wuthering Heights* (1847), or a book that deals with the minutiae of mental experience, such *as The Mezzanine* (1988) by Nicholson Baker. We expect the novel's use of chronology to reflect our own experience of time.

Shakespeare, by contrast, can cause problems for modern academics when they try to pin down the chronology of some of his plays. In *Hamlet* (circa 1601), the eponymous prince appears to be in his early twenties, until we are suddenly told, indirectly by the gravedigger, that he is thirty. Othello marries, travels to Cyprus, then murders his wife in a jealous fit, all in three days! While Shakespeare was certainly concerned with 'psychological realism' as we understand it, time-scale was not important to him. Indeed, he can happily include clocks in *Julius Caesar*, knowing that they didn't exist at the time. These anachronisms were not seen as such; indeed, the word anachronism was not used until thirty years after Shakespeare's death.

While Watt was describing realism in the literary novel, mainstream texts continue to focus on individuals in a clear contemporary or historical setting. However, from the earliest years of the twentieth century, at least, many artists were dissatisfied with the realist aesthetic. During the nineteenth century, naturalism became the favoured form for some 'realists', and in the twentieth century the modernists reacted against this. Before considering modernism, the next section considers a naturalist and a modernist take on the same subject.

Naturalism and distanciation: *The Jungle* and *Saint Joan of the Stockyards*

Emile Zola, one of the most famous exponents of naturalism, used the term in his preface to the second edition of his novel, *Therese Raquin*, in 1867. However, the term is not easily defined and has metamorphosed as different theorists put their own 'spin' on the idea.

Essentially, though, naturalism dealt with the materialist, rather than idealist, world. It often took working-class life as its subject, such as the miners in Zola's *Germinal*, or the railway worker *in La bête humaine* (memorably adapted as a film by Jean Renoir, 1938). In some ways, naturalists saw themselves as documentarists, objectively presenting a contemporary 'slice of life' – including sexuality and poverty – with which 'respectable' literature and theatre refused to deal. Because conditions caused by the ongoing industrialization of the times were often inhumane, one consequence of concentrating on working-class life was that naturalism had a didactic edge that was usually anti-bourgeois in nature.

Naturalism does not only describe a text's content. Many authors who saw themselves as naturalists experimented with form, such as the 'camera-eye' of John Dos Passos' trilogy *USA* (1930, 1932, 1936). In general, however, naturalism and modernism characterize opposite tendencies in art: one attempts to show the 'world as it is', while the other is concerned to highlight the 'text as it is'.

Upton Sinclair's *The Jungle* was first published in 1906 in the USA and is credited with forcing government legislation to improve health and safety in the Chicago stockyards (where animals were processed into meat). Bertolt

Brecht's play, *Saint Joan of the Stockyards* (1931), has similar subject matter – basically, the failure of unfettered capitalism to function to the benefit of society as a whole, in those stockyards. But while Sinclair uses a 'naturalist' technique, Brecht uses his 'epic theatre', modernist, approach.

Jurgis, the central character of *The Jungle*, is a twentieth-century Candide, Voltaire's naïve character, who investigates the world but fails to learn from his experiences and retains a faith in good that is patently out of step with the world. Sinclair used the character as a 'camera eye' – not the subjective eye of John Dos Passos in *USA*, but an objective lens through which the audience observes Jurgis's progress through Chicago society. He has very little character other than his stoicism.

The use of an objective camera eye is part of naturalism's project to represent the world through surface detail inspired by the idea that the dispassionate lens of the camera could show the world as it is. The meandering, picaresque structure of *The Jungle*, with its use of 'accidental' encounters, is also intended to signify 'ordinary life'.

The documentary-style attention to detail of the stockyards is also naturalist; though, unlike many naturalist projects, the details are not mundane, everyday life – at least, not to most of us – but refer to a particular industry, time and place. The details are so shocking that they do not need dramatic embroidery for Sinclair to make his point:

> Worse of any, however, were the fertilizer-men, and those who served in the cooking rooms. These people could not be shown to the visitor, for the odour of a fertilizer-man would scare any ordinary visitor at a hundred yards; and as for the other men, who worked in tank-rooms full of steam, and in some of which there were open vats near the level of the floor, their peculiar trouble was that they fell into the vats; and when they were fished out, there was never enough of them left to be worth exhibiting – sometimes they would be overlooked for days, till all but the bones of them had gone out to the world as Durham's Pure Leaf Lard! (1936: 120)

The Jungle is also a naturalist text in its didactic intent. Sinclair's picaresque adventure ends the radical statement:

> We shall have the sham reformers self-stultified and self-convicted; we shall have the radical Democracy left without a lie with which to cover its nakedness! And then will begin the rush that will never be checked, the tide that will never turn till it has reached its flood – that will be irresistible, overwhelming – the rallying of the outraged working men of Chicago to our standard! And we shall organize them, we shall drill them, we shall

marshal them for the victory! We shall bear down the opposition, we shall sweep it before us – and Chicago will be ours! Chicago will be ours! CHICAGO WILL BE OURS! (Ibid.: 411).

Brecht's intention in *Saint Joan of the Stockyards* was similar to Sinclair's. However, Brecht believed that naturalism offered only a static portrayal of the world that, he believed, took away the individual's power of political intervention; everything seems unchanging and unchangeable. Brecht rejected the Aristotelian notion of identification with the hero that sought to purge the audience of their emotions; his approach attempted to show the power relationships in society by distancing audiences from the text and forcing them to think about what they were experiencing. For Brecht it was these power relations that represented reality, and not the surface detail of naturalism.

In *Saint Joan of the Stockyards* the central character is Joan Dark, a latter-day Joan of Arc who is a lieutenant in the Black Straw Hats, a Salvation Army type of religious group. Joan believes in the inherent goodness of humanity and attempts to convince Pierpont Mauler, the meat king, of the error of his ways. Joan's effect on Mauler is simply to make him even more rich and powerful: when, in apparent remorse, he sells all his stock, he manages to avoid a crash in price; he is then begged to buy back stock to help the market and so gets back everything he sold for a fraction of the price.

To describe a play by merely referring to the printed text is to lose many of the artefact's channels of communication. A director can bring the same words to dramatic life in numerous different ways and, as it is live, it is not a media text. However, on the printed page we can comment on the play as a written media text.

Joan is similar to Jurgis in that she is naïve. However, she learns from her bitter experiences and reaches the conclusion that:

The truth is that
Where force rules only force can help and
In the human world only humans can help. (Brecht 1991: 108)

As can be seen from the characters' names Brecht uses, we are dealing with types (the corrupt major of the Black Straw Hats is called Snyder), and Brecht avoids any sense of 'novelistic' characters. The use of poetry, rather than everyday speech, serves to heighten the language's power and calls attention to its artifice.

While Sinclair draws us into his narrative through identification with Jurgis, Brecht distances us by 'scrapping the "well-made" limitations of the Aristotelian unities and substituting a montage based (as in the new visual arts) on cutting and selective realism' (Willett 1977: viii). Both authors had similar agendas – to expose the horrors of the Chicago Stockyards, and both were trying to represent a reality. Both texts are very powerful, and only ideologues would object to either on the grounds of their formal aspects.

Re-examining realism: modernism

Superficially, modernism refers to texts which are modern, often belonging to a specific period early in the twentieth century. However the elasticity of the term is such that the duration, beginning and end of this period are highly debatable. A more useful definition is that modernist texts, in contrast to realism, parade the fact that they are texts. For example, James Joyce's *Ulysses* (1922) highlights its use of words, which all novels must use, with unconventionally structured sentences and strange combinations of letters. Joyce not only plays with spelling but also creates words that are seemingly meaningless and rely, at least in part, on the sound they would make if read out loud. These devices are meant to mimic a character's 'unmediated' thoughts, their 'stream of consciousness', to convey the events of a single day. William Faulkner's *As I Lay Dying*, first published in 1930, included the 'stream of consciousness' from a corpse being carried to its resting place. Film director Carl Dreyer used the same device in *Vampyr* (*Vampyr – Der Traum des Allan Grey*, France–Germany, 1932), shooting a scene from the perspective of an 'undead' character in a coffin.

Similarly, *Citizen Kane* (US, 1941) begins by showing Kane's life in the form of an authentic-seeming newsreel (the cinematic equivalent of our television news), but then sets about deliberately casting doubt on its authenticity by drawing attention to the fact that 'newsreels' cannot be trusted to give a completely true picture.

In Chapter 3 we investigated the cinema of montage as an alternative to the continuity editing that dominates cinema in the West. This too was part of the project of modernism. Sergei Eisenstein and Dziga Vertov both drew attention to their texts as artefacts. Clearly, the conventional forms of any given era are likely to be considered the 'realistic' forms of the time. Modernist texts draw attention to themselves as texts through being formally unconventional for the time.

Their subject matter – the modern city and the masses within it – was also a common modernist theme. The thematic concerns of the city and the urban environment can be seen in T. S. Eliot's quintessential modernist poem, *The Waste Land* (1922):

Unreal City,
Under the brown fog of a winter dawn,
A crowd flowed over London Bridge, so many,
I had not thought death had undone so many. (Eliot 1974: 65)

Eliot uses a mixture of colloquial expressions, erudite allusion and German phrases in the poem, combined with traditional lyric, surrealism and satire, all serving to draw attention to it as a text. The theme of his poem – the intellectual aridity of Western civilization – is also a modernist concern. When he wrote it, apparently sophisticated civilization, with its dazzling technology and massive conurbations, had just indulged in the obscenity of the First World War. The year of Eliot's poem, 1922, is an important date in modernism. Joyce's *Ulysses* was published, as were novels by D. H. Lawrence and Virginia Woolf, and Brecht's first play, *Baal*, was staged. Brecht developed the theory of 'epic theatre', in which he constantly reminded the audience that they were watching a play, not reality. This had the effect of 'alienating' them and making impossible the catharsis of Aristotelian (Greek) theatre. Catharsis, in which the audience is emotionally purged by the experience of watching a play, is still the defining factor in nearly all entertainment today.

Brecht characterized 'epic theatre' as one that turned its spectators into observers rather than implicating them in the action. His objective was to rouse them to action, and, as Brecht's plays dealt with social inequality, he hoped the audience would be moved to fight for social justice. These ideas heavily influenced the political new wave of French cinema in the 1960s – see section 3.9.

Modernism was probably not the product solely of the social upheaval engendered by the First World War or the Soviet Revolution in 1917. Albert Einstein published his General Theory of Relativity in 1915 and received the Nobel Prize, for earlier work, in 1921. In effect, Einstein did away with the certainties of Newtonian physics by emphasizing that physical measurement was determined by the position of the observer; two observers in different positions observing the same object could produce different results. If science, which many still believed to be the objective way to observe reality, could not be relied on to give a coherent view of reality (quantum mechanics throws up many paradoxes, which, obviously, draw attention to themselves), then surely the project of realism was doomed.

Modernism was the expression of a 'paradigm shift' – a fundamental change in the social perception of reality. The certainties engendered by the Age of Enlightenment were no longer apparent, and the teleological progress of Western civilization was thrown into question by contemporary events.

Although realism is an exceptionally slippery term, one whose definition resides in the time and place in which it is used, it is a concept that has underpinned much of Western art since Homer (see Auerbach 1968). As noted in Chapter 3, the mimetic properties of the photograph seem to open up the possibility of representing the world as it is; what follows considers how realism has fared in film.

6.3 Realism and film

It's has been suggested that the circumstances surrounding the birth of cinema – with two of its pioneers making very different films at the same time – set up a tension between realism and fantasy that is still with us. On the one hand, there was the record of everyday life filmed in the Lumière brothers' 'actualities'; on the other, the fantastic artifice of Georges Méliès. The iconic nature of the film image appears to present reality in a recognizable form, yet at the same time also makes the fantastic believable, even if, to the modern audience, who are used to CGI (computer generated imagery), Méliès' effects now seem contrived and even risible.

From a scientific point of view, film appeared to offer a more powerful perception of reality that human beings were capable of producing through art. Eadweard Muybridge's series of photographs of running horses showed, for the first time, that artists had been portraying them incorrectly (the photographs showed all four feet off the ground at the same time). Films, by using microscopes, showed to a mass audience the world as humans cannot normally perceive it. Stop-motion photography, often used in nature documentaries, can show how a flower grows, and infra-red photography allows us to see in the dark. One of the first films to be banned was of the ripening of a piece of Stilton cheese: 'the prospect of customers gazing at the intricacies of bacterial movement magnified over a hundred times on to a wall-sized screen spurred the British cheese industry into virulent protest and the ninety-second film was withdrawn' (Mathews 1994: 7).

Narrative cinema is constructed in a similar way to the conventional novel, with the emphasis on individual actions, a specific time and place and so on. This cinema, in its fictional form at least, was developed most potently in Hollywood. It is useful to contrast the mainstream with oppositional discourse; Soviet Socialist Realism was an attempt to negate what was seen as the insidious tendencies of bourgeois cinema, exemplified by Hollywood.

Soviet Socialist Realism

Probably the first national movement that based itself on realism was Soviet Socialist Realism, the doctrine of which was set out by Andrei Zhdanov in

1932. The basic idea was that reality would be represented not as it is, but as it would become in a socialist state:

> Realism in this sense means art that sets out to present a comprehensive reflection and interpretation of life from the point of view of social relations; 'Socialist' means in accordance with the policy of the Communist Party. Socialist Realism is therefore based on a direct relationship between the artist and the process of building a new society; it is art coloured by the experience of the working class in its struggle to achieve socialism. (James 1973: 88)

What this meant in practice, as stated explicitly in the declaration on Socialist Realism made at the 1928 Congress on Film Questions, was that the film form used should be understandable by millions. Clearly the modernists, Eisenstein and Vertov, did not fit into this definition. In practice, Socialist Realism film form was very similar to that of Hollywood, though the content was very different, for example, films in support of Stalin's Five Year Plan.

While the remnants of this credo can still be seen in some totalitarian states – the idealism present in the numerous portraits of North Korea's Kim Il Sung, for example – it is arguable that Hollywood serves a very similar function. Though, of course, Hollywood does not serve communist ideology, it represents the values of bourgeois ideology.

The British Documentary Movement

The British Documentary Movement of the 1930s was established by John Grierson at the Empire Marketing Board. As the organization's title makes explicit, its aim was propaganda: 'When it came to making industry not ugly for people, but a matter of beauty, so that people would accept their industrial selves, so that they would not revolt' (quoted in Barnouw 1993: 91).

Grierson was a paternal propagandist, and his *Drifters* (1929) was a rare, and sympathetic, representation of the working class; and despite The Gas Light and Coke Company sponsoring *Housing Problems* (1935), directed by Edgar Anstey and Arthur Elton, for commercial reasons, the end result was a powerful indictment of the slums in which many poor people were forced to live.

Thirty-six years later, Nick Broomfield would return to the issue with *Who Cares* (1971):

> Where Elton's film identified urban terraces with dirt, poverty and unhappiness, Broomfield's Liverpudlians mourn the loss of community and

closeness the terraces brought, and find themselves unhappy and isolated in their brand new homes. (Birchall n.d.)

Housing Problems allows the inhabitants to speak for themselves (as does Broomfield) in their rat-infested homes, a considerable achievement given the bulky 35mm equipment that was used. Broomfield, on the other hand, used a wind-up camera, which meant that all the sound, as in 1935, had to be dubbed. Grierson believed that documentaries should be an educational tool as well as one that was aesthetically pleasing. His classic *Night Mail* (1935) is considered as an example of expository cinema (see p. 244).

While Grierson's films are likely to have had a social impact, they were none the less essentially conservative:

Grierson's vision of a documentary film movement [was of a] managerial elite, designed to provide the guidance the masses could not provide for themselves. Rather than the progressive, socially conscientious movement he styled himself as representing ... he might be better understood as 'authoritarian'. (Nichols 1991: 193)

Such authoritarianism was much more obvious in the work of Grierson's contemporary, Leni Riefenstahl's, in her documentaries glorifying Nazism, discussed in section 4.8.

Italian neo-realism and new wave cinema

Italian neo-realism was another national cinema that thrived, artistically if not financially, in Italy just after the Second World War. The premise of Italian neo-realism was that cinema should represent human reality, films being shot on location rather than in studios. This was a result of the material conditions of the time; the film studios were not available in any case, as they were being used by American troops.

Interestingly, the films produced now seem, in some aspects, peculiarly non-realistic: location shooting meant the soundtrack had to be dubbed later, and this was usually done by professionals rather than the performers themselves (to non-Italian speakers, the 'jarring' effect this creates is often lost as we are too busy reading the subtitles). Stylistically, there is little in common between them; rather, the films gain unity from their anti-fascist thematic. *Bicycle Thieves* (1948), directed by Vittorio di Sica and written by Cesare Zavattini, is probably the classic Neo-realist film.

The next 'leap forward' in cinematic realism occurred in the late 1950s, when lightweight equipment made it easier to shoot and synchronously record sound on location. Direct cinema and *cinéma vérité* are considered as examples of observational cinema (see p. 245).

Neo-realism is classed as a 'new wave' cinema. 'New waves' are usually characterized by their claim to a greater realism than the cinema they are seeking to supersede. This is often as much a political project – hence the febrile 1960s produced several 'new waves' – as a realist one. In other words, film-makers were seeking new 'ways of seeing' to overthrow the old order. In France, François Truffaut called the old order the 'cinéma du papa'; in Brazil, Glauba Rocha attempted to formulate an authentic Brazilian film 'untainted' by colonialist (Portuguese) or neo-colonialist (American) influences.

In 1995, Danish film-makers Lars von Trier and Thomas Vinterberg swore a 'vow of chastity' in the Dogme95 manifesto (http://www.dogme95.dk/menu/menuset.htm; accessed April 2008) for their film-making, including:

1. Location-only shooting
2. Synchronous sound
3. Hand-held camera
   and ...
8. No genre films

The Dogme95 manifesto certainly produced some interesting films, such as von Trier's *The Idiots* (*Idioterne*, Denmark, 1998). This manifesto was as much anti-Hollywood as pro-realist and was obviously polemical in nature, and von Trier went on to make the non-realist (European productions) *Dancer in the Dark* (2000) and *Dogville* (2003).

Documentary and television

In recent decades, while documentaries have increasingly been distributed first in cinemas, more recently television has been the prime medium for documentaries (and not forgetting radio documentaries). While many of these are expository, particularly the very popular natural history films, television has also been innovative. Paul Watson, for example, who was responsible for *The Family* (BBC, 1974), used 'fly-on-the-wall' techniques on a working-class family, which was controversial for its 'warts and all' representation. Watson also made the similarly acclaimed *Sylvania Waters* a decade later. Other TV documentaries to have made an impact include:

Roger Graef's *Police* (BBC, 1982) is a rigorous sociological study of the modern British bobby. Formally, the series adheres to the principles of Direct Cinema, the American movement which created a blueprint for the [fly-on-the-wall] documentary by championing the 'invisibility' of the film crew. In contrast, Leo Regan's *100% White* (Channel 4, tx. 17/7/2000), a study of neo-Nazis, echoes the concerns of the French cinéma-vérité movement by foregrounding the filmmaker's effect on his subjects. (Sieder, n.d.; accessed March 2008)

The most recent 'realist' innovation in television is 'Reality TV'. This has become very popular both with audiences and producers (it's relatively cheap to make) since the 1990s. Reality TV is more a hybrid in combining documentary techniques with the game show. From our perspective, the contrived nature of the situation the characters are in, and the 'demands' put upon them to stay in the show, make it more game show than documentary. The 'reality' aspect is mainly signified by the fact that it is ordinary people taking part and, in *Big Brother*, by the real-time mediation of people (often) doing nothing much.

While documentary is, primarily, a form, we can also consider it, particularly on television, in genre terms:

* instructional – how something works; how to do something
* educational – art, science, politics, social and cultural activity explained
* travelogue
* arts – artistic performance explored and represented
* historical, archival
* investigative – reportage
* expressive – documentary as art
* biographical – the story of a single person
* observational – representation of a community, institution, etc.
* 'wildlife'
* 'drama-docs' – dramatized documentaries
* 'docu-dramas' – fictions presented as if they were documentaries.

(Lacey and Stafford 2001: 8)

The next section attempts to define the different forms of documentary.

6.4 Formal realism in documentaries

Documentaries have a privileged place in the discourse of realism because they declare themselves to be non-fiction and, by extension, the truth. This is different from the claims to realism 'put forward' by fictional texts. Realist fictional texts do not claim to be representing actual events, but rather things which could happen, or might have happened.

However, the sign systems, narrative structure and performance within documentaries can be very similar to those used in fiction. Documentary is different from fictional discourse in its rhetorical pronouncement that it is representing *the* world rather than *a* created world; the pro-filmic event, in documentary, exists independently of the film-makers, whereas in fiction film the pro-filmic event exists only because the film-makers create it.

Documentary theorist, Bill Nichols, emphasizes the point: 'Documentaries ... do not differ from fictions in their constructedness as texts, but in the representations they make. At the heart of documentary is less a story and its imaginary world than an argument about the historical world' (1991: 111). Nichols develops this argument in stating that documentaries place evidence before others in order to convey a particular viewpoint, [and this] forms the organizational backbone of the documentary' (ibid.: 125).

Nichols describes six documentary modes, which he says are akin to sub-genres of documentary: poetic; expository; observational; participatory; reflexive; performative. These modes developed from the conditions of their time and so, to an extent, represent a history of documentary; Nichols suggests they can be seen as 'new waves' in documentary.

While this is useful from a textbook point of view as it allows a convenient alignment between types of documentary and a history of the form, Stella Bruzzi (2000) thinks that it oversimplifies the case. She suggests that the different modes have always co-existed, and it's far better to think of documentaries as being hybrids of different modes. So it is important to bear in mind that the modes are not mutually exclusive, and documentaries can inhabit more than one at a time, and films in the first mode, the 'poetic', are still being made.

The poetic mode

This mode foregrounds formal elements, particularly montage, which brings together both disparate images, for example the lines of the railway track and lines of telegraph wires, which are graphically edited together (that is, the editing emphasizes the similar shapes of the content of two shots) in *Berlin, Symphony of a Great City* (Germany, 1927). While it constructs a 'day in the life' narrative, the overriding aesthetic framework is the look of the images rather than any intrinsic documentary meaning. However, the final section, Act V, does include a montage of acts in theatre that do offer an insight into entertainment in 1920s Germany.

This mode thrived in the 1920s as part of the modernist avant-garde, and so it's not surprising that conventional film form was eschewed:

The poetic mode sacrifices the conventions of continuity editing and the sense of a very specific location in time and place that follows from it to explore associations and patterns that involve temporal rhythms and spatial juxtapositions. (Nichols 2001: 102)

Grierson, an important influence in the British Documentary Movement of the 1930s, didn't believe such films were classifiable as documentary, preferring the overtly pedagogical expository mode.

The expository mode

Expository documentary is characterized by a 'voice-of-God' narration, or intertitles, which address the viewer directly. The voice-over is God-like because it anchors the meaning of the images, explicitly states the text's preferred meaning and reduces the possibility of polysemy. The spoken word is the most important factor in the creation of meaning; the image is subordinate and merely emphasizes the 'objectivity' of the commentary; the images seem to show that the voice-of-God is speaking the truth. For example, in wildlife documentaries, we are usually invited, by the commentary, to interpret animal behaviour in anthropomorphic terms.

For example, *March of the Penguins* (*La Marche de l'Empereur*, France, 2005) was described by 'the conservative film critic and radio host Michael Medved [as] "the motion picture this summer that most passionately affirms traditional norms like monogamy, sacrifice and child rearing"' (Miller 2005). Clearly, this reading is greatly informed by Medved's conservatism, but considering the penguins to be similar to humans is encouraged by the commentary. The film, while being highly popular, was also extremely partial in that it ignored the impact of global warming on the penguins' habitat.

Interviews may be included in expository documentary, but are always less important than the voice-over that, in effect, is speaking on behalf of the text. These documentaries are usually structured by a conventional narrative and centre on a problem that needs solving. They also use dramatic techniques to heighten the suspense and so draw the audience into experiencing the text as entertainment. The editing serves primarily to give continuity to the argument.

John Grierson was instrumental in the development of this form of documentary in Britain during the 1930s. His project was in many ways similar to that of another Scot, his contemporary John Reith, the first Director-General of the BBC. Both had a mission to educate the masses; Reith developed the Public Service Broadcasting ethos, while Grierson made documentaries.

Grierson's first film, the silent *Drifters* (1929), was made for the Empire

Marketing Board, an organization dedicated to promoting the trade and engendering a sense of unity in the British Empire. Although *Drifters* is not an advertisement in the sense of selling a product or service, as Erik Barnouw notes:

> Final scenes depict quayside auctioning of the [herring] catch and project the herring business into international trade – 'a market for the world.' Grierson must have had the Empire Marketing Board in mind in his final subtitle: 'So to the ends of the earth goes the harvest of the sea'. (1993: 88)

Grierson's most well-known film is *Night Mail* (1934), which narrates the progress of a mail train from England to Scotland. Beautifully photographed and dramatically edited, it was a promotional film for the Post Office. The 'received pronunciation' of the voice-of-God voice-over, however, jars on the modern ear, particularly when contrasted with the local accents of the workers: the middle classes possess the voice of authority. There is still a hierarchy of accents in broadcasting in terms of the authority they signify; only local news is read by those with clearly recognizable regional accents.

Armed with the knowledge that recording synchronous sound was not possible until the 1950s, the Media Studies student will realize that all the sounds that appear to originate from the diegesis, the narrative world, are in fact post-dubbed (added later). The scene of sorters working on the train proved impossible to film because of the train's motion, and so was recreated as an eerily still environment in the studio. Such recreations are standard in documentaries, though they came under scrutiny, in the UK at least, in 2007, when the public's trust in television was shaken by a number of scandals – to the extent that Channel 5 news announced it was going to drop the use of 'noddies' (where film of the interviewer nodding is shot after the interview, but inserted throughout the interview).

One thing the poetic and expository modes have in common is that the film-maker's agenda holds primacy over events in the real world; though it could be argued that the expository documentary does present an accurate *view* if you happen to agree with, or are persuaded by, the film maker. The observational mode, on the other hand, asserts that the real world is the structuring factor.

The observational mode

The observational mode describes what is more commonly known as 'fly-on-the-wall' documentary *cinéma vérité* ('truth' cinema), Free Cinema or direct cinema. There is some confusion over definitions, and Nichols dispenses with the terms in favour of the 'observational' and 'participatory' modes. The defining aspect of the 'observational' mode is that the camera is as unobtrusive as possible, though not usually hidden. Hidden, and CCTV, cameras are usually used for humour or for investigative purposes, the latter often 'expository' in form. Ideally, participants of observational cinema should 'forget' the camera's existence and behave 'normally': 'The hand-held [camera] is the embodiment of human point-of-view image capture ... In contrast, the unblinking, mechanical eye of the wall-mounted surveillance camera betrays no investment in the recorded scene' (West 2005: 85).

The observational approach became viable after the introduction of light-weight 16mm cameras and the ability to record sound synchronously; Jean-Pierre Beauviala's crystal sychronization was crucial in this. The apparent capturing of reality as it happened encouraged observational exponents to eschew the rhetorical devices of the expository mode, and so the voice-of-God, titles and reconstructions, among others, were disavowed.

The 'observational' mode suggests that it is a 'window on the world'; it is as if the audience is allowed to see an unmediated reality. The techniques used to create this illusion are:

- indirect address to audience (speech is overheard and not directed to camera)
- synchronous sound (not post-dubbed)
- relatively long takes (shots) demonstrating nothing has been 'cut out'
- the camera follows the action so characters can walk out of the frame with the camera panning to 'catch up'.

Any sound, including music, must be diegetic, that is, originate from the scene being filmed. Continuity editing is used if a scene consists of a number of shots so the audience has a clear sense of narrative space. Just as in fiction, the editing will be seamless so as not to be noticed. As Karel Reisz said in *Cinéma Vérité: Defining the Moment* (Canada, 2002), observational film-makers worked by 'wanting what they got rather than getting what they wanted'.

In North America, observational cinema was cemented, in television, as Direct Cinema, exemplified by the Drew Associates' *Primary* (1960) made for Time Life Films. This observed the democrats electing John F. Kennedy to contest the presidency and involved the Maysles brothers and D.A. Pennebaker as well as the influential Richard Leacock – see Box 6.1.

Box 6.1   Direct Cinema: *Salesman* (1968)

The opening of Maysles brothers' *Salesman* shows a salesman failing to sell a Bible. The scene is constructed in eleven shots, with the dialogue usually beginning and ending at the same time as the shot ends, though there is one cut in the middle of a sentence, which suggests some post-dubbing. Because it is unusual to use more than one camera, it is likely that, if different camera positions are used within a scene, the documentary maker has requested participants to do the actions again and repeat what they have said, as is common in conventional documentaries. Clearly, in this sequence, *Salesman* is not following religiously the tenets of observational film-making, unless they are using more than one camera (which immediately doubles the obtrusiveness of the film-makers) and could be classed as an example of Beauviala's tenet that 'you have to tell lies to tell the truth' (*Cinéma Vérité: Defining the Moment*: Canada, 2002).

The Maysles brothers filmed four Bible salesmen when the footage was being edited, but the decision was made to follow one in particular:
'We took about four months trying to make a story about four people, and we didn't have the material. Gradually we realized we were dealing with a story about Paul, and that these other people were minor characters in the story' (Chapman 2007: 114).

Hence the film became a story about one man's rather desperate struggle to succeed, so while the observational mode stresses 'an empathetic, nonjudgmental, participatory mode of observation that attenuates the authoritative posture of traditional exposition' (Nichols 1991: 42), that doesn't mean the film-makers are not shaping the world they are showing. Because the 'observational' mode emphasizes 'showing' over the expository's 'telling', it can seem to be more realistic. However, just because the film-makers do not need a voice-over commentary to anchor the meanings of images, it obviously doesn't mean that they are not also *telling* us something.

No matter how unselfconsciously the subjects of a documentary may behave, the existence of the camera immediately turns them into actors. While it is possible that people will 'act naturally' in front of a camera – although most of us feel self-conscious – once behaviour has been recorded, then it is available for analysis to an extent that 'real life' never can be. An 'observational' documentary does not show 'real people', it shows 'social actors'.

In *High School 2* (1994) Frederick Wiseman creates a picture of an American inner-city high school through a mix of classroom scenes and teachers' interviews with students who have difficulties. The opening of the film shows students arriving at the school, creating a 'day-in-the-life-of' narrative framework, though what we see, clearly, must have been filmed over many weeks. Filming within an institution obviously requires the co-operation and permission of participants. Full access to 'reality' can be compromised by restraints on what can be filmed.

Wiseman produces a representation of the teachers as caring, liberal individuals that cannot be *the* truth, but is one representation of the school. If the young black male who states that he would respect the school more if there were more black teachers had made the documentary, then his portrayal of the institution is likely to have been very different.

Cinéma vérité is often confused with direct cinema as it shares a visual style. However, as Nichols suggests, it is more accurately part of the participatory mode.

The participatory mode

Originally, Nichols (1991) called this 'the interactive mode' but he changed it to the participatory mode (Nichols 2001) as the former is associated now with new media technologies:

> When we view participatory documentaries we expect to witness the historical world as represented by someone who actively engages with, rather than unobtrusively observes, poetically reconfigures, or argumentatively assembles that world. (2001: 116)

This mode was in many ways the dream of Dziga Vertov, the Soviet filmmaker of the 1920s discussed in Chapter 4. He created the idea of the Kino-Pravda and later Kino-Eye a 'wall newspaper (coming) out weekly or monthly; (illustrating) factory or village life' (Williams 1980: 25). It was not until the late 1950s that his ideal became practical, with the development of lightweight equipment that could make synchronous recordings.

Easily portable equipment meant that post-dubbing was no longer required and allowed the film-maker to speak directly to her/his subjects. The documentary makers could involve themselves in the scene and even interact with what was being filmed. Because of this, participatory documentaries focus on the exchange of information rather than on creating a coherent view. For example, Barnouw distinguishes between direct cinema and *cinéma vérité*, using Jean Rouch and Edgar Morin's *Chronicle of a Summer* (*Chronique d'un été*, France, 1961) as an example:

The direct cinema documentarist took his [*sic*] camera to a situation of tension and waited hopefully for a crisis; the Rouch version of *cinéma vérité* tried to precipitate one. The direct cinema artist aspired to invisibility; the Rouch *cinéma vérité* artist was often an avowed participant. The direct cinema artist played the role of uninvolved bystander; the *cinéma vérité* artist espoused that of provocateur. (Barnouw 1993: 254–5)

It could be argued that this mode is somewhat more 'honest' than previous modes, because no attempt is made to disguise the documentary-makers who, after all, must be present in order for the film to exist. But while the 'participatory' mode acknowledges the presence of film-makers, there remains the question of how far their presence influences what is being documented. After all, the fact that the rhetoric of all documentaries – that we are seeing the world as it is – is in reality unattainable, holds true for this mode. For example, in *Shoah* (France, 1985), how much are Claude Lanzman's promptings of Holocaust victims to talk about their experiences a result of the need for drama, rather than a documentarist's need for information?

Many 'participatory' documentaries use interviews that are, by their nature, a hierarchical discourse with the interviewer setting the agenda; anything can be proved by asking 'loaded' questions (and choosing who to interview). Similarly, while the 'vox pop' form of interviewing signifies itself as authentic, who, if anyone, checks up on the 'truth' of what is said?

However, the participatory mode

stresses images of testimony or verbal exchange and images of demonstration (images that demonstrate the validity, or possibly, the doubtfulness, of what witnesses) state. Textual authority shifts toward the social actors recruited: their comments and responses provide a central part of the film's argument. (Nichols 1991: 44)

For example, in *The Thin Blue Line* (US, 1988), directed by Errol Morris, various witnesses give their views of events, which often contradict each another, concerning the murder of a policeman. Despite the fact that Morris does not intrude as an interviewer, the audience is constantly reminded of the existence of multiple viewpoints because they are placed in the position of an investigating journalist questioning the main participants for the story. This is in sharp contrast to the 'voice-of-God' omnipotence offered by the 'expository' mode and the 'matter of fact' neutrality of the 'observational' mode. The use of montage to juxtapose one witness's statement, that she likes to help the police, with footage of an old movie showing a woman helping law enforcers, in fact undermines her trustworthiness as a witness, because the old footage looks ridiculous to us now. And that witness's testimony is, ultimately, shown to be invalid.

Inevitably, the 'participatory mode' is as constructed as those described earlier. Like the 'observational' mode, it appears to allow 'reality' to speak for itself, but simply because the mode acknowledges the film-maker's presence does not give it access to unmediated reality. The director still chooses where to place the camera, how to light the scene, and what to leave on the cutting-room floor.

The reflexive mode

The aim of the reflexive mode is not only to represent its subject but also to demonstrate itself in the act of representing (a characteristic of modernism); in other words, the mode draws attention to its own codes. A documentary about, say, an election campaign, would also be a documentary about making a documentary about an election campaign.

In a sense this is the direct opposite of the expository and observational modes, both of which attempt to convince us that we are not watching a carefully-constructed documentary, but rather have access to a 'window on the world'. The reflexive mode problematizes *what* we are seeing by drawing attention to the medium *through which* we are seeing.

Man with a Movie Camera (1929), Dziga Vertov's most famous work, is an excellent example of the reflexive mode. It is an ebullient and invigorating city tour, a mix of Moscow, Kiev and Riga, in which the hero (though Vertov professed to eschew such bourgeois conceptions), is the eponymous observer of events. Vertov's self-reflexivity consists of a number of techniques that draw attention to themselves. Vertov is even self-reflexive about the cinema experience: his film opens by showing an audience entering a theatre and watching the film begin.

Other sequences emphasize the constructed nature of the film by showing the cameraman filming events we see on the screen, sometimes as a reflection in a window or using eyeline-match editing; inanimate objects are animated using stop-motion photography; and an eye is superimposed on the camera's lens (the Kino-Eye indeed).

Another method of self-reflexivity can be seen in the work of avant-garde film and video maker, Jean-Luc Godard. Godard, in *Histoire(s) du Cinema* (France, 1988–98), in at least some of the parts, wrote directly on to the images he was using. This drew attention to the construction of the text (as the writing appears, we see the text being created) and at the same time cast doubt on the anchoring of the images, by showing the act of anchorage itself.

While the participatory mode emphasizes the relationship between the documentary maker and her/his subject, the reflexive mode is more concerned with the encounter between the documentary text and its audience. There is, of course, a danger that by drawing too much attention to its own mode of construction, a documentary may cause the audience to lose sight of its subject; the medium can obscure the message.

That said, at least this mode makes the clear statement that representing the world cannot be other than problematic, and that to suggest otherwise is a form of lie.

The performative mode

Nichols (1994) later added the 'performative' mode; though defining this is less straightforward than the other four. Stella Bruzzi suggests:

> A prerequisite of the performative documentary is the inclusion of a notable performance. Component performativity is based on the idea of disavowal that simultaneously signals a desire to make a conventional documentary (that is, to give an accurate account of a series of factual events) whilst also indicating the impossibility of [doing so] (2000: 155).

For example, Isaac Julien's *Looking for Langston* (UK, 1989) celebrates the life of black, gay poet Langston Hughes, not through a straightforward biography but with a collection of, often impressionist, scenes. Taken together they offer a 'meditation' (Julien's preferred term for the film – see http://www.screenonline.org.uk/film/id/541736, accessed December 2007), on the poet's life. For example a church, where a wake for Hughes is being held, is found to have a club in its basement that turns out to be a re-visioning of the Cotton Club in Harlem. The documentary challenges the idea that we can ever really fully represent Hughes's life while, at the same time, offering a portrayal of his importance as a black and gay poet. In doing so the film is obviously a personal portrayal of Hughes from Julien's point of view: 'performative films give added emphasis to the subjective qualities of experience and memory that depart from factual recounting' (Nichols 2001: 131).

The performative mode raises questions about knowledge: whether it is abstract or concrete, or typical or subjective. Like the reflexive mode it questions the possibility of offering a 'window on the world'. However, it does so not through drawing attention to its form but by offering a content that questions the epistemological basis of what we are seeing.

Table 6.1 A summary of Nichols's documentary modes

Documentary modes	Chief characteristics	Deficiencies
Hollywood fiction (1910s)	Fictional narratives of imaginary worlds	Absence of reality
Poetic documentary (1920s)	Reassemble fragments of the world poetically	Lack of specificity, too abstract
Expository documentary (1920s)	Directly address issues in the historical world	Overly didactic
Observational documentary (1960s)	Eschew commentary and re-enactment; observe things as they happen	Lack of history, context
Participatory documentary (1960s)	Interview or interact with subjects; use archival film to retrieve history	Excessive faith in witnesses, naïve history, too intrusive
Reflexive documentary (1980s)	Question documentary form, defamiliarize the other modes	Too abstract, lose sight of actual issues
Performative documentary (1980s)	Stress subjective aspects of classically objective discourse	Loss of emphasis on objectivity may relegate such films to the avant-garde; 'excessive' use of style

Source: Adapted from Nichols 2001: 138.

In addition to Nichols' modes, there is drama-documentary, which is usually structured formally in the same way as narrative cinema.

Drama-documentary

A drama-documentary (drama-doc) attempts to recreate, as accurately as possible, events that happened in reality. It is a form that often attracts controversy, because no matter how painstaking the recreation, it is a representation and therefore can never be precisely the same as the actuality. Complaints about drama-documentaries usually concern the text's lack of authenticity; the films *JFK* (US, 1991) and *In the Name of the Father* (Ireland–UK, 1993) were criticized for not being true to the events on which they were based. *Touching the Void* (UK, 2003) inserted talking heads of the two characters (mountaineers), whose experiences were being recreated, and their comments gave the reconstructions the stamp of authenticity.

As a consequence of such criticisms, in the 1990s, a group of drama-documentary makers constructed a self-regulatory charter.

a)   no version of events or conclusions should be offered as definitive if they cannot be substantiated through responsible journalistic methods;
b)   the nature of the programme must be spelt out to the audience very clearly before it begins;
c)   characters should not be portrayed having sex, smoking, drinking, swearing even, to enliven storylines unless such scenes can be substantiated;
d)   programmed-makers must inform people named in programmes that they are about to be screened. (Jim White 1994: 12)

A documentary-drama (docu-drama), on the other hand, is a drama shot in the style of a documentary (with use of hand-held cameras, interviews and so on). The classic of this genre is Ken Loach's and Tony Garnett's *Cathy Come Home* (BBC, 1966); more recent examples include *The Office* (BBC, 2001–3).

The use of dramatic techniques in documentary is not limited to drama-doc; however, its explicit use of fictional styles highlights the dramatic component. While the above charter seeks to avoid sensationalism, documentaries – in any of Nichols' modes – can sensationalize their subjects in much less obvious ways.

The agenda of most reconstructions is to be dramatic, and therefore the dominant discourse is narrative. It matters little if the reconstruction is about a rescue from a fire, or a race against time for an antidote to a snakebite; what is important is the dramatic resolution. The fact that these events really happened serves to make the text even more dramatic than a fictional representation might. Of course, the techniques used in reconstructions, such as cross-cutting between events, are those of narrative cinema.

Reconstructions are a relatively recent form of television drama. The most recent technological innovation has been the use of small-format video, enabling amateurs to make their own documentaries: video diaries.

Video diaries

Like observational cinema, video diaries became possible as a result of technological innovation. The arrival of S-VHS and Hi-8 formats allowed amateurs to create professional-looking videos. As digital video and editing software became cheaper, more people made their own films, and YouTube revolutionized the way home video could be accessed. Indeed, video diaries as a form are more likely to be found on the internet, such as England cricketer Matthew (Hoggy) Hoggard's on the tour of New Zealand early in 2008.

Initially, video diaries were a form of 'access television', where non-media professionals could take control of producing and editing representations; as the title suggests, video diaries are a particularly personal representation. This opportunity, however, was not as straightforward as it seemed. The BBC's 1990s Video Diaries series' editor, Jenny Gibson, stated:

> It's our job to identify (something very off-putting) and try to turn the diarist to take a less egocentric approach to something and less pushing of aspects of their personality which are difficult or confrontational. The other thing is they may be very much in love with a very contrived material, terribly in love with some parts that we know are a total contrivance. (Keighron 1993: 25)

So, despite the diarist's control of camera and editing, there are clearly institutional pressures that may compromise their ideas. Only one in fifty applications to create a diary got beyond the 'waste bin'. Clearly, it would be impossible to follow up and make all the proposals, so some gatekeeping is necessary, but the agenda of the gatekeeping organization, in this case the BBC's Community Programme Unit, would have a great influence on what is shown. In addition, the simplicity of filming and the relative cheapness of video means that far more footage is shot than would ever be shown. An average of 150 hours of recording was cut down to one hour for broadcast. And even if an individual is completely satisfied with the end product, it is highly likely that representations used, in terms of form, style and content, will be to some degree conventional and largely articulate the values of the dominant ideology.

Problems of getting one's videos seen have virtually disappeared in recent years, however. YouTube allows users to post their videos, within the guidelines set by the website such as 'no nudity', and Current TV encourages political engagement with both internet and cable/satellite television platforms.

Box 6.2 Constructing documentary realism

Life is not a conventional narrative unless you class life itself as a disruption (situation: you're born; resolution: you die). However, conventional narrative is predominantly used to structure documentaries. In some cases, such as following the progress of a trial in a law court, such narrative seems appropriate: the crime the defendant is accused of may represent the opening situation; the trial, the disruption; and the verdict, the resolution. In many cases, however, conventional narrative invites us into a fictional discourse, when what is being represented is reputed to be non-fictional.

This is not to accuse documentary-makers of lies. Any form of representation requires an agenda, even if it is often dictated by institutions (see section 4.8). In a fascinating article, journalist Robert Fisk describes the compromises made in the documentary series *From Beirut to Bosnia*, broadcast in Britain on Channel 4 in 1993. Fisk had reported on the Middle East and Balkans for seventeen years, in *The Times* and *The Independent*, but found the technology of television and the director's conception of the documentary's audience problematic:

> the technology of television would both trivialise and authenticate the world in which I had lived for 17 years. Even in a Palestinian hospital, a clapper-board – a real Hollywood-style chalk board with a black-and-white 'clapper' on top – had been clacked in front of wounded men. (1993: 24)

Michael Dutfield, the experienced director of the documentary, characterized the audience as his '82-year-old mum'; in other words, long and complicated political explanations had little role in the film. The problems inherent in representation were shown when interviewing an elderly Shia Muslim woman:

> when [she] was ready to tell [her son's] painful story on film, Michael did not like the sofa upon which she was sitting. It was second-hand, the only piece of bright colour in the room. 'It gives the wrong impression,' Michael said. 'She's poor but it makes her look rich. And she's not rich.'
> I objected to this. If the sofa gave the wrong 'impression', then so be it ... This woman's sofa was part of her identity. I loudly complained that to move the sofa would be like making a Hollywood film rather than a television documentary, a remark that at once angered Michael's cameraman, Steve. 'Come over here and look through the lens, Bob,' he said softly. I peered through it and understood at once. What was in reality a rather shabby second-hand sofa was transformed by the camera's lens into a heavily-embroidered, satin-covered chaise-longue. (Ibid.)

So in this case, the substitution of the sofa arguably created a more accurate representation than if the actual one had been used. However, in Fisk's view, the conventions of television, with its use of a particular technology and mass audience, certainly compromised the representation of the area. As Fisk said: 'It was not the theatricality I identified in documentary film-making [that troubled me] ... but the refusal to acknowledge it' (ibid.).

> An acknowledgement would have made *From Beirut to Bosnia* self-reflexive. Entertainment of the audience, including Dutfield's 82-year-old mother, is one of the requirements of most television texts. The genre of 'reconstructions', where real-life dramas are recreated using actors or the original participants, is the most evidently entertainment-based form of documentary.

While these six categories cover most documentaries ever made, there are always texts that do not conform to conventional outlines. For example, the form of two documentaries directed by Godfrey Reggio, *Koyaanisqatsi* (1983) and *Powaqqatsi* (1988), is heavily influenced by the use of time-lapse photography and slow motion.

Powaqqatsi is structured by montage, there is no voice-over, and chronicles the plight of the developing world (in contrast to its predecessor, *Koyaanisqatsi*, which portrayed the pointless speed of urban life). The images are linked graphically by the repetition of people as 'beasts of burden' labouring under sacks of sand, water containers or fuel. The especially composed score by Philip Glass mixes different musical vernaculars, thus giving a voice to non-Western sounds and peoples.

As the conclusion of *Powaqqatsi* nears, the subjects of Reggio's camera are found to stare more frequently at the audience with a gaze that can best be described as accusing.

While Reggio's movies occasionally seem similar in form to that most Western of art forms, the pop video (apart from being accompanied by minimalist music), the power of his imagery (and the accompanying soundtrack), with the subtlety of his rhetoric (the audience is forced to work for meaning), make him a documentary film-maker who has made political and stylistically avant-garde texts mainstream.

6.5 Representing the world in the news

Most documentaries have the 'luxury' of several months' gestation. However, the form that most immediately represents to world is news that often, in broadcasting, has to mediate the world virtually 'as it happens'. In order to structure this representation, news organizations employ particular agendas. For example, the news agendas of the mass market and quality press are different. The former will, for example, emphasize 'soft' news stories that focus on celebrities, trivia and entertainment, while the latter are more likely to emphasis 'hard' news, defined as stories focusing on politics and economics, for example. Of course, mass market newspapers, such as *The Sun* in Britain, also run hard news, just as the 'quality' press, such as *The Times*, include soft news.

In television news there are a number of news values that determine whether an event is defined as 'news for television'. Selby and Cowdrey (1995), in an adaptation of Galtung and Ruge's news model (in Cohen and Young 1981), describe eleven news values; if different then Galtung and Ruge's original formulations are in parentheses:

1. *Magnitude (F2: threshold)*   The event has to be 'big', which may be defined in terms of the number of people it influences, or the area it effects. For example, stories from sub-Saharan Africa normally revolve around hundreds of thousands of people facing starvation. This value is linked closely to ethnocentricity (item 3 below) in that a story requires far less magnitude to be defined as news the closer to home it is, so a car crash in which several people are killed is likely to be defined as national news.

2. *Clarity (F3: unambiguity)*   The story has to be relatively simple to explain. Arcane matters of economic theory are rarely aired on the news, while the nature of a aeroplane crash is easy to understand, so it is more likely to be reported.

If a story is complex, then it is likely to be reported in a simplistic fashion. For example, the news about the long-running Israeli–Palestinian conflict rarely clearly explained the military nature of the occupation. Audiences in a Glasgow University Media Group study often thought the Palestinians were occupying the 'occupied territories' and not the Israelis. The consequences of this are:

> it is difficult for viewers to understand why the conflict is so intractable. It can appear simply as two communities who 'can't get on' and who are squabbling over the same areas of land … [and] disadvantages the Palestinian perspective, as a key reason for their unrest and danger is left unexplained. (Philo and Berry 2004: 118)

3. *Ethnocentricity (F4: meaningfulness)*   The closer the story is to the home audience, the more likely it is to be covered. In 1995, in Pakistan, 600 people died in floods that received barely a mention. From 1 September 1993 to 31 August 1994, about 75 per cent of ITV's *News at Ten* was concerned with domestic news (Cleasby 1995: 9).

Similarly, ethnocentricity can lead to large numbers of people simply being ignored. As BBC correspondent Mark Doyle described:

When it was announced that most of the foreigners had been evacuated from Kigali (in Rwanda), it meant that most of the white people had gone. On the day the announcement was broadcast in Europe, I came across about 5,000 Zairean nationals at their embassy, desperate to leave. (Doyle 1994: 100)

Ethnocentricity can define the news in the case of local bulletins that are unlikely to cover anything outside their area. Also, nations that are deemed politically close to those of the broadcasters' are more likely to be covered, which goes some way to explaining the amount of reporting of American Presidential elections in the UK.

4. Consonance (F5)   Where stories are covered in a way that reflects journalists' expectations of what normally happens in such situations. For example, a demonstration involving racists is expected to involve violence, and this will be foregrounded in the report even if violence does not dominate the event; an example of this is the anti-fascist march that took place in Welling, Kent, in 1993.

However, journalists' expectations sometimes do not reflect changing society. For example, when five women were murdered in late 2006 in Ipswich by a serial killer, the press referred to them as prostitutes, implying that their deaths were less tragic because of their occupation: 'But public attitudes to women in the sex industry have changed, as the press quickly discovered. In Ipswich and elsewhere, people were outraged by TV and radio bulletins that baldly announced five "prostitutes" had been murdered in Suffolk' (Smith 2008).

Consonance also refers to way a story is communicated. For example, research showed that if a female scientist was quoted, her appearance was far more likely to be commented upon than if a male scientist was being cited:

Comments included: 'The 55-year-old academic's mane of blonde hair, her short, navy, voluminous skirt teamed with a Vivienne Westwood jacket and knee-length boots sets a high benchmark' (*Sunday Times*) as opposed to the rather more cerebral musings on the appearances of male scientists such as 'His full white beard is worn more in homage to Charles Darwin than the Almighty' (*Observer*). (Levenson 2008: 2d)

There is a (patriarchal) expectation that a woman's attractiveness is important; whereas, for the male scientist, his gravitas is emphasized.

5. *Surprise (F6: unexpectedness)*   Extraordinary stories are more likely to get coverage than commonplace ones. For example, early in 2008 it was reported that a window cleaner had survived a 47-storey fall in New York.

6. *Elite centredness (F10: reference to elite people)*   Well-known people are more likely to be reported on than unknown ones. Film star Hugh Grant's arrest on Sunset Boulevard for 'lewd conduct in a public place', in summer 1995, was only a news story because of his film star status. Similarly, politicians often dominate 'hard' news agendas, and celebrities the 'soft' ones.

7. *Negativity (F12: reference to something negative)*   Most news covered is 'bad news' because 'good news' takes longer to happen and is less likely to be surprising; 'there were no train crashes today', while a pleasing piece of news, is hardly worthy of being broadcast.

The focus on negative news can have adverse consequences in the developing world. The fact that 48 per cent of all news reports by British television news in the period 1 September 1993 to 31 August 1994 about the developing world in the South concerned 'conflict and disaster' (Cleasby 1995: 13) gives a distorted view of the world.

8. *Human interest (F11: reference to persons)*   How a news story affects people's lives is deemed important; often vox pop interviews with people affected by the event or 'the person in the street' are included to give a human angle to events. These are usually carefully selected to give a cross-section of views. In recent years, in Britain, it has been more common to see ethnic minorities being able to offer their opinion, suggesting that they might have been excluded earlier.

9. *Composition (F8)*   In order to maintain audience interest, television news will be structured to give variety. Numerous 'talking head' interviews may bore an audience, so the programme is composed to give a mix of anchor, location footage, computer graphics and so on.

Composition is also evident in the mix of hard and soft news stories, particularly the convention that the final story should be humorous, allowing the anchor, who looked stern at the start of the programme, to smile at its close. The main headlines may be repeated, usually when there is bad news, but this time the context is more relaxed.

10. *Location reporting*   The reporter is filmed as close as possible to the events, thus signifying that the story is accurate, because the reporter is present. The contrived nature of this was highlighted during the first Gulf War, in

1990, when journalists filed their reports from the region with material supplied from London. News was managed so tightly by the military that journalists could only 'act out' their role and not actually fulfil it. The fact that journalists in this situation were performing their roles was emphasized by Mimi White in her investigation into CNN's reporting: 'with reporters and crew sporting gas masks ... a reminder of the risks to the correspondents are taking to both *tell* and *be* the story' (1994: 137). The journalists, rather than becoming conduits of news, were themselves the story; something that often disguised the fact that they didn't really know what was going on.

The first Gulf War also saw the introduction of the embedded reporter. On the face of it, allowing journalists to travel with the army would allow them direct access to events; however, journalists found that they struggled to be objective because they were part of the troop. In addition, non-embedded journalists were denied access to official news releases and indeed, according to BBC journalist, Kate Adie, were threatened by the military (Hales 2003).

11. Actuality reporting   Ideally, the events of the story should be *seen*. Stories without pictures get a very low priority in news coverage.

In addition to Selby and Cowdrey's selection, there are four other factors:

12. Inheritance factor (F7: continuity)   Once a story has hit the headlines, this in itself defines it as news. For example, in early 1997, a number of outbreaks of food poisoning, caused by *E. coli*, were reported after several people died in Scotland. It is likely that *E. coli* causes problems every year, but once it hit the headlines because of the number (magnitude) of deaths in Scotland then other cases were far more likely to be reported.

At the start of the twenty-first century, in Britain, it seemed that 'road rage' was becoming endemic and, more recently, knife crime seems to be spiralling out of control. Whether these perceptions are simply a result of higher-profile reporting or are in fact occurring is often difficult to determine.

13. Frequency (F1)   Events that happen on a daily basis are far more likely to be reported than those that develop over weeks. Many news stories are 'diary events', such as the Opening of Parliament, the Pope's Christmas Day address, and the monthly announcement of interest rates.

14. Impartiality   In Britain, the law obliges broadcasters to report impartially. In practice, this has meant giving two sides to any contentious story; political news usually features comment from the government and an opposition party. This ignores the fact that often there are more than two perspectives on a story and can have a severely unbalancing effect on the way that news is communicated. For example, any story that emphasized evidence of 'global warming', such as receding glaciers, would be balanced by a 'climate change' naysayer casting doubt on the evidence. In many cases, the 'balance' view is supplied by a special interest group:

> thirteen of the most senior doctors in Britain ... wrote a public letter calling on the government to stop funding homeopathy and other 'unproven or disproved treatments'. The journalists immediately reached for a homeopath who denounced the doctors' letter snappily as 'medial apartheid'.
> (Davies 2008: 131)

The need for balance, in effect, can give equal weight to sources of information of widely varying levels of robustness. In 2007, the BBC revised its impartiality guidelines – see pp. 266–7.

15. Sources   Press releases from official sources, such as the government or emergency services, are likely to be reported as news. News management, by political and business organizations, has grown massively since the early 1970s; the Central Office of Information (the British government's press office) increased its spending from £27m in 1979 to £189m in 2003.

The immense time pressure that news organizations are under, coupled with the greater demand for profitability from modern news proprietors, means that press releases, and news agency copy, is increasingly likely to be defined as news – see Davies (2008). This has also led to a rise in the use of PR (public relations) sourced information (see section 4.8). For example, the police, when reporting crime statistics, are likely to present this information in a light favourable to themselves. Some organizations issue video news releases (VNRs), and this could be used as part of the news broadcast without acknowledgement. In 1995, the environmental pressure group Greenpeace issued VNRs as part of their successful campaign to prevent the Brent Spar oil rig being dumped at sea.

In an overview of factors that define events as news, Jackie Harrison included two other variables:

- there are pictures of film available (television news)
- they contain short, dramatic occurrences that can be sensationalized (2006: 137)

We can add to this the 'tabloid' mantra: 'if it bleeds, it leads'; indicating that the more sensational the story – the bleeding can be physical or emotional – the more prominence it will be given. It should be apparent, by now, that what is packaged as news is a result of numerous factors that many journalists either don't recognize or don't acknowledge, which can lead many to suggest Media Studies, as a subject, does not know what it is talking about.

Box 6.3 Historical background of television news in Britain

In Britain, the BBC was the pioneer of broadcast news. While the BBC has become the touchstone of public service broadcasting (PSB) it was originally a commercial company, licensed by the government, and created by a cartel of radio manufacturers. The manufacturers needed to have programmes broadcast so that consumers would be encouraged to buy radios.

Despite its commercial origin, the BBC soon became, under the aegis of its first Director-General, John Reith, an organization dedicated to public education rather than private profit (for more detail on PSB, see Lacey, *Media Institutions and Audiences*).

The first news bulletins on the BBC used material provided by news agencies. Unless the agency is state controlled, news agency bulletins are often couched in neutral terms in order to appeal to, and be bought by, a large number of news organizations. This makes it easier for organizations to incorporate agency material into their own news agendas. However, this isn't necessarily the harmless exercise it might appear to be:

> Because news agencies must please all news editors, everywhere, they must work … to create the appearance of objectivity and neutrality. In so doing, they manufacture a bland and homogeneous, but still ideologically distinctive, view of the world; stories challenging the ideological [*sic*] of the dominant political players on the world scene (in agency eyes, the US and UK) receive little attention. (Davies 2008: 136)

This neutrality in news presentation was easily compromised. The reporting of the 1926 General Strike saw the Corporation faithfully following the government's line, even to the extent of refusing to allow the Leader of the Opposition to speak to the nation. In 1927 – as a reward for good behaviour during the previous year? – the BBC was awarded a Royal Charter that basically allowed Reith to continue his crusade to educate, rather than entertain, the masses. News was also seen as a public service, and the emphasis was on honesty rather than entertainment, even to the extent of announcing 'there is no news tonight'!

During the 1930s, the news function was expanded and split from current affairs, a division that is still in place. For the first time, the BBC used its own reporters, and Richard Dimbleby pioneered 'on the spot reporting'; giving radio news an immediacy that newspapers could never have. The political and economic turmoil of the decade, particularly the rise of fascism, stimulated reporting from abroad. Events in distant places were important to a general public concerned that there might be another war.

It was probably the need for widespread coverage of the Second World War that stimulated a worldwide system of reporting, something we now take for granted. Unsurprisingly, during the war, the BBC acted as an unofficial 'Ministry for Propaganda', allowing itself voluntarily to be censored by the government. At this time, the Nine O'Clock News became a national institution, with over half the nation listening to the broadcasts.

BBC TV news was first broadcast in 1954; however, it was little different from radio news. In order to give the impression of objectivity, it was thought necessary to show a picture of Nelson's Column, and the audience merely heard the newsreader's voice.

Clearly, news coverage has developed greatly since the 1950s. However the notion that television news is impartial is still commonplace and, indeed, enshrined in British law. The alleged neutrality applies to ITV as well as to the BBC. This 'impartiality' is possibly unique to Britain. In the USA, for example, it is common for reporters and anchors (the newsreaders) to editorialize: in other words, to give their own particular slant on events. This is also common in Europe; in Italy, television stations are even explicitly aligned with political parties.

News values in action

Many, if not all, of these values are structured by the dominant ideological discourses of our society. For example, by dealing only with stories that can be represented with 'clarity', the complexity of society as a structure is glossed over. In consequence, social problems (dealt with under 'negativity') are represented as relatively simple, which does not allow a 'full' picture of potential social dysfunctions. When, for example, homelessness is covered in the news (often a popular Christmas story, or motivated by prolonged cold weather – both examples of consonance, the problem of housing shortage and the government-imposed financial restrictions on local councils and social housing organizations is rarely addressed. Instead, we are often left with the impression that more charitable beds will alleviate the problem.

Ethnocentricity encourages audiences to consider themselves, and their fellow-countrymen and women, before people of other nations. A news agenda that emphasized, say, the notion of Spaceship Earth (a metaphor for the fact that we all have an interest in looking after our planet) may consider certain events thousands of miles away as relevant as those that are local.

The use of location reporting, in particular, frequently gives 'trivial' information a high status. A device television news often uses is to go live for an update on a breaking story. These 'updates' are usually nothing more than a restatement of what's already known, but give the impression that the audience is receiving vital information because the report is being filed from 'on the spot'.

From a broadcasting perspective, the definition of the legal requirement for impartiality in their reporting as necessitating (only) two points of view means that binary oppositions (see section 2.5) are used to structure the report. Often implicit within such a structure is 'right' and 'wrong' – the 'right', of course, representing the values of the dominant ideological system.

There should be no sense of a conspiracy in what is described above; the professional practices that lead the dominant ideological discourse to structure the news are institutionalized. The notion of gatekeepers (who are the people, such as news editors, who make decisions about whether to 'run' a story or 'spike' it) emphasizes that individuals in a news organization are less important than the position they fill. To an extent, it doesn't matter *who* makes the decision, only *what* decision they make, and this is invariably determined by the institution's agenda.

The ownership of the organization producing the news is also very important, though in the case of broadcast news in Britain, the legal requirements of balance are more powerful determining factors. In newspapers, knowing who is the owner and what is their political orientation is essential. Fox News's motto, 'We report, you decide', attempts to disguise the right-wing agenda of its proprietor, Rupert Murdoch – see *Outfoxed: Rupert Murdoch's War on Journalism* (US, 2004).

Conventions of British broadcasting news

Broadcasters present their news framed by the anchor in the studio. The news itself is shown through a mix of interviews, reportage and commentary. Interviews are usually with eyewitnesses to the event, a vox pop of what 'the person on the street' thinks, or with known individuals such as politicians or named experts (the elite). The reporter will give 'factual' detail about the story; comment usually comes from a 'correspondent' who will normally offer a consensus interpretation of events. Both the report and the comment may be provided by the same journalist, but are clearly signed as different; the anchor may ask for the correspondent's opinion after we have being given the 'story'.

All the main news stories include a filmed report that is usually shot on location. On television, this is often spoken 'to camera' and 'signed off' in front of a significant location (stakeout); for example, the White House for US political stories, thus signifying that the report is authoritative.

The terms 'report' and 'news stories' are often used interchangeably, because reports can be narratively structured. Dramatic tension is often invoked by the use of a binary opposite; for example the 'nature versus humanity' of the reporting of natural disasters. This tension is the narrative disruption that needs to be resolved, and without which there is no story. The report may not carry the resolution; this may occur later and be reported in future broadcasts. However, news bulletins, often no more than a collection of headlines that are broadcast, particularly on radio, 'on the hour' can be so totally shorn of context as to be meaningless. For example, when BBC radio reported that the 'Beijing' Olympic flame would be leaving Greece on 24 March 2008, it was stated that '1,000 police would be deployed'; but there was no explanation as to why.

Clearly, the most important story of the day, as defined by the news agenda, will be the 'lead'. The running order of stories demonstrates the priority the news agenda is giving to them. In 'hard' news channels, political and economic stories are common leads, followed by domestic issues. A foreign story will normally only take the lead if it involves a disaster, 'preferably' with some home nationals involved. Sport, as in newspapers, is commonly positioned toward the end.

On television, filmed reports are usually a mixture of montage and continuity editing, and will contain reaction shots and other techniques of continuity editing. This 'transparency' of construction reinforces the notion that the news is a 'window on the world'. Geoff King, analysing the reporting of the aeroplanes crashing into the Twin Towers in New York on 11 September 2001 noted how footage used in the news, in the days that followed, was combined according to the rules of continuity editing:

> Just as the first part of the impact becomes visible on the other side of the tower, a cut is made to a new angle, in which a fuller view is given of the fireball coming through the far side of the tower. A match-on-action ... is used to establish a seamless cut from one image to the other. (2005: 51)

As in all mainstream media texts, the dominant ideology is the structuring feature, always working to create a preferred reading that reflects (bourgeois) consensus values. Despite this, the BBC, in particular, comes under regular attack from politicians who find its 'balanced' reporting not to their liking. For example, conventions that – during the Iraq War – emphasized the BBC's impartiality by referring to 'British troops' rather than 'our troops', led it to be dubbed, by some, as the Baghdad Broadcasting Corporation.

While the BBC is a state broadcaster, funded by the licence fee, it is not an arm of government. This status means it has be particularly careful in its editorial policy (see http://www.bbc.co.uk/guidelines/editorialguidelines/; accessed March 2008). In 2003, in the run-up to the Iraq War, a report on BBC Radio 4's breakfast news programme, *Today* (a programme that is extremely influential in setting the political news agenda for the day), broadcast a report in which it was stated that the government had exaggerated the threat from Iraq's 'weapons of mass destruction' (which did, in fact, turn out to be non-existent). Despite the fact that the reporter, Andrew Gilligan, reworded his report in later contributions to the programme, the government, then struggling to convince the nation that it was necessary to go to war with Iraq, responded very aggressively, led by the prime minister's press officer, Alistair Campbell. The BBC refused to apologise; the government instigated an enquiry, led by Lord Hutton, who found 'for' the government and 'against' the BBC. Greg Dyke, the Director-General, was forced to resign; however, the government's triumphalism was tempered by the widespread perception that the Hutton Inquiry was a whitewash that favoured the government.

The aftermath of the Hutton Inquiry led to many changes at the BBC. In 2007, it acknowledged that the 'two sides of the story' idea of balance was no longer viable:

Impartiality in broadcasting has long been assumed to apply mainly to party politics and industrial disputes. It involved keeping a balance to ensure the seesaw did not tip too far to one side or the other.

Those days are over. In today's multi-polar Britain, with its range of cultures, beliefs and identities, impartiality involves many more than two sides to an argument. Party politics is in decline, and industrial disputes are only rarely central to national debate. The seesaw has been replaced by the wagon wheel – the modern version used in the television coverage of cricket, where the wheel is not circular and has a shifting centre with spokes that go in all directions. (BBC Trust 2007: 5)

What this means for its news reporting remains to be seen. However, as noted in section 3.3, in our consideration of dialogic communication, the acknowledgement that the institution has to be aware of its own perspective is encouraging:

> Impartiality involves breadth of view, and can be breached by omission. It is not necessarily to be found on the centre ground ... Impartiality requires the BBC to examine its own institutional values, and to assess the effect they have on its audiences. (The BBC's Impartiality Values, http://news.bbc.co.uk/1/hi/entertainment/6764279.stm; accessed March 2008)

The BBC published the following guidelines for the May local elections in Britain:

> Overall balance of the parties
> Each bulletin, programme or programme strand, as well as online and interactive services, covering each election, must achieve an appropriate and fair balance over an appropriate period. Whilst the majority of coverage is likely to be about the main parties care must be taken to ensure that other political parties and independent candidates also receive appropriate coverage. (http://www.bbc.co.uk/guidelines/editorialguidelines/advice/election/balance.shtml; accessed April 2008)

In recent years, even news organizations as well funded as the BBC have come under pressure to break news more quickly, as they are competing with 24-hour rolling news channels and the internet. The rolling news channels tend to structure themselves on an hourly basis and so start the hour with the news headlines – which may be the same as those of the previous hour.

Audience readings of TV news

In Britain, television news has greater credibility than printed news, and the BBC more so than ITN. This is probably because of a combination of a press that is too obviously partisan and the strength of the myth that 'seeing is believing'. Even in a multi-channel environment, flagship news programmes on the BBC have an audience of around seven million viewers, and clearly still have a great influence on people's perception of the world.

It is likely that most of this audience make a 'dominant' reading of the representation, though both negotiated and oppositional readings are also, of course, possible. Political stories are most likely to receive readings that are not 'dominant', depending on the individual viewer's political orientation.

Because news often deals with issues removed from the immediate concerns of the general public, audiences frequently have no first-hand knowledge of stories covered. When stories concerning, say, a particular locality are carried, then an 'oppositional' reading may be made, especially if – as is quite probably – the content is negative.

The press are more likely to be seen by audiences to be biased, or inaccurate, in their representations, as they have no requirement for balance. For example, when nine-year-old Shannon Matthews went missing in Dewsbury, Yorkshire, only to be found hidden at her uncle's house, the apparent attempt, by Shannon's family, to hoodwink the public led the press to represent negatively the whole housing estate. For example *The Sun* ran the headline, 'Estate is like a nastier Beirut' (9 April 2008) and compared the area to the fictional drama *Shameless* (Channel 4, 2004–). Needless to say, many people who lived there disagreed (Wainwright 2008).

The internet has made it much easier for audiences to share their views of broadcasts by commenting on stories on the news providers' websites. This is usually a mix of comment on stories, or other contributors' comments, or eyewitness accounts of the events being reported.

EXERCISE 6.1

Videotape a whole news programme and consider the extent to which it follows the news conventions described above. (A comparison of different stations' news bulletins can also be revealing about news agendas.)

As noted at the start of this section, a news organization's agenda structures what, and how, it reports the world, and this agenda can be influenced greatly by the proprietor. For example, Rupert Murdoch, head of News Corporation, supported the invasion of Iraq in 2003:

'Rupert Murdoch argued strongly for a war with Iraq in an interview this week. Which might explain why his 175 editors around the world are backing it too' (Greenslade 2003).

The following sections looks at representations of the Iraq conflict made in the years following the invasion. The focus is on cinematic representations, using a variety of devices to convey a particular message.

6.6 Representing the war in Iraq

Unlike the situation during the Vietnam War, when Hollywood barely noted the war's existence in its films, the conflict in Iraq, which started with the (primarily) American–British invasion in 2003, has seen many films released on the subject. Most of these films have been, in some way, critical of the way the conflict was being managed by the American government, and virtually all of them were box office disappointments. These fictional features were preceded by a large number of documentaries; these too failed to find much of an audience.

We can only speculate as to why audiences weren't interested in seeing representations of such an important event. It is possible that, as cinema is seen primarily as an entertainment medium, audiences didn't want to be reminded of the death and destruction occurring in Iraq. The films, as is usual, received a mixed critical reaction, from 'lukewarm' – to be polite – for *Lions for Lambs* (2007) to generally positive – for example, *In the Valley of Elah* (2007). Unsurprisingly, given the divided nature of the support for the war in Iraq, a number of these films, such as *Redacted* (2007), were seen as being particularly controversial.

Most of the films, typical of Hollywood, use generic conventions. *Rendition* (2007) works as a political thriller focusing on two narratives: the 'rendered' Egyptian-born El-Ibrahimi, who is taken to another country to be tortured, and his American wife who desperately tries to find out why he hadn't returned home. In political thrillers, 'The basic plot is an ordinary man pulling an innocent thread which leads to a mess of corruption. The corruption should be political or governmental in nature' (Lundegaard 2006). It is usual in the genre for the 'ordinary man' to succeed, at least to an extent, in revealing the corruption to the world, as is the case in *The Interpreter* (UK–US–France, 2005), though this may be tempered by a suggestion that the corruption will continue, as in *Three Days of the Condor* (1975). In *Rendition*, the ordinary man is simply a victim, powerless to do anything, while his wife, though resolute in her attempts to find her husband, similarly fails to achieve anything. Although, as a mainstream film, it is unsurprising that there is a 'happy' ending, courtesy of a disgusted CIA officer, the twist on the genre of making the protagonists powerless is a powerful indictment of the current political climate, where torture appears to be official policy in America.

In the Valley of Elah is a mix of thriller, melodrama and police investigation. The protagonist, Hank Deerfield, played by Tommy Lee Jones, is a patriotic ex-serviceman who supports the war. Early in the film he helps an immigrant put right an American flag that is flying upside down, saying that an upside-down flag means the country is in mortal danger. However, his investigation into his son's death, just after he'd returned from Iraq, reveals to him how war dehumanizes soldiers, and the film concludes with him deliberately flying the flag upside down.

Melodrama is a non-realist genre, and so consciously uses both characters and settings symbolically. Deerfield, the name itself evoking the American pastoral, represents someone who naturally supports the country in times of war. He is a deeply repressed male, contrasted with his sometimes-desperate wife, played by Susan Sarandon. Deerfield's investigations reveal the 'dark heart' at the core of this war and, even though he is patriotic, he realizes that the war is wrong.

Elah uses the device of a corrupted mobile phone video, which is slowly revealed throughout the film, as part of unravelling the mystery of what had happened to Deerfield's son. *Redacted*, the most unconventional of the 'Iraq films', also uses new media technologies to represent the rape of a 15-year-old girl and the murder of her and her family by US marines. The film starts with a disclaimer that the film is 'a fiction inspired by true events'. The writer-director, Brian DePalma, uses a mix of texts to show what (might have) happened: a 'home video' made by one of the marines; a pastiche of a French (intellectual) documentary about Iraq; CCTV cameras; internet postings; a video made on a mobile phone; photojournalism. While it might seem that it is a realist text, the multi-media mixing instead draws attention to the artifice of what is shown. This may suggest that such horrendous events *cannot* be convincingly rendered by realism. Indeed, DePalma also deploys melodrama; the one good guy, who tries to publicize what's happened, is called Lawyer McCoy. This melodrama extends to the use of an aria from Puccini's opera *Tosca*, the protagonist of which murders the man who is trying to rape her. This highly passionate aria could be seen as an ironic comment on the Iraqi teenager's inability to kill her rapists. However, the last image of the film is an actual photograph of the dead girl which needs no melodramatic heightening to appal its audience, and so, ultimately, DePalma's films comes across as exploitative.

One British film to deal with a similar topic is *The Battle of Haditha* (2007). This is a drama-doc that recreates the massacre of twenty-four men, women and children in Haditha by (allegedly) US marines. Director Nick Broomfield's intensely realist aesthetic, signified by the hand-held camera and utterly convincing performances, manages to humanize both the perpetrators of the atrocity – we understand that these are young men, badly led, and out of their depth – as well as getting to 'know' the victims. It also features a sex scene between a Muslim husband and wife, where the woman removes her veil; this in itself should not be remarkable, but such representations are extremely rare. From a Western perspective, the lifting of the veil individualizes the character and makes it easier to identify with her.

All these films are critical of America's conduct in the war; it would be difficult to offer a gung-ho representation of events while the victory, heralded by George Bush in May 2003, had still failed to materialize. *The Kingdom* (2007) was one mainstream film (all the others were independently produced) that was actually set in the Middle East, albeit Saudi Arabia. Here, Jamie Foxx plays an FBI investigator, Ronald Fleury, who bulldozes his way through political objections to investigate, and bring to justice, the perpetrators of a terrorist attack against American families. The film is progressive in its casting of an African-American as a lead where his ethnicity is absolutely irrelevant; however, its portrayal of backward foreigners needing American assistance plants its perspective as being firmly of the view that 'the West is best'.

It certainly isn't wholly simplistic. An opening montage succinctly lays out the geopolitical history of the region, and sites oil as the driving force behind America's involvement in the region, and not 'freedom', as politicians suggest. And Foxx's 'local' helper is a well-drawn character, though the fact that 'a sequence showing Al Ghazi's family's evening Salah in parallel [with] Fleury phoning his son was almost cut from the film during the editing process' (Miller 2007: 63b) is evidence of Hollywood's reluctance to humanize non-Western characters. Because of the nature of international cinema, it is rare that we get to see how other cultures represent both themselves and the West.

6.7 Other representations

For many years in the West, accessing Third (or developing) World film and television programmes was very difficult. However, the internet has encouraged the distribution of both; almost certainly, they appeal primarily to various diaspora. In comparison, non-Western music does appeal to Western audiences. The catch-all term 'world music' has been used as a marketing tool since the 1980s, and it seemed that Salif Keita's crossover hit, *Soro* (1987), would herald a blossoming of world music in the West. However, it is only in the twenty-first century that the 'genre' (though as it encompassing so many different cultures and styles it cannot be really classified as such) established itself as a niche in Western music markets, evidenced by the rebirth of *Songlines* magazine in 2002.

Despite films being made in the early twentieth century in many non-Western countries – India's first feature *Raj Harishchandra* was produced in 1913 – the lack of economic infrastructure and the colonial status of many countries made it difficult to produce indigenous films in many places. For example, in Tanzania:

In 1935 the British Colonial Office embarked on the Bantu Educational Cinema Experiment, financed by the Carnegie Corporation and the northern Rhodesia copper mines. The purpose was to educate the Africans, perpetuate colonial traditions and provide entertainment. (Ngayane 1993: 13)

Obviously, these films were propagandistic in nature, and Africans' involvement was only at a menial level. Unlike music, where Westerners can hear
more or less (if not actually understand) what the musicians are saying, the
highly expensive nature of both film and television makes it difficult to
produce texts in great numbers. Even the musicians are dependent on Western
record labels for the distribution and marketing of their music, such as Nick
Gold's World Circuit company responsible for the Buena Vista Social Club.

The first African film by an African, *Borom Sarret* (Senegal), wasn't
produced until 1966. During the 1960s, a decade of worldwide political
ferment, the idea of Third (World) Cinema was developed. While Third
Cinema could simply describe films made by Third-World countries, from the
perspective of looking at alternative representations, the ideological conception of Third Cinema is most interesting:

> The term was launched as a rallying cry in the late 1960s by Fenando
> Solanas and Octavio Getino, who define Third Cinema as 'the cinema that
> recognizes in [the anti-imperialist struggle in the Third World and its
> equivalents within the imperialist countries] ... the decolonization of
> culture'. (Shohat and Stam 1994: 28)

Like the term 'world music' (and the term 'world cinema' is also used as a
marketing device), Third Cinema encompasses many different film-makers,
and so any generalization can only be indicative and not absolute. In
attempting to summarize the differences between Third World and Western
societies, Teshome H. Gabriel suggests that 'the former aims at changing the
individual through community, the latter wants the community changed by
the individual' (1989: 41). Gabriel goes on to suggest stylistic differences
between Western and Third Cinema; for example:

> *The long take*: It is not uncommon in Third World films to see a concentra-
> tion of long takes and repetition of images and scenes. In the Third World
> films, the slow, leisurely pacing approximates the viewer's sense of time
> and rhythm of life. (ibid.: 44–5)

In other words, the chronotope of Third Cinema is distinctive. Mikhail
Bakhtin (see 3.3) describes the chronotope as 'particular combinations of
time and space as they have resulted in historically manifested narrative
forms' (Holquist 2002: 109). While the chronotope is similar to diegesis (the
narrative world created by the text), it highlights how the representation of
time is as important as the representation of *space*. In the West, our concept
of time is highly linear whereas, in Africa, for example, tradition is much

more important to the extent that, instead of forging on to the (bourgeois) future, the past remains in the present. Hence the 'rhythm of life' portrayed in African films tends to be very different from Western narratives, which tend to be fast-paced and eschew narrative redundancy. As the title suggests, there is a lot of 'waiting' in *Waiting for Happiness* (*Heremakono*, Mauritania, 2002). In *Abouna* (Chad, 2002), a story of two brothers who wish their father would return, while the narrative does progress, it doesn't come to a conclusion at the end; there is, simply, a sense that life will go on.

Gabriel also suggests that the close-up is used differently. Its use is less frequent and has an informational purpose rather than allowing us access to a (bourgeois) individual's psychological state as it is conventionally used in the West. Of course, these are generalizations, but we should not be surprised that Third Cinema, when allowed to speak with its own voice, should speak in different ways from the West.

Third Cinema is not the same as counter cinema (see section 3.9), as that was constructed in opposition to the dominant cinema; Third Cinema practitioners were not going to allow dominant (Western) cinema to determine, even if in opposition, their way of showing. Third Cinema's highly politicized project was at its most evident in the 1960s, with films such as *Hour of the Furnaces* (*Hora de los hornos*, Argentina, 1968) and *Blood of the Condor* (*Yawar Mallku*, Bolivia, 1969) films that, respectively, opposed government oppression in Argentina and revealed America's role in the sterilization of the Bolivian Indian population.

The decades following, exacerbated by globalization, has seen a reduction in overtly political cinema, but not in other ways of representing the world. For example, director Ousmane Sembene's film *Moolaadé* (Senegal, 2004) is a strong protest against female circumcision:

> The story, with its exploration of the power relations between men and women, is fascinating in itself. But Sembene also uses it to explore the whole fabric of village life, with its songs and rhythms and ambivalent relationship to the outside world, symbolized by the radios that the women love to listen to. This is not the usual Western-style film with dramatic pace – we are gradually immersed, instead, through the collection of little details that eventually accumulate into a poetic world-view. The wide-screen composition and color give the picture a contemplative beauty even as the story's conflict becomes more and more intense. (Dashiell 2005)

In section 3.8 we considered how discourse is a powerful way of defining power relations; Said's discussion of Orientalism showed how the East is characterized, by the West, as its Other. Similarly, overcoming colonialist discourse – that is, to 'speak' with one's own voice – is very difficult, especially in the early years of independence. Western cinema was, by default, *the* cinema, and so a new cinema had to be developed in its wake; such was the project of Third Cinema. One way of operating is to silence cinema completely by banning it, the preferred option in the years following the Islamic Revolution in Iran in 1979. In the intervening years, through negotiation and pragmatism, Iranian cinema developed to become among the most vital in the world (see Naficy 2002).

Another national cinema that produces an extraordinary quantity of films (though the concept of nation states is a Western one), is Nollywood – a term given to Nigerian video films. Chukwuman Okoye argues that, despite the often low production values that characterize these films:

> They invent a progressive African aesthetic which undermines the cultural imperialism of the West and underscores the possibility of formulating both an African postcolonial identity, a mode of seeing and knowledge production, as well as an independent entrepreneurial framework. (2007: 28a)

In the films considered in this section so far, there are few direct representations of the West. In *Waiting for Happiness*, moving to France is seen as an escape to a better life, though the film certainly casts a great deal of doubt on whether this is the case. *Lagaan: Once Upon a Time in India* (India, 2001) is a melodrama celebrating a village's triumph – in a cricket match – against the imperial British. The two main Western characters are Captain Andrew Russell and his sister. The captain is a strict stereotype, an upper-class, arrogant, callous Englishman convinced of his superiority. His sister, however, is far more sympathetic to the locals and is 'in love' with the hero, who organizes a cricket match as a way of getting rid of an iniquitous tax (the 'lagaan'). The two-dimensional Western characters give Western audiences a clue as to how non-Westerners have been represented for years. The film itself, however, as Rebecca Brown argues:

> presents a colonial past in which resistance to the colonizer 'unifies' the villagers, but only under the banner of Hinduism. From the conservatism of the film's depiction of the village to its token inclusion of Muslims, Sikhs, and untouchables, *Lagaan* unwittingly reasserts the primacy of Hinduism in India, and does so through the two-pronged approach of recasting both Indian history and Hindu gods. (2004)

Another film that contests Western history is *The Opium Wars* (*Yapian zhanzheng*, Japan–China, 1997), representing Britain's role as a drug trafficker at the time it annexed Hong Kong. The film had propagandistic timing, being released when Hong Kong was returned to China after 99 years of colonial rule. Despite this, the film is notable in *not* crudely stereotyping the British; as in *Lagaan*, a female character is shown to be the one with the most conscience. I suppose the criminal acts of imperial Britain were sufficient in themselves to convey the film's message.

Conclusion

I hope that readers of this book now have a greater understanding of how media texts communicate their meaning and how ideological concerns always structure what is being said. It was noted, in the Introduction to the Second Edition, that the internet has led to greater opportunities for the production of texts without the mediation of media organizations. This obviously offers a greater freedom of expression for people of wildly varying ideological viewpoints. It has also led to an increasing interest in governmental control over communications:

> A new generation of surveillance technologies, population databases, identity management systems, 'dataveillance', data-sharing and data-mining tools are providing the state with the capacity to construct an almost unimaginably detailed picture of our private lives. (Hayes 2008: 14a)

The extent to which the general population is aware of this is debatable; it is highly likely that many will know more about the latest fashions being paraded by the likes of Paris Hilton than the threat to their privacy. Others may argue that such information is required for our security against threats such as 'Islamist fundamentalism'. And, of course, our viewpoint and knowledge will be largely based on information provided by the media, and, despite the internet, the major corporations are still by far the dominant forces in constructing world-views for their audiences. And, as these corporations are invariably businesses, these world-views are unsurprisingly bourgeois in nature, with possibly one exception: publishing, and it is one section of the media that is under-represented in this book.

Publishing is one media industry that does offer left-wing views that criticize both governments and capitalism. In the UK, the following books have been published since 2006:

- *Chinese Whispers: The True Story Behind Britain's Hidden Army of Labour* (Penguin) by Hsiao-Hung Pai

- *Eat Your Heart Out: Why the Food Business Is Bad for the Planet and Your Health* (Penguin) by Felicity Lawrence
- *Flat Earth News* (Chatto & Windus) by Nick Davies
- *Going to Extremes* (Granta) by Barbara Ehrenreich
- *Hungry City: How Food Shapes Our Lives* (Chatto & WIndus) by Carolyn Steel
- *Live Working or Die Fighting: How the Working Class Went Global* (Harvill Secker) by Paul Mason
- *Risk: The Science and Politics of Fear* (Virgin) by Dan Gardner
- *The Shock Doctrine* (Penguin) by Naomi Klein
- *Standard Operating Procedure: A War Story* (Picador) by Philip Gourevitch and Errol Morris (also a documentary film).

Three of the books are published by Penguin, part of the Pearson group that owns the *Financial Times*. Both Chatto & Windus and Harvill Secker are part of the Random House Group, which is owned by multinational media corporation Bertelsmann. Virgin is part of Richard Branson's venture capital organization, and Picador is part of the Palgrave group that also published the book you are reading. Granta is the only independent publisher.

The views represented in these books are very rarely aired on television or in mainstream cinema; however, they do find a voice in print – in magazines such as *Red Pepper* as well as the books cited above. Of course, the main difference in consumption of audio-visual texts compared to print ones is that the former are often viewed collectively, whereas reading is usually a solitary process. As mentioned in Chapter 3, the radical press of the nineteenth century was effective as it was often read out to illiterate workers and so was a collective experience. The modern equivalent might be to read the book – for example, Naomi Klein's *The Shock Doctrine* (2007); visit the website (www.shockdoctrine.com), which offers more recent evidence supporting the book's thesis; and then view the video posted on YouTube, which has a link from the website (in early August 2008, over 600,000 viewings of the video had taken place). The video, by Klein and Mexican film-maker, Alfonso Cuaron, was commissioned by the publisher; no doubt as a way of publicizing the book. Readers are invited to subscribe to Klein's newsletter and find out about events happening in their area.

One thing is certain: knowledge is power, and ignorance merely allows us to be exploited, so it is crucial that everyone learns about the power of the media and how to use that power themselves.

Bibliography

Achbar, Mark (ed.) (1994) *Manufacturing Consent: Noam Chomsky and the Media*, Montreal and New York: Black Rose Books.

Adams, Esther (1997) 'Approaches to "the North": Common Myths and Assumptions' in O'Sullivan and Jewkes (eds) *The Media Studies Reader*.

Althusser, Louis (1971) *Lenin and Philosophy*, New York and London: Monthly Review Press.

Altman, Rick (ed.) (1981) *Genre: The Musical*, London: Routledge & Kegan Paul.

Alvarado, Manuel, Robin Gutch and Tana Wollen (1981) *Learning the Media,* Basingstoke: Macmillan.

Ameli, Saied R., Syed Mohammed Marandi, Sameera Ahmed, Seyfeddin Kara and Arzu Merali (2007) 'The British Media and Muslim Representation: The Ideology of Demonisation'. Available at: http://www.ihrc.org.uk/show.php?id=2493; accessed February 2008.

Anderson, Benedict (1991) *Imagined Communities* (revd and extended edn), London and New York: Verso.

Appadurai, Arjun (1990) 'Disjunction and Difference in the Global Media Economy' in Featherstone, *Global Culture.*

Argyle, Michael (1983) *The Psychology of Interpersonal Behaviour* (4th edn), Harmondsworth: Penguin.

Attwood, Feona (2005) 'Tits and Ass and Porn and Fighting': Male Heterosexuality in Magazines for Men', *International Journal of Culture Studies*, 8: 1, 87–104. Available at: http://digitalcommons.shu.ac.uk/ccrc_papers/20/; accessed April 2008.

Auerbach, Erich (1968) *Mimesis: The Representation of Reality in Western Literature*, Princeton, NJ: Princeton University Press.

Barnes, Rachel (1994) 'Desperately Seeking an Identity', *The Guardian*, 24 October.

Barnouw, Erik (1993) *Documentary* (2nd revd edn), New York: Oxford University Press.

Barthes, Roland (1973) *Mythologies*, St Albans: Granada.

Barthes, Roland (1977) 'Introduction to the Structural Analysis of Narratives' in Roland Barthes *Image-Music-Text*, Glasgow: Fontana.

Barthes, Roland (1990) *S/Z*, Oxford and Cambridge: Basil Blackwell.

Bazin, Andre (1967) *What is Cinema?* Vol. 1, Berkeley and Los Angeles: University of California Press.

BBC Trust (2007) 'From Seesaw to Wagon Wheel: Safeguarding Impartiality in the 21st Century'. Available at: news.bbc.co.uk/1/shared/bsp/hi/pdfs/18_06_07impartiality bbc.pdf.

Beder, Sharon (1997) *Global Spin: The Corporate Assault on Environmentalism*, Dartington: Green Books.

Beltran, Mary (2004) *'Mas Macha*: The New Latina Action Hero' in Tasker (ed.) *Action and Adventure Cinema*.

Benjamin, Walter (1979) 'The Work of Art in the Age of Mechanical Reproduction' in Mast and Cohen (eds) *Film Theory and Criticism*.

Bennett, Tony and Jane Woollacott (1987) *Bond and Beyond: The Political Career of a Popular Hero*, London: Macmillan.

Bennett, Tony, Susan Boyd-Bowman, Colin Mercer and Janet Woollacott (eds) (1981) *Popular Television and Film*, London: British Film Institute.

Berger, John (1972) *Ways of Seeing*, London and Harmondsworth: BBC and Penguin.

Birchall, Danny (n.d.) 'Who Cares (1971)'. Available at: http://www.screenonline.org.uk/film/id/820087/index.html; accessed March 2008.

Bordwell, David (2006) *The Way Hollywood Tells It: Story and Style in Modern Movies*, Berkeley, Los Angeles and London: University of California Press.

Bowker, Julian (ed.) (1991) *Secondary Media Education*, London: British Film Institute.

Bradbury, Malcolm and James MacFarlane (eds) (1976) *Modernism*, Harmondsworth: Penguin.

Brando, Marlon, with Robert Lindsay (1994) *Songs My Mother Taught Me*, London: Century.

Branston, Gill and Roy Stafford (2006), *The Media Student's Book* (4th edn), London and New York: Routledge.

Brecht, Bertolt (1991) *Saint Joan of the Stockyards*, London: Methuen.

Brooker, Will (ed.) (2005) *The Blade Runner Experience: The Legacy of a Science Fiction Classic*, London: Wallflower.

Brown, Rebecca M. (2004) 'Lagaan: Once Upon a Time in India', *Film & History: An Interdisciplinary Journal of Film and Television Studies*, 34:1, 78–80. Available at: http://muse.jhu.edu/demo/film_and_history/v034/34.1brown.html; accessed April 2008.

Brownlee, John (2007) 'Political Correctness Destroys Ming the Merciless'. Available at: http://blogs.amctv.com/scifiscanner/2007/07/political-corre; accessed November 2007.

Brunsdon, Charlotte (ed.) (1986) *Films for Women*, London: British Film Institute.

Brunsdon, Charlotte (1998) 'Structure of Anxiety: Recent British Television Crime Fiction', *Screen*, 39:3, Autumn.

Bruzzi, Stella (2000) *New Documentary: A Critical Introduction*, London and New York: Routledge.

Bryce, Derek (2007–8) 'The 2007 Iranian "'Hostage Crisis"': An Orientalist Captivity Narrative', *Media Education Journal*, 42, Winter.

Bukatman, Scott (1990) 'Who Programs You? The Science Fiction of the Spectacle' in Kuhn (ed.) *Alien Zone*.

Buscombe, Edward (2006) *100 Westerns*, London: British Film Institute.

Butler, Judith (1999) *Gender Trouble* (2nd edn), London and New York: Routledge.

Byars, Jackie (1991) *All That Hollywood Allows*, London: Routledge.

Cantoni, Lorenzo and Stefano Tardini (2006) *Internet*, Abingdon and New York: Routledge.

Carr, Diane, David Buckingham, Andrew Burn and Gareth Schott (2006) *Computer Games: Text, Narrative and Play*, Cambridge and Malden: Polity Press.

Casey, Bernadette, Neil Casey, Ben Calvert, Liam French and Justin Lewis (2002) *Television Studies: The Key Concepts*, London and New York: Routledge.

Cawelti, John G. (1976) *Adventure, Mystery and Romance*, Chicago: University of Chicago Press.

Chapman, Jane (2007) *Documentary in Practice*, Cambridge and Malden: Polity Press.

Choong, Teo Kia (2004) *Hero* (*Ying xiong*). Available at http://www.scope.nottingham.ac.uk/filmreview.php?issue=may2004andid=651andsection=film_rev; accessed March 2008.

Cleasby, Adrian (1995) *What in the World Is Going On?*, London: 3WE – Third World and Environment Broadcasting Project.

Clover, Carol J. (1992) *Men, Women and Chainsaws: Gender in the Modern Horror Film*, London: British Film Institute.

Cohan, Steven (1993) '"Feminizing" the Song-and-Dance Man' in Cohan and Hark (eds) *Screening the Male*.

Cohan, Steven and Ina Rae Hark (eds) (1993) *Screening the Male*, London: Routledge.

Cohen, Stanley and Jock Young (eds) (1981) *The Manufacture of News – Social Problems, Deviance and the Mass Media* (revd edn), London: Constable.

Collins, Jim, Hilary Radner and Ava Preacher Collins (eds) (1993) *Film Theory Goes to the Movies*, New York: Routledge.

Coulthard, Lisa (2007) 'Killing Bill: Rethinking Feminism and Film Violence' in Tasker (ed.) *Action and Adventure Cinema*.

Creeber, Glen (ed.) (2004) *Fifty Key Television Programmes*, London: Arnold.

Creed, Barbara (1993) *The Monstrous-Feminine: Film, Feminism, Psychoanalysis*, London and New York: Routledge.

Curran, James (ed.) (2000) *Media Organisations in Society*, London: Hodder Arnold.

Curran, James and Jean Seaton (1991) *Power Without Responsibility: The Press and Broadcasting in Britain* (4th edn), London: Routledge.

Curran, James and Jean Seaton (2003) *Power Without Responsibility: The Press and Broadcasting in Britain* (6th edn), London and New York: Routledge.

Curran, James, David Morley and Valerie Walkerdine (eds) (1996) *Cultural Studies and Communications*, London: Arnold.

D'Acchi, Julie (2002) 'Gender, Representation and Television' in Miller (ed.) *Television Studies*.

Danesi, Marcel (2006) *Brands*, New York and Abingdon: Routledge.

Dashiell, Chris (2005) 'Moolaadé'. Available at: http://www.cinescene.com/dash/moolade.htm; accessed April 2008.

Davies, Nick (2008) *Flat Earth News: An Award-winning Reporter Exposes Falsehood, Distortion and Propaganda in the Global Media*, London: Chatto & Windus.

Doane, Mary Ann (1987) *The Desire to Desire: The Woman's Film of the 1940s*, London: Macmillan.

Doane, Mary Ann (2000) 'Film and the Masquerade: Theorizing the Female Spectator' in Stam and Miller (eds) *Film and Theory*.

Dolby, Nadine (2006) 'Popular Culture and Public Space in Africa: The Possibilities of Cultural Citizenship', *African Studies Review*, December (quoted from http://findarticles.com/p/articles/mi_qa4106/is_200612/ai_n19197926/pg_8; accessed November 2007).

Doyle, Mark (1994) 'Captain Mbaye Diagne', *Granta 49*, Harmondsworth: Penguin.

Drummond, Phillip (1997) *High Noon*, London: British Film Institute.

Dyer, Gillian (1982) *Advertising as Communication*, London: Routledge.

Dyer, Richard (1979) *Stars*, London: British Film Institute.

Dyer, Richard (1981) 'Minnelli's Web of Dreams', *The Movie*, 58.

Dyer, Richard (1985) 'Taking Television Seriously' in Lusted and Drummond (eds) *TV and Schooling*.

Dyer, Richard (1993) *A Matter of Images*, London: British Film Institute.

Eagleton, Terry (1983) *Literary Theory*, Basil Blackwell Oxford.

Eimer, David (2008) 'Tibet Protest Crackdown Claims up to 100 Lives'. Available at: (http://www.telegraph.co.uk/news/main.jhtml?xml=/news/2008/03/15/wtibet715.xml; accessed March 2008.

Eisenstein, Sergei (1979) 'A Dialectical Approach to Film Form' in Mast and Cohen (eds) *Film Theory and Criticism*.

Eliot, T. S. (1974) *The Waste Land*, London: Faber & Faber.

Ellis, John (1982) *Visible Fictions*, London: Routledge & Kegan Paul.

Elsaesser, Thomas and Warren Buckland (2002) *Studying Contemporary American Film*, London: Arnold.

Engdahl, William (2008) 'Risky Geopolitical Game: Washington Plays "Tibet Roulette" with China'. Available at: http://www.indymedia.org.uk/en/2008/04/396124; accessed April 2008).

Evans, George (1998) 'Sex, Lies and Democracy: The Press and the Public – Review', *Contemporary Review*, December (quoted from http://findarticles.com/p/articles/mi_m2242/is_1595_273/ai_53590225; accessed November 2007.

Evans, Harold (1997) *Pictures on a Page* (Pimlico edn) London: Pimlico.

Falcon, Richard (1994) *Classified!*, London: British Film Institute.

Faludi, Susan (2007) *The Terror Dream: What 9/11 Revealed About America*, London: Atlantic Books.

Fanon, Frantz (2001) *The Wretched of the Earth*, London: Penguin Classics.

Featherstone, Mike (ed.) (1990) *Global Culture: Nationalism, Globalization and Modernity*, London, Thousand Oaks, CA and New Delhi: Sage.

Featherstone, Mike, Scott Lash and Roland Robertson (eds) (1995) *Global Modernities*, London, Thousand Oaks, CA and New Delhi: Sage.

Fisk, Robert (1993) 'Through a Lens, Fuzzily', *Independent on Sunday* (Review section), 5 December.

Fiske, John (1989) *Reading the Popular*, London and New York: Routledge.

Forster, E. M. (1976) *Aspects of the Novel*, Harmondsworth: Pelican.

Fowler, Roger (1991) *Language in the News*, London: Routledge.

Freedan, Michael (2003) *Ideology A Very Short Introduction*, London and New York: Oxford University Press.

French, Sean (1996) *The Terminator*, London: British Film Institute.

Gabriel, Teshome H. (1989) 'Towards a Critical Theory of Third World Films' in Pines and Willeman (eds) *Questions of Third Cinema*.

Gelder, Ken (2007) *Subcultures: Cultural Histories and Social Practice*, Abingdon and New York: Routledge.

Geraghty, Christine (1991) *Women and Soap Opera: A Study of Prime Time Soaps*, Cambridge: Polity Press.

Gibson, Ben (1988) 'Powaqqatsi', Monthly Film Bulletin, 55 (655), August.

Gibson, Owen (2005) 'Abusive Calls Give BBC Chiefs a Jerry Springer Moment', The Guardian, 10 January. Available at: http://www.guardian.co.uk/media/2005/jan/10/broadcasting.bbc; accessed April 2008.

Gilbert, Keith (2003) 'Small Faces: The Tyranny of Celebrity in Post-Oedipal Culture', Mediactive, 2.

Gill, Rosalind (2007) Gender and the Media, London and Malden: Polity Press.

Gillmor, Dan (2008) 'The Tools of Citizen Journalism', New Scientist, 15 March.

Glasgow Media Group (2005) 'Media Coverage of the Developing World: Audience Understanding and Interest'. Available at: http://www.gla.ac.uk/centres/mediagroup/debate.htm; accessed March 2008.

Goffman, Erving (1979) Gender Advertisements, London: Macmillan.

Goldsmiths Media Group (2000) Media Organisations in Society: Central Issues in Curran (ed.) Media Organisations in Society.

Gombrich, E. H. (1989) The Story of Art (15th edition), London: Phaidon Press.

Gough-Yates, Anna (2003) Understanding Women's Magazines: Publishing, Markets and Readerships, London and New York: Routledge.

Grant, Barry Keith (ed.) (1996) The Dread of Difference: Gender and the Horror Film, Austin, TX: University of Texas Press.

Greenslade, Roy (2003) 'Their Master's Voice', The Guardian, 17 February. Available at: http://www.guardian.co.uk/media/2003/feb/17/mondaymediasection.iraq; accessed April 2008.

Greenslade, Roy (2004) Press Gang: How Newspapers Make Profits From Propaganda, London: Pan Macmillan.

Gregory, R. L. (1966) Eye and Brain, London: Weidenfeld & Nicolson.

Hales, Paul (2003) 'US Threatens to Eliminate Independent War Journalists', The Inquirer, 11 March. Available at: http://www.theinquirer.net/en/inquirer/news/2003/03/11/us-threatens-to-eliminate-independent-war-journalists; accessed March 2008.

Hall, Stuart (ed.) (1997a) Representation: Cultural Representations and Signifying Practices, Sage: London, Thousand Oaks, CA and New Delhi.

Hall, Stuart (1997b) 'The Work of Representation' in Hall (ed.) (1997a) Representation.

Hall, Stuart, Dorothy Hobson, Andrew Lowe and Paul Willis (eds) (1980) Culture, Media, Language, London and New York: Routledge.

Hallam, Julia and Margaret Marshment (1995) 'Framing Experience: Case Studies in the Reception of Oranges Are Not the Only Fruit', Screen, 39(1), Spring.

Hand, Richard J. (2005) 'Aesthetics of Cruelty: Traditional Japanese Theatre and the Horror Film' in McRoy (ed.) Japanese Horror Cinema.

Haraway, Donna (1991) Simians, Cyborgs and Women: The Reinvention of Nature, New York: Routledge.

Harker, Joseph (2008) 'Too Much Purley and Not Enough Peckham', MediaGuardian, 3 March. Available at: http://www.guardian.co.uk/media/2008/mar/03/pressandpublishing.raceandreligion; accessed March 2008.

Harrison, Jackie (2006) News, Abingdon and New York: Routledge.

Harvey, Sylvia (1980) May '68 and Film Culture, London: British Film Institute.

Harwood, Sarah (1997) Family Fictions: Representations of the Family in 1980s Hollywood Cinema, London: Macmillan.

Hatzfeld, Jean (1994) 'The Fall of Vukovar', *Granta*, 47, pp. 197–222.

Hayes, Ben (2008) 'Surveillance Society', *Red Pepper,* 157, December/January. Also available on http://www.redpepper.org.uk/-Dec-2007-Jan-2008-.

Heath, Stephen (1981) *Questions of Cinema*, London: Macmillan.

Hebdige, Dick (1979) *Subculture: The Meaning of Style,* London: Methuen.

Henderson, Brian (1976) 'The Long Take', in Nichols (ed.) *Movies and Methods.*

Herman, Edward S. and Noam Chomsky (1994) *Manufacturing Consent: The Political Economy of the Mass Media*, London: Vintage Books.

Hill, Amelia (2008) 'North versus South: The Old Divide Just Got Wider', *The Observer*, 24 February. Available at: http://www.guardian.co.uk/uk/2008/feb/24/britishidentity. communities; accessed March 2008.

Hoberman, J. (1993) *42nd Street*, London: British Film Institute London.

Holmes, Andrew (2002) 'Let There Be Blood', *The Guardian*, 5 July. Available at: http:// film.guardian.co.uk/censorship/news/0,11729,749447,00.html#article_continue; accessed March 2008.

Holmes, Tom (2006) 'Magazine Design' in McKay (ed.) *The Magazine Handbook.*

Holmlund, Chris (1993) 'Masculinity as Multiple Masquerade' in Cohan and Hark (eds) *Screening the Male.*

Holquist, Michael (2002) *Dialogism* (2nd edn), London and New York: Routledge.

Holton, Robert (1992) *Economy and Society*, London and New York: Routledge.

Irons, Glenwood (ed.) (1995) *Feminism in Women's Detective Fiction,* Toronto, Buffalo and London: University of Toronto Press.

Jackson, Peter, Nick Stevenson and Kate Brooks (2001) *Making Sense of Men's Magazines*, Cambridge: Polity Press.

James, C. Vaughan (1973) *Soviet Socialist Realism*, London: Macmillan.

Jeffords, Susan (1993) 'Can Masculinity Be Terminated?' in Cohan and Hark (eds) *Screening the Male.*

Jeffords, Susan and Lauren Rabinovitz (eds) (1994) *Seeing Through the Media: The Persian Gulf War*, New Brunswick, NJ: Rutgers University Press.

Jenkins, Henry (1992) *Textual Poachers: Television Fans and Participatory Culture*, New York and London: Routledge.

Jennings, Ros (2004) 'Cagney and Lacey' in Creeber (ed.) *Fifty Key Television Programmes.*

Jerslev, Anne (n.d.) 'Sally Potter's "ecrands seconds": A Reading of Sally Potter's Work'. Available at: www.nordicom.gu.se/common/publ_pdf/45_Jerslev.pdf; accessed March 2008.

Jones, Sarah Gwenllian (2002) 'Gender and Queerness' in Miller (ed.) *Television Studies.*

Keighron, Peter (1993) 'Video Diaries: What's Up Doc?', *Sight and Sound,* 3(10), October.

Kerr, Paul (1981) '*Gangsters*: Conventions and Contraventions' in Bennett *et al.* (eds) *Popular Television and Film.*

King, Geoff (2002) *New Hollywood Cinema: An Introduction*, New York: Columbia University Press.

King, Geoff (2005a) '"Just Like a Movie"?: 9/11 and Hollywood Spectacle' in King (2005b).

King, Geoff (ed.) (2005b) *The Spectacle of the Real: From Hollywood to Reality TV and Beyond*, Bristol: Intellect Books.

Kitses, Jim (2004) *Horizons West: Directing the Western from John Ford to Clint Eastwood* (new edn), London: British Film Institute.

Kracauer, Siegfried (1979) 'Basic Concepts', in Mast and Cohen (eds) *Film Theory and Criticism*.

Krutnik, Frank (1991) *In a Lonely Street: Film Noir, Genre and Gender*, London and New York: Routledge.

Kuhn, Annette (1985) *The Power of the Image*, London: Routledge & Kegan Paul.

Kuhn, Annette (ed.) (1990) *Alien Zone: Cultural Theory and Contemporary Science Fiction Cinema*, London and New York: Verso.

Lacey, Nick (1996/7) 'Loaded Lads and Lasses', *in the picture*, 29, Winter, pp. 16–17.

Lacey, Nick (2000) *Narrative and Genre*. Basingstoke: Palgrave Macmillan.

Lacey, Nick (2002) *Media Institutions and Audiences*. Basingstoke: Palgrave.

Lacey, Nick (2005) 'Postmodern Romance: The Impossibility of (De)centring the Self' in Brooker (ed.) *The Blade Runner Experience*.

Lacey, Nick and Roy Stafford (2001) 'Documentary', *in the picture* publications.

Lavery, David (ed.) (2006) *Reading Deadwood: A Western to Swear By*, London and New York: I. B. Tauris.

Lehman, Peter (1993) '"Don't Blame This On A Girl": Female rape-revenge films' in Cohan and Hark (eds) *Screening the Male*.

Levenson, Ellie (2008) 'Women, Science and Representation', *MediaGuardian*, 25 February. Available at: http://www.guardian.co.uk/media/2008/feb/25/television.pressand publishing

Lister, Martin, Jon Dovey, Seth Giddings, Iain Grant and Kieran Kelly (2003) *New Media: A Critical Introduction*, Abingdon and New York: Routledge.

Lundegaard, Erik (2006) 'The Manchurian Movie: Who Took the Politics Out of the Political Thriller?'. Available at: http://www.msnbc.msn.com/id/7547900; accessed April 2008.

Lusted, David (ed.) (1991) *The Media Studies Book*, London: Routledge.

Lusted, David and Philip Drummond (eds) (1985) *TV and Schooling*, London: British Film Institute Education Dept.

MacCabe, Colin (1980) *Godard: Images, Sounds, Politics*, London: Macmillan.

Macdonald, Myra (2003) *Exploring Media Discourse*, London: Arnold.

Manovich, Lev (2001) *The Language of New Media*, Cambridge, MA: MIT Press.

Mast, Gerald and Marshall Cohen (eds) (1979) *Film Theory and Criticism* (2nd edn), New York: Oxford University Press.

Mathews, Tom Dewe (1994) *Censored*, London: Chatto & Windus.

McCabe, Janet (2006) 'Myth Maketh the Woman: Calamity Jane, Frontier Mythology and Creating American (Media) Historical Imaginings' in Lavery (ed.) *Reading Deadwood*.

McCloud, Scott (1994) *Understanding Comics: The Invisible Art*, New York: Harper Perennial.

McGreal, Chris (2004) 'BBC Accused of Bias against Israel', *The Guardian*, 1 April. Available at: http://www.guardian.co.uk/media/2004/apr/01/bbc.israel; accessed April 2008.

McGuigan, Jim (1992) *Cultural Populism*, London: Routledge.

McKay, Jenny (ed.) (2006) *The Magazines Handbook*, London and New York: Routledge.

McKeon, Matt and Susan Wyche (n.d.) 'Life Across Boundaries: Design, Identity, and Gender in SL'. Available at: www.mattmckeon.com/portfolio/second-life.pdf; accessed April 2008.

McRobbie, Angela (1996) 'More!: New Sexualities in Women's Magazines' in Curran, Morley and Walkerdine (eds) *Cultural Studies.*

McRobbie, Angela (2004) 'Reflections Upon Young Women in Consumer Culture'. Available at: http://www.goldsmiths.ac.uk/media-communications/staff/mcrobbie.php; accessed April 2008.

McRobbie, Angela (2006) 'Female Celebrities Must Work Just as Hard Off Stage' *The Guardian,* June. Available at: http://www.guardian.co.uk/commentisfree/story/0,,1792628,00.html; accessed April 2008.

McRobbie, Angela (2007) 'Postfeminism and Popular Culture: Bridget Jones and the New Gender Regime', in Tasker and Negra (eds) *Interrogating Postfeminism.*

McRoy, Jay (ed.) (2005) *Japanese Horror Cinema,* Edinburgh: Edinburgh University Press.

Miller, Henry K. (2007) '*The Kingdom*', *Sight & Sound,* 17(11), November.

Miller, Jonathan (2005) 'March of the Conservatives: Penguin Film as Political Fodder', *New York Times,* 13 September. Available at: http://www.nytimes.com/2005/09/13/science/13peng.html; accessed March 2008.

Miller, Toby (ed.) (2002) *Television Studies,* London: British Film Institute.

Minns, Adam (1999) 'Four Goes East', *Screen International,* 1233, 5 November.

Morley, David (1992) *Television Audiences and Cultural Studies,* London: Routledge.

Mulvey, Laura (1985) 'Visual Pleasure and Narrative Cinema' in Bill Nichols (ed.) *Movies and Methods.*

Murphy, Desmond (2006) *Buffy the Vampire Slayer: Study Guide,* Aberdeen City Council.

Naficy, Hamid (2002) 'Islamizing Film Culture in Iran: A Post-Khatami Update' in Tapper (ed.) *The New Iranian Cinema.*

Napier, Susan J. (2005) *Anime from Akira to Howl's Moving Castle,* (updated edn), New York and Basingstoke: Palgrave Macmillan.

Neale, Stephen (1980) *Genre,* London: British Film Institute.

Neale, Steve (1977) 'Propaganda', *Screen,* 18(3), Autumn.

Neale, Steve (1993) 'Masculinity as Spectacle' in Cohan and Hark (eds) *Screening the Male.*

Neale, Steve (2000) *Genre and Hollywood,* London and New York: Routledge.

Neale, Steve (ed.) (2002a) *Genre and Contemporary Hollywood,* London: British Film Institute.

Neale, Steve (2002b) 'Westerns and Gangster Films Since 1990' in Neale (ed.) (2002a).

Newman, James (2004) *Videogames,* Abingdon and New York: Routledge.

Ngayane, Lionel, (1993) 'For Africans, With Africans, By Africans' in Shiri (ed.) *Africa at the Pictures.*

Nichols, Bill (ed.) (1976) *Movies and Methods,* Berkeley, Calif. and Los Angeles: University of California Press.

Nichols, Bill (1981) *Ideology and the Image,* Bloomington: Indiana University Press.

Nichols, Bill (ed.) (1985) *Movies and Methods,* Vol. 2, Berkeley, CA and Los Angeles: University of California Press.

Nichols, Bill (1991) *Representing Reality,* Bloomington and Indianapolis: Indiana University Press.

Nichols, Bill (1994) *Representing Reality*, Bloomington and Indianapolis: Indiana University Press.

Nichols, Bill (2001) *Introduction to Documentary*, Bloomington: Indiana University Press.

Nowell-Smith, Geoffrey, 'Why Realism?' unpublished?.

O'Day, Marc (2004) 'Gender, Spectacle and Action Babe Cinema' in Tasker (ed.) *Action and Adventure Cinema*.

O'Donnell, Hugh (2007–8) 'Girl Meets World: *Ugly Betty* and the Internationalisation of the *Telenovela*', *Media Education Journal*, 42, Winter.

Okoye, Chukwuma (2007) 'Looking at Ourselves in Our Mirror: Agency, Counter-Discourse, and the Nigerian Video Film', *film international*, 5(4).

O'Reilly, Tim (2005) 'What Is Web 2.0: Design Patterns and Business Models for the Next Generation of Software'. Available at: http://www.oreillynet.com/pub/a/oreilly/tim/news/2005/09/30/what-is-web-20; accessed February 2008.

Orwell, George (1971) *The Collected Essays*, Vol. 1, Harmondsworth: Penguin.

O'Sullivan, Tim, Brian Dutton and Philip Rayner (1994) *Studying the Media*, London: Edward Arnold.

O'Sullivan, Tim and Yvonne Jewkes (eds) (1977) *The Media Studies Reader*, London: Hodder Arnold.

Paik, E. Koohan (2004) 'Is Lost in Translation Racist?'. Available at: http://www.asianamericanfilm.com/ archives/000602; accessed November 2007.

Page, Adrian (2000) *Cracking Morse Code: Semiotics and Television Drama*, Luton: University of Luton Press.

Panofsky, Erwin (1979) 'Style and Medium in the Motion Pictures' in Mast and Cohen (eds) *Film Theory and Criticism*.

Perkins, Tessa (1997) 'Rethinking Stereotypes' in O'Sullivan and Jewkes (eds) *The Media Studies Reader*.

Philo, Greg and Mike Berry (2004) *Bad News From Israel*, London: Pluto Press.

Pines, Jim and Paul Willeman (eds) (1989) *Questions of Third Cinema*, London: British Film Institute.

Pink, Daniel (2007) 'Japan, Ink: Inside the Manga Industrial Complex', *Wired*, 15(11), 22 October.

Robertson, Pamela (1996) *Guilty Pleasures: Feminist Camp from Mae West to Madonna*, London and New York: I. B. Tauris.

Robertson, Roland (1995) 'Glocalisation: Time–Space and Homogeneity–Heterogeneity' in Featherstone *et al.* (1995).

Roth, Mark (ed.) (1981) 'Some Warners Musicals and the Spirit of the New Deal' in Altman (ed.) (1981).

Rubin, Martin (1999) *Thrillers*, Cambridge: Cambridge University Pres.

Ruh, Brian (2004) *Stray Dog of Anime: The Films of Mamoru Oshii*, New York and Basingstoke: Palgrave Macmillan.

Said, Edward (2003) *Orientalism*, London: Penguin Books.

Scharf, Aaron (1983) *Art and Photography*, Harmondsworth: Penguin.

Selby, Keith and Ron Cowdrey (1995) *How To Study Television*, London: Macmillan.

Shakir, Shanaz (2006) 'Investigate and Critically Reflect on the Ways in Which Viewers React to Same-Sex Romantic Screen Kisses'. Available at: www.aber.ac.uk/media/Students/szs0405.pdf; accessed March 2008.

Shiri, Keith (ed.) (1993) *Africa at the Pictures*, London: British Film Institute.

Shohat, Ella and Robert Stam (1996) 'From the Imperial Family to the Transnational Imaginary: Media Spectatorship in the Age of Globalization' in Wilson and Dissanayake (eds) *Global/Local*.

Sieder, Joe (n.d.) 'Fly on the Wall TV'. Available at: http://www.screenonline.org.uk/tv/id/698785/index; accessed March 2008.

Sinclair, Upton (1965) *The Jungle*, Harmondsworth: Penguin.

Slotkin, Richard (1973) *Regeneration Through Violence*, Middletown, CT: Wesleyan University Press.

Smith, Joan (2008) 'The Same Old Story', *The Guardian*, 22 February. Available at: http://www.guardian.co.uk/uk/2008/feb/22/ukcrime.gender; accessed March 2008.

Smith, Paul Julian (2004) 'Tokyo Drifters', *Sight and Sound*, 14 (1), January.

Sontag, Susan (1976) 'Fascinating Fascism' in Nichols (ed.) *Movies and Methods*, Berkeley, CA: University of California Press.

Stafford, Roy (1995) 'Sound on Film – What to Teach?', *in the picture*, 25, Spring.

Stam, Robert (1992) *Subversive Pleasures: Bakhtin, Cultural Criticism, and Film*, Baltimore, MD and London: Johns Hopkins University Press.

Stam, Robert and Toby Miller (eds) (2000) *Film and Theory: An Anthology*, Malden and Oxford: Blackwell.

Stam, Robert, Robert Burgoyne and Sandy Flitterman-Lewis (1992) *New Vocabularies in Film Semiotics*, London: Routledge.

Steemers, Jeanette (2004) *Selling Television: British Television in the Global Marketplace*, London: British Film Institute.

Stein, Atara (1998) 'Xena: Warrior Princess, the Lesbian Gaze, and the Construction of a Feminist Heroine', *Whoosh!'*, 24, September. Available at: http://www.whoosh.org/issue24/stein1a.html; accessed April 2008.

Stephenson, Hugh (1994) *Sex, Lies and Democracy: British Press and the Public*, London: Longman.

Storey, John (2001) *Cultural Theory and Popular Culture: An Introduction* (3rd edn), Harlow: Pearson Education.

Sturken, M. and L. Cartwright (2001) *Practices of Looking: An Introduction to Visual Culture* (London and New York: Oxford University Press).

Surowiecki, James (2005) *The Wisdom of Crowds: Why the Many Are Smarter Than the Few*, London: Abacus.

Swanson, Gillian (1991) 'Representation' in Lusted (ed.) *The Media Studies Book*.

Tapper, Richard (ed.) (2002) *The New Iranian Cinema*, London and New York: I. B. Tauris.

Tasker, Yvonne (1993) *Spectacular Bodies*, London and New York: Routledge.

Tasker, Yvonne (ed.) (2004) *Action and Adventure Cinema*, Abingdon and New York: Routledge.

Tasker, Yvonne and Diane Negra (eds) (2007) *Interrogating Postfeminism: Gender and the Politics of Popular Culture*, Durham, NC and London: Duke University Press.

Taylor, T. L. (2003) 'Multiple Pleasures: Women and Online Gaming', *Convergence*, 9(1). Available at: www.cyberfest.us/Women%20Gamers/Taylor-WomenAndGaming.pdf; accessed April 2008.

Thill, Scott (2006) 'Expanding the Possibilities', *Bright Lights Film Journal*, 51, February. Available at: http://www.brightlightsfilm.com/51/chungiv.htm; accessed April 2008.

Thwaites, Tony, Lloyd Davis and Warwick Mules (1994) *Tools for Cultural Studies*, South Melbourne, Macmillan.

Tolson, Andrew (1998) *MEDIAtions: Text and Discourse in Media Studies*, London: Hodder Arnold.

Tomc, Sandra (1995) 'Questing Women: The Feminist Mystery after Feminism' in Irons (ed.) *Feminism in Women's Detective Fiction*.

Tudor, Andrew (1989) *Monsters and Mad Scientists: A Cultural History of the Horror Movie*, Oxford and Cambridge, MA: Basil Blackwell.

Tulloch, John (1995) '"But He's a Time Lord! He's a Time Lord!": Reading Formations, Followers and Fans' in Tulloch and Jenkins, *Science Fiction Audiences*.

Tulloch, John and Henry Jenkins (1995) *Science Fiction Audiences: Watching* Doctor Who *and* Star Trek, London and New York: Routledge.

Wainwright, Martin (2008) 'The Real Moorside Story', *The Guardian*, G2, 11 April.

Ward, Lucy (2007) 'Childcare Locks Women into Lower-paid Jobs' *The Guardian*, 6 December.

Watt, Ian (1972) *The Rise of the Novel*, Harmondsworth: Pelican.

West, Amy (2005) 'Caught on Tape: A Legacy of Low-tech Reality' in King (ed.) *The Spectacle of the Real*.

White, Jim (1994) 'Drama: The Last Resort', *The Independent*, 12 November.

White, Mimi (1994) 'Site Unseen: An Analysis of CNN's *War in the Gulf*' in Jeffords and Rabinovitz (eds) *Seeing Through the Media*.

Willett, John (1977) *The Theatre of Bertolt Brecht* (3rd edn), London: Methuen.

Williams, Christopher (1980) *Realism and the Cinema*, London: Routledge & Kegan Paul.

Williams, Raymond (1974) *Television, Technology and Cultural Form*, London: Collins.

Williams, Raymond (1976) *Keywords*, Glasgow: Fontana.

Williams, Raymond (1977) *Marxism and Literature*, Oxford: Oxford University Press.

Williamson, Judith (1983) 'Images of "Woman" – the Photographs of Cindy Sherman', *Screen*, 24(6) November–December.

Wilson, Rob and Wimal Dissanayake (eds) (1996) *Global/Local: Cultural Production and the Transnational Imaginary*, Durham, NC and London: Duke University Press.

Winship, Janice (1987) *Inside Women's Magazines*, London and New York: Pandora.

Winston, Brian (1995) *Claiming the Real*, London: British Film Institute.

Wollen, Peter (1972) *Signs and Meaning in the Cinema* (3rd edn), London: Secker & Warburg/British Film Institute.

Wollen, Peter (1985) 'Godard and Counter Cinema: *Vent d'Est*' in Nichols (ed.) *Movies and Methods*.

Wood, Robin (1985) 'An Introduction to the American Horror Film' in Nichols (ed.) *Movies and Methods*.

Wu Jiao (2008) 'Tibet Chairman: Police Exercised "Great Restraint"', *China Daily News*, March 2008. Available at: http://www.chinadaily.com.cn/china/2008-03/18/content_6543572.htm; accessed March 2008.

Index

Printed and bound by CPI Group (UK) Ltd, Croydon, CR0 4YY